I Become Part of It

Bird's Head Shield, 1981 KEVIN RED STAR

I Become Part of It

Sacred Dimensions in Native American Life

D.M. Dooling and Paul Jordan-Smith, eds.

A Parabola Book

HarperSanFrancisco
A Division of HarperCollins*Publishers*

With the cooperation of
The Colorado Historical Society
200 Fourteenth Avenue, Denver, Colorado

PARABOLA BOOKS are developed by the Society for the Study of Myth and Tradition, a non–profit organization devoted to the dissemination and exploration of materials relating to the myth, symbol, ritual, and art of the great religious traditions. The Society also publishes PARABOLA, The Magazine of Myth and Tradition.

FIRST HARPERCOLLINS PAPERBACK EDITION PUBLISHED IN 1992

Library of Congress Cataloging-in-Publication Data

I become part of it : sacred dimensions in native American life / D.M. Dooling and
    Paul Jordan–Smith, eds.— 1st HarperCollins paperback ed.
      p. cm.
    ISBN 0–06–250235–2
    1. Indians of North America—Religion and mythology. 2. Indians of North
America—Legends 3. Tales—North America I. Dooling, D.M.
II. Jordan–Smith, Paul
E98.R3I19   1992
299'.7—dc20   91–58397
                                                     CIP

---

92   93   94   95   96   MAL   10   9   8   7   6   5   4   3   2   1

This edition is printed on acid–free paper that meets the American National Standards Institute Z39.48 Standard.

Contents

· I Become Part of It ·

Illustrations

·I Become Part of It·

Introduction

*L*ong ago, when Tabaldak finished making the world, that Great Being still had some of the dust of Creation on his hands. So, just as one does after finishing planting, Tabaldak began to brush that dirt from his hands. That dirt, the dust from the making of all, all that came to be as Tabaldak, the Owner/Creator thought of it and made it, that dust sprinkled like rain onto the earth. There, where it fell, the earth began to move. It moved as if with breath. The shape of a head and then a torso formed in the loose red earth. The shapes of arms and hands, of waist and hips formed. Then that shape sat up. It opened its mouth. It spoke words of greeting. These were the first words heard on the new earth, but the language was the language of the earth which shaped itself into a being. Tabaldak understood those words.

Tell me your name, the Owner/Creator said.

I am Odzihozo, the being said. I am the One Who Gathers Himself.

You are wonderful, Tabaldak said.

Nda, said Odzihozo. It is you who are wonderful. You sprinkled the earth with the dust of creation.

Then Odzihozo looked about, wide-eyed, and Tabaldak also looked in that same way. All of creation was around them.

So the western Abenaki story of creation begins. It is only one of many such stories told about this land which is now called North

America, this land known by many Native Americans as the earth on Great Turtle's back. Like most of those stories of creation, it teaches a lesson. We are part of the earth, one with creation. We are a part of it all.

When I was asked to write an introduction for this book, I was not certain where to start. As I read these powerful stories and essays, however, as I felt the way they were as connected to each other as skin to flesh, as flesh to bone, I began to think of this not as a book, but as a living and breathing being. Words, when spoken with reverence and attention to their true meaning, are alive. I realized then that the only way to begin was at the beginning.

When we consider the sacred dimensions of Native American life, we do well to begin at creation for that is the root of everything in the native world. The spirit of creation, the strength of the sacred, interpenetrates every aspect of traditional (and, to a large degree, contemporary) American Indian life. When stories are told—stories such as those in this volume— they always serve a double purpose. Stories entertain and they instruct. They delight and they teach. Stories work best when they are told either to the very young or to those who have not forgotten the child within them, who open themselves without preconceptions to the possibility of other worlds than their own everyday reality, who accept that even everyday life—if seen through different eyes—may be suffused with magic.

American majority culture has been characterized for a long time by an ethnocentric bias which has made it impossible for most—scholars and laypeople alike—to appreciate and respect the many different cultures which were and still are found among the native peoples of this continent. All too frequently, books written about Indians have been by experts who were certain they knew more about the native people they studied than the native people themselves. They often took apart native life in their books the way a high school biology student dissects a frog. The result, as with that unfortunate frog, was something static and dead. Interesting, perhaps, but without life. That is particularly ironic when one considers that American anthropology might be said to have had its birth in a volume which was truly a collaboration between a Native American and a non-native. *The League of the Iroquois* by Lewis Henry Morgan was published in 1851. It was based almost entirely on the accurate and detailed information supplied by a young Iroquois man named Ha-sa-no-an-da, to whom the volume was inscribed. (Ha-sa-no-an-da, Ely Parker, would go on to even greater things, becoming an inspired defender of the rights of his people, a civil engineer, and a general in the Union army during the Civil War, the right-hand man of U.S. Grant.) Although Morgan felt that the only hope for the Indians to survive lay on their being "elevated and christianized," he saw in the Iroquois League conclusive proof of the "superior acuteness and profundity of the Indian intellect." Morgan also recognized the tenacity of Native American culture, stating that "in the depths of Indian society there is a spirit and a sentiment to which their minds are attuned by nature; and great must be the power, and constant the influence which can overcome the one, or eradicate the other." The profundity of Morgan's insight can be measured by the final essay in *I Become Part of It.* It is a statement by a contemporary Iroquois member of the Great League, Oren Lyons, which draws its power from an unswerving dedication to those same still-living Iroquois traditions eulogized by Morgan.

I mention both Morgan and the self-centeredness of much of American anthropology because I feel this book to be a true descendent of the best impulses found in Morgan and an antidote to the poison of bad scholarship about Native American ways. All of those, both native and non-native, who have contributed to this book are connected in one way or another to what may be called — for lack of a better word — "traditional" Native American culture. Those who are non-native, such as Joseph Epes Brown and Thomas Buckley, have lived and studied with native elders in a non-judgmental way. Brown's work with Black Elk, for example, was done over a period of many years during which he lived and traveled with the old man and his family. Considering the openness of most Native American cultures to sincerely interested outsiders, I am amazed that more anthropologists have not taken this path to understanding, accepting the opportunity to truly "become a part of it." (But I suspect that the popular phrase and mindset of "participant-observer" has enabled a great many to still remain aloof and judgmental while supposedly taking part.)

When the first Europeans reached this hemisphere, they recorded their impressions of the people and cultures they encountered. Columbus, in his journals, speaks of their having "as much lovingness as though they would give their hearts . . . they remained so much our friends that it was a marvel." Later descriptions of Native Americans as fierce fighters and cold-hearted savages came after, after Columbus and his cohorts introduced slavery and tyranny, killing as many as six million Arawaks and Caribs as the Spaniards virtually extinguished the native populations of the Antilles. The traditional cultures of North America, like those of the West Indies, tended to be stable, life-affirming, and open to friendly outsiders. Evidence for this can be found in the chronicles from the times of early contact and, amazingly (considering nearly 500 years of repression), among Native American peoples today. There is a long history of the adoption of non-natives into Native American societies. This is not the sign of childlike, naive people, as some have written. It is, instead, the mark of security, of nations and people who knew so clearly who they were that they could allow outsiders to join them.

I Become Part of It is part of that tradition, also. It invites the reader into native cultures, to see things with a native eye, in a different way. Most contemporary Americans have seen Native American art, usually in museums or in a color plate in a book. Sam Gill's essay, "It's Where You Put Your Eyes," offers another approach. To truly see a mask, you must see from within it, see the world through its eyeholes. But that is only one example of many. Lakota writer Arthur Amiotte's descriptions of his own experiences of initiation in a vision quest are both private and generous at one and the same time and the reader has been prepared to better understand those experiences through the perspective offered by earlier essays in the book.

Linked together by traditional tales, which act both as bridges and as opportunities to hear the words of storytellers from a number of native cultures, all of the essays in this book are like the Pomo basket mentioned in Brown's "Becoming Part of It." They are utilitarian and beautiful. They have been sung into existence. One of my favorites is Vine Deloria's "Out of Chaos." I have Hi-Lited so many lines of it that it looks as if it has more gold than the Black Hills. It is an essay which should be read by anyone who, with starry eyes, wishes to go among the Indians and "learn from their ways." I have never read a better summation of the forces which lead to the destruction of the cultural life of Indians. That destruction begins when the imposition of western constraints results in the loss of "ceremonial time," and prevents the people from pursuing, without interference, traditional rituals within that sacred and timeless time and in those sacred places. The facts Deloria points to have gone unrecognized by all too many in recent years, Indian and non-Indian alike. This world is more than just a physical thing. An awareness of its spiritual, sacred dimensions is vital not only for the survival of cultural life, but for the continuance of life itself on an earth now clearly threatened by forces which western cultures have set into motion.

Handsome Lake, the Iroquois prophet, spoke of a time to come when the Maple, the leader tree of the woodlands, would begin to die from the top down. Then, he said, we would be close to the end of the world. Today, in New York, in New Hampshire, in Vermont, the maples are dying from the top down. The greenhouse effect which was only theory a decade ago appears to have begun as the earth's climate grows hotter, the cycles of drought grow deeper, the unforgivable pollution of air and water become everyday headlines. When the life of the intellect and the life of the spirit grow apart, terrible things become possible. When we no longer perceive the Earth as a living being, speaking to the Creator and to those who take time to listen, then we are all threatened with destruction. *I Become Part of It* is more than just another interesting book about Indians. It is both lesson and reminder. Native people understood that they had to live within the balance. When you are no longer part of it, the world goes out of balance. It is, however, not yet too late to listen and to learn. This book is a good place to begin.

The ten Native American artists whose works have been selected to accompany these texts have been well chosen. Each of their pieces shows a deep understanding of the relationships between visible world and spirit, human being and the vast circle of life. The influences of their individual native traditions — from the Plains and the desert southwest to California and the Alaskan coast — add special meaning to their images, which serve as excellent complements to these essays and stories. Like the folk traditions and introductions to native ceremonial awareness given us in written words, their visual representations may open our eyes further to those ways of seeing which do not place people at the exclusive center. Carl Beam's eagle and moon lift us above the earth. Dan Namingha's "Longhair Kachina" appears to flow out of the land, vibrant as dancing. Kevin Red Star's "Bird's Head Shield" gives us the picture of man and shield as one, the decorations of the human and his shield shaping a prayer.

Some of these artists are ceremonial people themselves. David Paladin's "Blue Winter Kachinas" is a statement of living faith from a man who was both artist and "shaman." Frank La Pena, whose Wintu name is Tauhindauli, once spoke with me at great length about the importance of taking an active part in the ceremonies of his people, of the many times he has made the tough climb to the top of Mount Shasta—both alone and with his children—to place prayer feathers. His "Deer Rattle—Deer Dancer" is tremulous with the knowledge lent by that way of life, by the mystery of human and deer skull as one, the staff and the circle, the continuance of death and life. That connection between humans and animal beings opens from the old ways in the winged shape and metamorphosing face in the paintings of Yurok, Rick Bartow, and in the contemporary legend shaped by the spirit mask of Tlingit artist Edna Jackson, its left eye another face.

Jaune Quick-to-See Smith deserves special mention. Her work has always delighted me and it has been used to illustrate the work of many contemporary Native American poets. Child-like at first glance, especially to an uninformed viewer, the pictures actually display exceptional skill. Their lines are as basic and powerful as those of ancient cave paintings and petroglyphs. Their figures seem linked to those of the winter counts which were painted on buffalo skins to record the significant events of each new year. They also remind me of the drawings I saw in a captured ledger book where the Cheyenne warrior

Little Fingernail, killed in battle as he and his people tried to escape from the U.S. Army and return to their own land, recorded his impressions with handmade paints as they made their long flight. He saw a life continuously full of beauty, even in the midst of hardship and battle. Jaune Quick-to-See Smith's balance of shapes and shadings and her understanding of the heart of those symbols she uses—whether Indian cowboy or glyph of walking spirit—make her work worthy of long study.

But that is true of each of these pictures. Each deserves unhurried consideration and careful seeing, the kind of attention which every essay and tale in this volume recommends— completing the circle.

Gah ne goh he yoh / Joseph Bruchac
Skamonkas Kisos / Corn Harvest Moon

Becoming Part of It

Joseph Epes Brown

*I*n talking about sacred dimensions in Native American life, I must proceed not just as a descriptive ethnographer but also as a historian of religion, and with what I hope is a basic humanistic concern; that is, I believe it important to ask about the relevance of these primal values to a dominant contemporary world with life-ways which are oriented towards very different directions and with contrasting priorities. One notices very clearly today our increasing malaise and sometimes even fear, which—at least in certain segments of our society—is leading to a growing mood for re-evaluation and reassessment, a wish even to take a backward look, so to say, at "progress," that concept which for so long has been an unquestioned quasi-religious dogma in our lives. Many of those early studies of Native American peoples and cultures suffered from the kinds of prejudices that came out of this prevailing concept of progress.

An expression of this new and growing mood is found in an increasing concern to seek out our ancient origins, with a view to rediscovering and perhaps even identifying with what is our own proper heritage. I put the question in this manner because very often when I speak about the relevance and the reality of American Indian values, I am misunderstood, especially by students who like to believe that what I am trying to say is that they should go out and be and live like American Indians; this is not my point at all, because for those of us who are non-Indians it is an impossibility. One has to be brought up in these cultures and traditions, one has to live the languages, in order truly to identify with the ethos of an American Indian people. What I am trying to say is that these traditions could be taken as models which might provide us with answers to some of the dilemmas with which we are currently struggling in our own society.

In the 1960s, in our restlessness with where we found ourselves, we began to turn to the religions and methods of the Orient, with all the attractions and mystique which distance provides. By the 1970s, however, with our rapidly growing ecological concerns, there developed an increasing awareness that certain answers could be found in the spiritual traditions of the Native Americans; for here the sacred values which so many of us were seeking out were actually rooted in this land, where they have survived through some sixty to eighty thousand years. Out of this mood there has come a vast array of new literature, both genuine and spurious, relating to Native American lifeways and world view; and even if the approach has often been overly romantic, there is here a change from earlier attitudes and prejudices, which is a positive sign even if it is only a beginning.

Although greatly oversimplified and generalized, let me give at least a brief sampling of what I think are some of the core Native American values and perspectives, through which we can perhaps come to relearn a little bit about ourselves and about our own proper spiritual heritage, the hope being that what has been lost can still be rediscovered. Certainly the Native American people themselves, especially the younger ones today, are trying to regain and revitalize their own traditions which may have been lost, or taken from them through a variety of pressures and prejudices. We have, I suggest, in this struggle a model for our own proper quest. What are some of its contours?

Tribal cultures, it seems to me, present a model of what a religious tradition *is*; and this is a basic reality which we have lost sight of. That is, what really is a true religious tradition? What does it encompass, what are its dimensions? These cultures demonstrate how all components of a culture can be interconnected: how the presence of the sacred can permeate all lifeways to such a degree that what we call religion is here integrated into the totality of life and into all of life's activities. Religion here is so pervasive in life that there is probably no Native American language in which there is a term which could be translated as "religion" in the way we understand it. As Peter Nabokov tells us in his book, *Indian Running*, when you track down a seemingly isolated or minimal feature of Indian life, such as running, the whole system opens before your eyes; and this is true because of the interrelatedness of all the components of a genuine tradition. Obviously in such a system life cannot be fragmented, due to that binding and interconnecting thread of the presence of the sacred.

In terms of interconnections, a dominant theme in all Native American cultures is that of relationship, or a series of relationships that are always reaching further and further out; relationships within the immediate family reaching out to the extended family, to the band, outward again to the clan, to the tribal group; and relationships do not stop there but extend out to embrace and relate to the environment; to the land, to the animals, to the plants, and to the clouds, the elements, the heavens, the stars; and ultimately those relationships that people express and live, extend to embrace the entire universe.

In the Plains area, to give an example, one of the most profound rites is that of the smoking of the pipe. In this ritual

smoking of the pipe, all who participate are joined in a communal ritual, and when it is finished, everybody who has shared in
the smoking of the pipe recites the phrase, in Lakota in this
case, "*mitakuye oyasin*" — "we are all relatives." We *are* all related, because in this rite we have all become one within a
mystery that is greater than any of its parts. I shall talk more
about the general importance of rituals and ceremonies later.

Associated with relationship there should be mentioned the
theme of reciprocity which permeates so many aspects of North
American cultures. Put very simply, reciprocity here refers
again to that process wherein if you receive or take away you
must also give back. This is a living statement of the importance
of the cycle permeating all of life. Everything in their world of
experience is conceived in terms of such cycles or of the circle;
everything comes back upon itself. Black Elk so often said that
all the forces of the world work in cycles or circles; the birds
build their nests in circular form, the foxes have their dens in
circles, the wind in its greatest power moves in a circle, and life
is as a circle. I recall once how this reality was beautifully
expressed in a living manner, when I noticed how this dignified
old man would relate to little children. He would get down on
his hands and knees and pretend he was a horse, and the
children would squeal with joy on the old man's back. Here
there obviously was no generation gap; he was one with the
child. I once asked him how it was that he could so relate to the
child, and he replied: "I who am an old man am about to return
to the Great Mysterious" (*Wakan Tanka*, Lakota) "and a young
child is a being who has just come *from* the Great Mysterious; so
it is that we are very close together." Because of such cyclical
understanding, both are very nearly at the same point.

Such attitudes could be spelled out in terms of any number of
cultural expressions, but the point I want to draw from this is that
we have here an example which contrasts with our own dominant

concept of process which is in terms of linearity—the straight line which moves from here to there and onward indefinitely. Indeed, this theme of linearity permeates all aspects of our life. The way we read, for instance, is in lines; we have sayings in our vocabulary that tell us to "Line up!" "Let's get this straight!" Or if we refer to somebody who is a little bit crazy, we make a circular motion alongside our head, by which we indicate the reason is going in circles. There is something here from which we can learn, something about ourselves and our concept of progress, with all the loaded meanings which this term bears.

One must mention also the special nature of Native American languages, which contrasts with our understanding of language and our use of words. In Native languages the understanding is that the meaning *is* in the sound, it *is* in the word; the word is not a symbol for a meaning which has been abstracted out, word and meaning are together in one experience. Thus, to name a being, for example an animal, is actually to conjure up the powers latent in that animal. Added to this is the fact that when we create words we use our breath, and for these people and these traditions breath is associated with the principle of life; breath is life itself. And so if a word is born from this sacred principle of breath, this lends an added sacred dimension to the spoken word. It is because of this special feeling about words that people avoid using sacred personal names, because they contain the power of the beings named, and if you use them too much the power becomes dissipated. So usually one has to refer to a person in a very circuitous manner, or use a term which expresses relationship.

In this context one must also emphasize the positive values that could be attached to non-literacy. I use that term rather than illiteracy, which connotes the *inability* to read and write, which is negative and derogatory. Too often we have branded people as being backward and uncivilized if they are *illiterate*, whereas one can make a strong case for the advantages of growing up and living in a society which is *non-literate*. For in such a society all the lore which is central and sacred to the culture is borne *within* the individual in a living manner; you do not have to go outside of yourself, for all that is essential to life is carried with you, is ever-present. It seems that where you have people who are non-literate in this positive sense, you tend to have a special quality of person, a quality of being that cannot be described—a very different quality from that of the literate person. It has been my experience when among primal peoples in many parts of the world that there is something here that is very special.

Paralleling this primal concept of language, and of the word not as "symbol" but as an immediate event, is the quality of experiencing the visual arts and crafts. I should stress first of all that for primal peoples generally there is no dichotomy between the arts and crafts, in the manner that our art historians insist on, where art is one kind of thing that can be placed on a mantel-piece or hung on the wall, and the craft item is inferior because it is made for utilitarian ends. This seems to me a most artificial distinction and I think it is time that we outgrew it; indeed there is today evidence that we *are* re-evaluating such prejudiced dichotomies. For why cannot a utilitarian object also be beautiful? All necessary implements, utensils, and tools in Native American life-ways are of technical excellence and are also beautiful. They must be made in special sacred ways, and the materials of the tools and objects made have to be gathered with prayer and offerings. Beauty and truth are here one! When a Pomo basketmaker, for example, goes out to collect the grasses for her basket, she prays to the grasses, she enters into a relation-ship with them as she gathers, and makes offerings in return for having taken their life. When a woman weaves a basket she will pass the grass between her lips to moisten it, but also to breathe upon it, to give her life breath into the grass and thus give to the basket a special sacred quality that is always present in its use and tangible presence.

Through these few selected examples which have been given, I am suggesting that, where such traditions are still alive and spiritually viable, there tend to be present, within all of life's necessary activities, dimensions and expressions of the sacred. Actions of such quality could therefore be considered to manifest a ritual element in the sense that they tend to *order* life around and toward a Center. In this context, however, one must also speak of those special great rites and ceremonies, many often related to the seasonal cycles, which serve not just to support continuing orientations toward the sacred in everyday activities, but work for the *intensification* of such Presence and experience; such rites may also be the source and origin of new rites, ceremonies, and other sacred expressions through the visual arts, songs, or special dance forms.

One example of a ritual complex which is central to the lives of Plains people is the well known "vision" or "guardian spirit quest." This ritualized retreat is for the benefit of the individual man and woman, and yet means are present for the eventual sharing of received vision powers or messages with the larger community. After rigorous preparations, which always include the rites of the purifying sweat lodge and instructions by a qualified elder, the candidate goes to a high and remote place with the resolve to fast and pray continually and to suffer through acts of sacrifice and exposure to the elements for a specified number of days. The ordeal is highly ritualized and may involve the establishing of an altar, or the setting out of poles at the center and to the four directions of space. The person may also be instructed to remain within this established space and not to move about casually but to walk only out from the center to each of the poles in turn, always returning to the center. Prayers may be addressed to the powers of the four directions, and one may also use repetitive prayers such as the one the Lakota Black Elk has given us: "Grandfather, Great Mysterious, have pity on me." One may also remain silent, for it has been said that "silence *is* the voice of *Wakan Tanka*, the *Great Mysterious.*" If tired, one may sleep, for dreams of power may come to the candidate in this manner; yet it is understood that the true vision is of greater power than the dream. Often the sacred experience comes in the mysterious appearance of an animal or a winged being, or perhaps in one of the powers of nature. A special message is often communicated to the seeker, and this will serve as a guide and reminder throughout the person's life. After three or four days one returns to camp where a sweat lodge has again been prepared; within this lodge the candidate will explain the vision or dream which will be interpreted by the guiding elder, who will then give instructions as to what should now be accomplished in order to insure the continuity of the participation of the spiritual throughout the person's life. From such experiences have come the "medicine bundles" with rich and complex rites specific to each bundle and their ceremonial opening on special occasions. They have also been the origin of sacred types of art forms, such as the painted shields, or special songs of power, or even the great ritual dances, such as the horse dance, involving four groups of eight horses not representing, but *being* the powers of the four directions of space. It is in this manner that something of the sacred experience which had come to a particular individual is shared by all members of the larger community.

What is remarkable about the rites of the vision quest among the Plains peoples is that it is accomplished not just by special people as is the case in the Arctic, but that every man or woman after the age of puberty is expected to participate either once or

Untitled, 1984 JAUNE QUICK-TO-SEE SMITH

even repeatedly throughout his or her life.

What concerns us in this example is not just the detailed pattern of the ritual elements of the quest as such, which can encompass a multitude of very diverse possibilities, but that here we have one sample as a model of traditional ritual structures and acts which must involve initial purification, choice of appropriate site, the defining and delimiting of a special sacred place, and the fixing of a center. Further, ritualized *actions* are prescribed for the participant, which means that participation is not just with the mind, or a part of one's being, but with the totality of who one is. Also provided are means for continuity and development of the sacred experiences received, and the eventual responsibility for sharing something of them with the larger community.

As complement to the individually oriented "vision quest," one could mention the great communal "Sun Dance," referred to in different terms across the Plains groups. For this great complex of solemn rites, ceremonies, fasting, sacred song and dance fulfills not just the particular spiritual needs of the actively participating individuals, but also those of the entire tribal group gathered in circular camp for the occasion. The event is indeed for the welfare of the entire world. These are ceremonies, interspersed with special sacred rites, which celebrate world and life renewal at the time of spring. The ritualized dance forms again involve orientation around and towards a center which is either the sun itself or the cottonwood tree as axis of the world, standing at the center of a circular frame lodge carefully constructed in imitation of the cosmos. The ritual and ceremonial language of the total celebration speaks to and encompasses a plurality of spiritual possibilities at the levels of microcosm, macrocosm, and metacosm. It is believed by many that should the sacrificial rites of this "thirst lodge" be neglected or forgotten, the energy of the world will run out and the cycle in which we are living will close. It is an example to the world that these rites and ceremonies are far from being neglected, for today in ever increasing numbers the people are participating and are finding renewed strength and spiritual resolve.

All spiritually effective rites must accomplish three cumulative possiblities which may be termed purification, expansion—in wholeness or virtue—and identity. A ritual means which embodies these possibilities may be found in the sacred nature and use of the Plains Indian tobacco pipe, the smoking of which constitutes a communion. The shape of the pipe with its stem, bowl or "heart," and foot, is identified with the human person. In purifying the pipe before a ritual smoking there is an analogy to man's own purification; for in concentrating on the hollow of the straight stem leading to the bowl comes the understanding that one's mind should be this straight and pure. In filling the bowl of the pipe a prayer is said for each grain of tobacco in such a manner that everything in the world is mentioned. The filled bowl or the heart of man, in thus containing all possibilities, is then the universe. Finally, the fire which is put to the tobacco is the Presence of the ultimate all-inclusive Principle, *Wakan Tanka*, the "Great Mysterious." In smoking the pipe, through the aid of breath the totality of all creation is absorbed within this ultimate Principle. And since in the pipe there is a grain of tobacco identified with the one who smokes, there is here enacted a sacrificial communion of identity. With this understanding, the phrase "we are all related," recited by the individual or group after the smoking, takes on the deepest possible meaning.

I will sum up by simply saying that in all that I have tried to speak of in such brief fashion, we have expressions through different means of a special quality among traditional peoples

that could be called oneness of experience: a lack of dichotomiz-
ing or fragmenting, a unity in the word and in visual image. In
the painted image, for example, the understanding is that in the
being that is represented, or even in a depicted part of that
being—the paw of a bear, let us say—all the power of the animal
is present. One can draw from all Native American cultures
examples to reinforce such interpretation. One final example I
will use is that of the Navajo dry painting or "sand painting" as it
is sometimes called. These are made in a rich ceremonial context for the curing of individuals who have gotten out of balance
with their world. They are long ceremonies which can go on for
four or five or up to ten days, during which time sacred chants are
used with all the meaning of the *word* as I have tried to explain it.
At a certain moment during the ceremony the ill person is placed
at the center of one of the dry paintings; the understanding is
that the person thus becomes identified with the power that is in
the image painted on the earth with colored sand and pollen.
And the singer takes some of the painted image and presses it to
the body of the ill person, again to emphasize this element of
identity: the painting is not a symbol of some meaning or power,
the power *is* there present in it, and as the person identifies with
it the appropriate cure is accomplished.

I conclude with this portion of a Navajo chant:

> The mountains, I become part of it . . .
> The herbs, the fir tree, I become part of it.
> The morning mists, the clouds, the gathering waters,
> I become part of it.
> The wilderness, the dew drops, the pollen . . .
> I become part of it.

And in the context of other chants, there is always the conclusion that indeed, I *am* the universe. We are not separate, but are
one.

The Trees Stood Deep Rooted

Sam Gill

Some time ago, I went to hear Indian elders speak about public education programs for Indians. An old Papago man was among them. When his turn came he rose slowly, and with deliberation began to speak. His style was formal and bore an air of certainty, though for his meaning I had to await the English interpretation. He began with the creation of the Papago world, by telling how Earthmaker had given the Papago land its shape and character. He identified the features of that creation with the land on which he had always lived, as had his father and all his grandfathers before him. Pausing in his story he asked how many of us could locate our heritage so distinctly. Then he went on to tell the stories of Iitoi, who had acted as protector and teacher of the Papago under the name Elder Brother. He told of the way of life of the Papago people, a way of life they have always enjoyed.

It was perhaps fifteen minutes before he began to speak directly to the subject of education, but the old man had been talking about education all along. He was demonstrating to his audience a basic principle in education: knowledge has meaning and value only when placed within a particular view of the world. He was utilizing the way of his people by consulting the stories of the creation for the proper perspective from which to speak. There was power in his words and his statement was convincing.

As a Papago elder, this old man understood the power of relating the stories of creation. Papago culture abounds in songs and poems ritually uttered in order to provide sustenance and to maintain the Papago way of life. They are the gifts of the gods, not the works of man. Some are attributed to Iitoi, who used them to win battles against enemies. The Papago identify the ruins which are found throughout their southern Arizona desert homelands as the villages of these enemy peoples. The Papago people have songs and poems which they recognize as capable of affecting nearly every aspect of life. The feeling of the power the people find in these words is captured in the beautiful lines of one of their sacred poems:

> With my songs the evening spread echoing
> And the early dawn emerged with a good sound.
> The firm mountains stood echoing therewith
> And the trees stood deep rooted.[1]

The Papago are not unique among Native Americans in recognizing a kind of performative power in the language of their songs, prayers, and poems. In his eloquent address, "The Man Made of Words," N. Scott Momaday said, "Whenever the Indian ponders over the mystery of origin he shows a tendency to ascribe to the word a creative power all its own. The word is conceived of as an independent entity, superior even to the gods." According to Momaday, the Native American "locates the center of his being within the element of language . . . It is the dimension in which his existence is most fully accomplished. He does not create language but is himself created within it. In a real sense, his language is both the object and the instrument of his religious experience."[2]

The repetitive nature of Native American prayer and song has caused some observers to declare them to be merely the recitation of magical formulae. This is a view to be guarded against. The magic of the word lies mainly in the fact that it is capable of placing the speaker in communication with his own being and with the whole world. Native Americans do not restrict language to its capacity to describe the world: they recognize that, from one perspective, it is the world.

There seems to be a remarkable link between the stories of origin and the life-ways of Native Americans. It seems to me that this link is the language of ritual that constitutes Native American religious traditions. The events of creation are somehow paradigmatic, and the knowledge given in the creation stories permeates the life of the people.

To the Navajo, the world was not created by some powerful earth-making god, but through the creative powers of thought and the ritual language of song and prayer. Indeed, thought and speech were personified prior to the creation of the world. They arose from the medicine bundle out of which all creation was to come and they were said to embody the powers of the bundle. They took the form of a young man and woman of such radiance and beauty that they could scarcely be looked upon. While they were to be present in this form for only a brief time, it was told that they would always be near to the world, for theirs are the powers that sustain life. Their names are often rendered in English as Long Life Boy (thought) and Happiness Girl (speech), reflecting the Navajo view that their names are synonymous with the highest measure of life.

The Navajo ceremonial, Blessingway, demonstrates how the Navajo envision the way thought and speech became manifest in the creation of the world and in the sustenance of life. Of the twenty-five or thirty major ceremonial ways known to the Navajo, Blessingway is generally recognized as fundamental to all others; it is an indivisible body of story and ritual and a whole religious ideology. The Navajo name for Blessingway, *hozhooji*, reflects the pervasive ideology of creation that supports this ceremonial; a literal translation would be something like "the way to secure an environment of perfect beauty." The occasion for the first performance of a Blessingway ceremonial was the creation of the Navajo world; consequently, the ways of creation are the model for all versions and all performances of Blessingway. It is because Blessingway is the way of creation that it is called the backbone of Navajo religion and is recognized as the source and pattern of the Navajo way of life and thought.

In Blessingway stories, the first act in the creation of the world was the building of a ceremonial structure in which the ritual acts of creation could be performed. A version of Blessingway, therefore, is performed on the occasion of the construction of a new Navajo house. But Blessingway is also incorporated into all other ceremonials as the first-performed rite in order to "bless" the structure in which the rituals are to be carried out—whether the occasion be marriage, the need for rain, or difficult or imminent childbirth. In the story prototype, the humanlike beings who were performing the ritual began to construct the ceremonial house. Significantly, these humanlike beings who preceded the creation of the world are known by the Navajo word *yałti'ii*, which means "speaker." They readied the support poles and leaned them into position. As the support poles were readied and dropped into place, songs named them and described their placement and significance.

> Along below the east, Earth's pole I first lean into position
> As I plan for it it drops, as I speak to it it drops, now it
> listens to me
> As it drops, it yields to my wish as it drops.
> Long life drops, happiness drops into position *ni yo o.*[3]

And below the south, Mountain Woman's pole is leaned into position, followed by Water Woman's pole below the west and Corn Woman's pole below the north.

The house described in this ceremony provides the pattern for the common Navajo conical-style hogan. It serves the Navajo both as a place of residence and as a ceremonial structure. But the song identifies this simple four-pole substructure with the pillars that support the Navajo world. The foundations of the poles are located below the horizon in the four cardinal directions. Each pillar is named and given the power to sustain life through its identification with long life (thought) and happiness (speech). The commonplace Navajo home is at the same time the structure of the entire Navajo world.

This linkage between the most commonplace and the most ethereal, made through ritual language, is illustrated even more powerfully in the imagery, found in a Navajo Nightway prayer, of the house whose structure is composed of the life forms of the earth:

> House made of dawn
> House made of evening twilight,
> House made of dark cloud,
> House made of male rain,
> House made of dark mist,
> House made of female rain,
> House made of pollen,
> House made of grasshoppers.[4]

Each line focuses the mind on an image of the finite, material, domestic dwelling only to explode that image into fantastic dimensions by identifying its composition with unexpected building materials. A unity is achieved through the lines in their creation of an image of a living universe.

The ideology of Navajo sand painting also illustrates the way in which creation is fundamental in Navajo life. Paintings made of crushed vegetal materials or ground minerals and rocks are ritually constructed and used as part of several Navajo ceremonials. Hundreds of them have been recorded and their designs and meanings are remarkably complex. Without accounting for all the occasions in which sand paintings are used, the ritual acts performed upon them, or the various scholarly interpretations made of them, it can be shown that the efficacy of the sand painting act is derived from the events in the creation of the Navajo world.

In the Blessingway story it is told that after the "speakers" built the creation hogan, they entered it and proceeded with the creation. From the medicine bundle they took pieces of white shell, abalone, turquoise, and jet. With these materials they constructed representations on the floor of all forms of life that were to be in the Navajo world. These forms of life were personified as holy people having humanlike forms. The ritual construction was like a sand painting. Each holy being represented was given identity by its dress and placement relative to the others. The resulting design was not a physical model of Navajoland, but rather a map of the Navajo religious conception of the world.

The creation concluded with the intoning of a long prayer to these holy people, who represented the life forms of the earth. The prayer associated and identified them with the physical universe and consequently effected an indivisible unity between the ritual world of the ceremonial hogan of creation and the physical world of the Navajo, a unity of the spiritual and the material. A world had been made using only simple materials and the creative powers of thought and speech. Based on this model, Navajos continue to perform acts of creation through the power of ritual representation in sand paintings and the ritual language of song and prayer.

Following the creation, the life forms known as Dawn and Evening Twilight went on a tour to inspect the new world. Upon ascending mountaintops to gain a vantage point, they found the scene around them to be extremely beautiful. This state of pristine creation is articulated by the Navajo people in many ways and it stands as the inspiration and measure of Navajo life. Life is envisioned as a journey down a road. It is deemed a good life if the traveler is surrounded by an environment of beauty comparable to that of the newly created world. Most Navajo prayers conclude with a passage describing this good life:

> With beauty before me may I walk
> With beauty behind me may I walk
> With beauty above me may I walk
> With beauty below me may I walk
> With beauty all around me may I walk
> As one who is long life and happiness may I walk
> In beauty it is finished.
> In beauty it is finished.

Through the utterance of the prayer one is placed once again on the good road, so that it may be said with confidence and feeling, "In beauty it is finished."

There is yet another way to show how the events of creation are paradigmatic for Navajo life-ways. This centers on the importance in Navajo culture of the possession of a mountain-soil bundle. After the world was created, but before it was made suitable for habitation by Navajo people, a girl-child was created. Her parents are said to be the beautiful youth and maiden, Long Life Boy and Happiness Girl. This child had the remarkable ability to grow older through time, to reach old age and to repeat the cycle of life again and again. Because of this she was called Changing Woman. Changing Woman was given a medicine bundle containing objects and powers that created the world. The bundle was the source of her own existence, since her parents were the personification of the powers it held. Changing Woman was also taught the creation rituals. With the bundle and the Blessingway songs and prayers, Changing Woman at once holds and represents the powers of creation. She personifies the perfect beauty secured in the creation. She is identified with the newly created earth. She is the source and sustenance of all life. She is time. She is the mother of the Navajo people.

After her birth, Changing Woman used her creative powers to make the earth ready and suitable for the Navajo people. She created the plants and animals and cleared the world of the monsters who had come to threaten human life. Having made the earth a suitable place, she created the Navajo people. Her final act before departing from the Navajo world was to pass the knowledge of Blessingway on to the Navajo people. In doing so, she charged them with the responsibility to maintain the world in its state of perfect beauty by the use of Blessingway. She warned them that the Blessingway songs must never be forgotten, for Navajo life depends upon them.

Changing Woman is wholly benevolent and of such beauty that she is rarely represented in any visual form in Navajo ceremonials. But she did show the Navajo how to make a bundle modeled on hers; this was the origin of the mountain-soil bundle. It is made with soil ritually collected from the four mountains which stand in the quarters of the Navajo world. The soil from each mountain is wrapped in buckskin. Maintaining the directional orientations, these four bags are placed around stone representations of Long Life Boy and Happiness Girl. A buckskin is wrapped around all this and the bundle is secured.

The mountain-soil bundle is the nuclear symbol in Blessingway. Many Navajo families keep them as guides to the Navajo way of life and as sources of long life and happiness for the family. The bundle represents the powers of creation, the source of life, and the perfect beauty established by Blessingway.

Navajo people often refer to the relationship of their many ceremonial ways as the branches of a tree which extend over every occasion, bearing and protecting the Navajo way of life. They identify Blessingway as the trunk of this tree which supports all other ceremonial branches. This tree stands deep rooted in the creation of the world.

Certainly the Navajo are not representative of all Native American peoples, nor should they be considered typical. Even in the American Southwest, the Navajo are only one among many cultures which contain a wide variety of life-ways and religious practices. While there is tremendous diversity within Native American cultures, certain general observations may be drawn from the Navajo example.

We have seen that the Navajo find in the story of their origin a paradigm for their life-ways and religious practices. The story of origin serves at once as a prototype for a ceremonial performance and as a wellspring of philosophy and world view. A distinctive characteristic of this paradigm is the way in which it unifies the mythical and physical geographies, the ethereal and the commonplace, and the spiritual and the material. Frequently the best-known passages from Native American literature are ones that illustrate this correlation. Often these passages describe an association of four or six directions with colors, animals, birds, eras, and certain qualities or temperaments. Such well-defined patterns have suggested that Native Americans live in simple harmonious integration with the world around them.

In light of the Navajo views of creation, we should re-examine the common assumption that Native Americans are simple children of nature. I believe we will find this view erroneous. Native Americans have shown themselves to be masters of survival in an environment which has often been reluctant to nurture them, but their life-ways can scarcely be called the simple following of natural instincts. It seems almost the opposite. The Navajo, for example, look upon no living thing as simply natural, as a product of some impersonal system of natural law. Life is dependent upon holy people who were created in the beginning and who stand within all living things. Native Americans can hold a person-to-person relationship with their environment because in their view of creation the power of life, which is a person, is united with and identical to the physical living world. The nature of these personal relationships is not determined by the aspirations of ego as much as by patterns established in the stories, songs, and prayers which comprise their traditions.

There is also a tendency to assume that the paradigms which arise from the stories of creation represent the Native American view of the permanent status of their world. But these patterns of perfect beauty serve more as an objective and a measure in life than as a description of it. Underlying these global representations of the ideal are infinitely complex principles of relationship which determine and direct the life-ways. In the whole range of human action nothing is exempt. In other words, for Native Americans all human action is continually measured against traditional patterns so that the way life is experienced is dependent upon how it is lived.

It is through a tradition of formal ritual acts that Native Americans relate to the world, find the significance of life, and uphold the responsibility for maintaining order as it was given to the world in the beginning. From the Native American view, their ritual acts are creative acts of the highest order, since the object of their creation is the world itself. This may well be the greatest contrast between native and non-native American views of life. A prevalent non-native attitude is to associate ritual and tradition with lack of innovation and creativity. Twentieth-century art forms illustrate this attitude. It is an age of happenings, chance events, and shapeless forms designed to be independent of the past and tradition. It is an ego-centered culture seeking noble achievements and separate realities. This view is alien to Native Americans for they have accepted the charge of responsibility for performing the acts upon which life and reality depend.

The Native American view of human creativity is based in religion, which is inseparable from art. Such a stance is that of the creative genius of the Native American way of life to see the uncommon in the common, to find the ethereal in the mundane. Theirs is the way longed for by Artur Sammler, the protagonist in Saul Bellow's novel, *Mr. Sammler's Planet*, who said, "And what is 'common' about 'the common life'? What if some genius were to do with 'common life' what Einstein did with 'matter'? Finding its energetics, uncovering its radiance."[5] Deep rooted in creation, Native American traditions energize the common life.

The Roots of Peace

Iroquois

*T*here was a dark time before the great Confederacy, when all the nations of the Iroquois were at war with each other, and the people were weak, and the Mahicans and the Adirondacks attacked and slew them at will. Then the Peace Maker came out of the west.

He came in a canoe made of glittering white stone which was very heavy, yet it did not sink, but flew swiftly over the water of the lake. He was a messenger from the Master of Life, who had revealed to his grandmother in a dream that a child would be born to her virgin daughter, and he would bring the good news of peace and power to the people, and that his name would be the Peace Maker. And so he was born, and grew, and came out of the west in his white stone canoe.

The first people he met were hunters, and he gave them the message to take back to their chiefs that the fighting must cease. And he went to the house of a woman, who fed him, and he gave her the message of peace and power in its three parts: justice, health, and law. And he told her there would be a longhouse, and a council of nations, and unity between them. The woman was glad and embraced the message, and the Peace Maker made her the mother of nations.

Then he continued eastward and came to the house of the Man Who Eats Humans, who had just put a kettle on the fire with the meat of a human body in it. The Peace Maker climbed to the roof and looked down the smoke hole, and his face was reflected in the water of the kettle. The Man Who Eats Humans saw the reflected face and was amazed, for it was his own face, and yet it was wise and noble.

"I didn't know that I was like that," he said. "This is not the face of a man who eats human flesh. I see it is not like me to do that, and I shall not do it anymore," and he took the kettle outside and emptied it. Then the Peace Maker came to him and entered the house with him and gave him the message of peace and power, and the man embraced it. The Peace Maker went out and killed a deer and brought it back for their food. "It is the meat of deer that men must eat," he said, "and their antlers placed on men's heads shall be the sign of authority," and ever since that day the chiefs of the Five Nations have worn the horns of the deer.

The Peace Maker told the man that he was to be his messenger, and that he was to spread the news of the Great Peace and to convert the chiefs of the people. The hardest part of his task would be to convert a magician-chief of the Onondagas whose name was Atotarho, and who was so strong and cruel and evil that all men and animals feared him. His body was twisted seven times, and his hair was a mass of writhing snakes. For this reason, the Peace Maker gave the man who was to be his messenger the name of Hiawatha, He Who Combs, because he would prevail over Atotarho and comb the snakes from his hair.

The Peace Maker went among the people, and the first he converted to the Great Law were the Mohawks. Hiawatha went to begin his struggle with Atotarho, but Atotarho mocked him and put evil spells on all three of his daughters and on his wife, so that they died. Hiawatha was so overcome with grief that he could no longer bear the land of the Onondagas, and he went south and sat on the shore of the lake to mourn. He made strings of shells and sang songs of grief, begging for someone to come and make the shell strings into words of consolation. At last the Peace Maker came and listened, and he also made strings of shell and put them with Hiawatha's, and spoke words of consolation that are still used with the wampum strings by the people; and Hiawatha was freed from his grief.

After this, the Peace Maker and Hiawatha went to the Oneidas and the Cayugas and the Senecas and converted them all to the Great Law of Peace, and also all the chiefs of the Onondagas except Atotarho. The Peace Maker told him that he would be the chief of all the Council and the Keeper of the Council fire. Atotarho wished for this and for peace but asked where was the power. Then the Peace Maker called all the chiefs of all the nations, and they came together and were as one; and the Peace Maker said, "Here is power." Then Atotarho's mind was changed, and Hiawatha combed the snakes from his hair, and the seven twists came out of his body. The Peace Maker placed the antlers on his head and on the heads of the other chiefs and taught them the words of the law.

And he planted a pine tree, and called it the Tree of Peace; and four roots spread out, to the four directions. Then he uprooted the tree, and took all the weapons of war and threw them in the hole under the tree, and then he planted the tree again. In the topmost branches he placed an eagle, to watch and cry out if any evil approached the people.

> Roots have spread out from the Tree of the Great Peace, one to the north, one to the east, one to the south, and one to the west. These are the Great White Roots, and their nature is Peace and Strength.

If any man or any nation shall obey the laws of the Great Peace . . . they may trace the roots to their source . . . and they shall be welcomed to take shelter beneath the Tree . . .

Doing Your Thinking

Thomas Buckley

We look at each other, but we do not see each other anymore. Our perception of the world has withered away; what has remained is mere recognition.

—Viktor Shklovski

The Yurok Indians live where they always have, in north-western California along the lower reaches of the Klamath River and both above and below its mouth on the Pacific coast near the present-day Oregon border. Numbering somewhat more than three thousand individuals, the Yurok are but one of several groups indigenous to the area that are at once unique and of similar cultures. Much has changed in the region since 1850, when the Gold Rush brought a massive and devastating influx of non-Indians into the lower Klamath drainage. Yet cultural change cannot be simply dealt with as "acculturation." Aspects of European-American culture have been adopted, voluntarily and otherwise, by Indians. Usually, however, these have been taken up in a particular, culturally specific way, to be woven into the inclusive fabric of contemporary Indian life. This has been true in education as in every undertaking and expression. It is apparent, at a gross level, in the efforts of college-educated Yurok intellectuals towards expressing traditional esoteric values and practices in terms of Jungian and transpersonal psychologies, and in the presence of a young man among the neighboring Hupa who began his training as an Indian doctor, a "shaman," at about the same time that his exceptional facility in mathematics was hitting the local papers. Perhaps the more important and more interesting signs of the persistence of traditional educational ways in contemporary Indian culture are the far more subtle ones; the particular gesture or silence or phrase that a person uses, a specific sort of glance directed at a child or visitor, a certain shared understanding that is present in a group; reactions and recognitions and attitudes that are manifested at the extreme limits of description yet which are distinctly palpable.

I am interpreting aspects of the earlier stages in traditional Yurok education—up through what some Indians consider, today, the old equivalent of a high-school diploma; that is, through the acquisition of the necessary tools for higher education. After this point, although studies become increasingly complex and sophisticated, they still rest on the same theories, principles, and techniques. In discussing these aspects of an ever-changing cultural pattern I use the present tense. The "now" thus indicated is to be understood as representing only a part of present Yurok realities—very often and for a great many individuals a submerged, even unconscious part. Nevertheless, the aspects described as occurring in the present are indeed ongoing ones, shifting and entering into new relationships, taking on new guises, as ever throughout the Yurok's long history. Somehow, these things continue to make sense in a context of grammar schools and graduate professional schools, Christian churches and television, home economics and modern hard knocks.

The Universe, *ki wes'onah*, is energy. It moves against itself and creates waves and these waves go through everything. Each person receives and is part of the Universe in this way and, too, each is unique. The energy that enters a human fetus ten weeks after conception is the "life" of that being, its spirit, *wewoloček*. Occasionally this spirit is augmented through the favor and intervention of another human being or a spirit being. In any case, a person's spirit is unique, and to deny this unique life is against the law.

The Universe incorporates, manifests, is one with, the law, and everything occurring in the world is subject to this law while expressing it. To guide human beings there are many, many laws that interpret the (finally unspeakable) law and apply it to specific situations in the form of rules for conduct. Thus, there is a correct way to behave in every situation, a correct answer to every question; there is truth. Most simply, the truth is what has been known to work, every time. (Some people say that *skuyeni*, "good," really means "successful," *kimoleni*, "bad," "unsuccessful"; but both words have many meanings.)

These things being so, all education and training must move in respect of each unique person's individuality while at the same time insuring the success of the results as far as this is possible. That is, the interface between individual and society is specified by culturally defined truth expressed in a legal idiom.

The direct study of the law itself is advanced study, far beyond the scope of this introduction to "secondary education." One approaches it gradually through study of specific laws as these are encountered in attaining mastery of various sorts of specialized activities. One who has acquired knowledge of many laws and of the law is *teno·wok*, a "well-educated one," a member of an intellectual and spiritual elite minority. One must begin at the beginning and few go that far. To even begin to study the laws pertinent to one's chosen activities one must be able to perceive the "facts" involved in those activities. Thus, before one can learn to think, to define the facts inherent in situations, one must learn to perceive, to "see."

Thoughts-and-feelings, being parts of situations, of actions, are simply another sort of *thing*, to be seen and defined. Explanation is largely useless, because a person can only see for himself, and must be both encouraged and allowed to do so.

Thus, a young child is actively taught very little; it learns by watching and copying when it has enough interest. Most things are not explained, since people can only learn by and for themselves, learn to sort out facts, to draw conclusions about what works and what does not. For example, among certain families there is a great emphasis on table manners, a very definite etiquette. Nothing much is said: a young one watches and learns. When it is old enough to know right from wrong but still misbehaves at meals, its meal-basket is turned over, upside down. Hungry or not, no more food. It's up to the child to figure out what's wrong and to fix it, and thus to start learning about the laws concerning food and the respect for both resources and other human beings that underlie them.

To explain too much is to steal a person's opportunity to learn, and stealing is against the law.

Children grow when they grow, as they learn to see, learn to learn, according to their spirits. A famous man of the last century learned very early to observe the men of his village carefully. After a while, using his toy bow, he killed a bird with valuable feathers. He made a small wooden storage box, as he'd seen done, put the feathers in this, and showed the men. One of them made him a real hunting bow, a small and light one, and from then on he was free to join hunting parties, with all of the rights and responsibilities of a hunter. He had done what a man does and, in this respect, was treated like a man. He was six at the time.

This man was very unusual, leaping to the top of his class in high school, as it were, while most of his age-mates were still in first grade. Most children grow more gradually, spending most of their time with other children, older and younger, helping to take care of the younger ones and learning from the older ones. Usually there is a strong bond with a "grandmother" and, perhaps, a "grandfather"—sources of comfort in a hard world, people who may occasionally explain things. So it goes until puberty. Children are not handled roughly, not scolded severely unless there is really no alternative. They are, after all, only children.

At puberty things change. The person is an adult now and must act it, or find out about his shortcoming in an emphatic way. Fathers and mothers may occasionally teach their sons and daughters after this point, but it is deemed best to have an "uncle" or an "aunt" do it. Parents and grandparents are considered too emotionally involved to exercise the necessary rigor and objectivity. The leisurely and affectionate learning situation under "grandmothers" and "grandfathers" becomes a thing of the past, although these relatives often remain confidantes. "Uncles" and "aunts" are tougher.

Girls who have been watching their mothers and other older women make baskets and do other household tasks are now expected to do these things well themselves: no more play-baskets. They are helped, taught. A basket is started for the young woman and given to her to finish. The teacher watches, rips out a mistake and hands the workpiece back to be done again. There is very little credit given for "trying"; you can't eat soup out of a good try. If a girl has it in her to be a good basket maker (not all do) she will be one, spending the necessary effort to see how it's done; others are maybe meant to be doing something else.

Once, this was the pattern:

The young man leaves the women's house at puberty (or before if he's ready earlier) and moves into the "sweat house," the men's house. He no longer plays with the girls and younger children. His education is now largely up to him, and there is a great deal to learn.

Perhaps he decides that it's time to have a real bow, something a man should have—both a weapon and wealth. He finds a man, an "uncle," who is making himself a new bow (maybe not so coincidentally) and he follows this man around, seeing all that he possibly can: where the tree grows, what sort of tree it is, how it's split and what wood's selected, how this is scraped and fashioned, how the glue is made and the sinew applied. Very little is said. Having seen the whole process, he starts out alone. Maybe he shows his work to this teacher. The older man maybe asks, "Which end of the bow grew towards the top of the tree?" Or, maybe, he just takes the workpiece, scrapes it in the direction opposite to the young man's efforts, hands it back: let him figure it out. He either does or he doesn't, and if he doesn't, there's no point in trying to teach him more yet.

I asked an old man canoe maker on the River today if someone had taught him how to build the beautiful old boats. "Naw, nobody taught me nothing. I just watched and picked it up. That's how you used to learn everything; you watched and figured it out and went ahead and did it. Nobody taught you." This man makes fine redwood canoes of a very pure, traditional style. It takes many months, after the tree is felled, and it's a fairly complicated business.

Thoughtful people will tell you that two important things are learned through this process of watching and doing, beyond the actual skill that is acquired. First, one learns to see things as they are, to see the facts. Secondly, seeing the facts, one sees that one must start everything at its beginning and see each necessary step in an action, each constituent part of a situation,

Coyote Running, 1985 RICK BARTOW

clearly, leaving nothing out. If something is left out—like re-
membering which end of the bow was highest on the tree from
which it was cut—one has no choice but to go all the way back to
the beginning and start over. The same will be found to be true
in thinking through complex problems, in unraveling situations,
thinking being an action. One proceeds slowly, in small incre-
ments of progress.

If you do leave anything out, if you don't start at the very
beginning, or go back to it when you should, your efforts are
considered to be out of control. You have reason to doubt yourself and thus, by definition, you are afraid. The process of
education is seen as a process of gaining absolute self-
confidence, of vanquishing doubt, and thus fear. "Don't you be
fearing too much!" are the instructions from the *wo·gey*, the
Immortals. The only way to remove all doubt is to begin at the
beginning and follow through, on your own. (An old man to his
student who must do something difficult: "Can you do it? Yes or
no? Are you doubting? If you have doubts they'll just get in your
way when you get out there.")

To see the facts is to see the meaning of the facts: no distinction can be made; a fact *is* a meaning.

I was once sitting with another older man by our fire. When
we'd eaten he held up a piece of the wood that we'd gathered.
"What's this?" he asked. "Piece of firewood," I answered. He
looked sad, disgusted; put down the stick, silent. I thought
more. "It's wood, a piece of a tree." He brightened a shade:
"That's a little better. What's a tree?"

Later that evening, turning in, he offered a rare bit of direct
teaching: "When you can see each leaf as a separate thing, you
can see the tree; when you can see the tree, you can see the
spirit of the tree; when you can see the spirit of the tree you can
talk to it and maybe begin to learn something. Goodnight."

"There are two sides to everything. What a real Man does is

to define these and keep them in balance."

A tree is a tree, and it is each of its parts. This is the physical tree, a fact, and there is a spiritual tree as well, another fact, a potential object of perception. This spiritual tree has two sides, a side that can be seen, as the physical is seen, and another side, completely different, as spirit is completely different from matter. These two sides have two sides, too. To know a tree, to be in control of your relationship to trees, is to define all of these sides, these facts, and to act from the totality of this knowledge. But one can only begin at the beginning. Learning to see material things, then, is basic to learning to see nonmaterial things, simply because the former are more obvious, more easily perceivable facts; not because they are, finally, qualitatively different. Seeing the physical is the beginning of a continuum that includes more advanced orders of perception and of definition. One must explore the entire continuum in order to find its middle, the point of balance from which all truly controlled action springs, and at which all fear is rendered irrelevant.

Thoughts, as well as spiritual things, are facts that can be seen. Contemplating, "doing your thinking," *kočpoks, leponol owenkip*, means seeing mental and emotional facts and defining them. Speculation is something quite different, and native-educated Yurok are consistently careful, in conversation, to discriminate between what they've seen to be a fact, and what they think or surmise to be a possibility.

(A simple technique begins to teach one how to define thoughts as facts. One has, let's say, family trouble. He's confused and prey to uncontrolled emotion, to doubt. He should pick up a stone and see it. He shouldn't just look at it, but see it, as though no one were there behind his eyeholes. Now he looks at the situation at home in the same way, defines the facts as they are, as though no "he" were looking at them.)

Every person, again, has a unique spirit or potential. In northwestern California, as elsewhere, "be true to yourself" is, finally, the ultimate expressible law. The question becomes, then, *who* you are, all of you, each aspect clearly defined. Knowing this exactly, doubt vanishes and one becomes capable of living a balanced life. In the Yurok view, only a fool tries to be other than what he potentially is, and only a fool fails to take responsibility for his full potential. Fools are laughed at and usually come to a bad end.

Of course, who one is has two sides to it, a personal and a social one, and each of these has two sides, and so on. Education moves to both illuminate and to integrate these aspects and the succession of paired aspects inherent in each. Female puberty offers a succinct example.

Traditionally, when a girl menstruates for the first time she undertakes a ten-day period of seclusion and ritual activity, an amplified version of the routine she'll follow during each of her periods until menopause. One side of menstruation is seen to be polluting and dangerous, even poisonous. The other, balancing side is seen to be that of great, female energy, menstruation marking the time at which a woman is at the peak of her powers, closest to realizing her full potential. It is, thus, a very "pure" and "beautiful" thing, too.

Experienced women instruct the young woman in the laws pertaining to menstruation, socializing her as it were. At the same time, because a young woman is close to her potentials at this time, it is a time for her to "do her thinking," to engage in the most focused sorts of reflection and self-definition. Meditation and contemplation are thus strongly urged by her teachers and supported by various routines and rituals. For example, after a certain period of ritual austerity, the new woman is given an abalone shell to see. (The abalone is identified as both female and as sun- or spirit-like.) In the polished whorls and patterns she sees her own life's trail, her direction, unique and individual.

Again, scratching-sticks are used, it being against the law for a woman to touch her own body while menstruating. The standard anthropological explanation of this practice, widespread in native North America, is that one is so highly charged with pollution that, touching oneself, one poisons oneself. The analysis of Yurok women has a more satisfying logic: one makes scratching and touching difficult, keeping it conscious and intentional, they say, so that a woman is encouraged to perceive all of her body exactly as it is, every itch included. Coming to know the body more intimately during this time of heightened access to the truth, the facts, one comes to know oneself more intimately.

Another side of who one is is, of course, who one is not. As for the menstruating woman the body is utilized as an organ of perception richly implicated in a process of contemplation, so a young man's body may be used in "doing his thinking" about who he is and who he is not.

A Yurok teacher:

"My nephew was so angry! So mad at the world. I told him, 'Do like they used to do in the old days. You're mad, you think you're pretty tough? Well, go down to the beach in the high surf, you'll find out. You go fight with the waves for a while, kick them and beat them and try to knock them down. Your Father, the ocean, will show you something. Now when you've had enough, when you can't stand up any more, go lie on the beach, that's your Mother. Kick her and pound her and yell at her too. She'll forgive you. When you're done in, just lie still and cry. She'll tell you something you need to know.' "

Body and mind, then, are both mobilized in "doing one's

thinking," in defining facts. To seek perception with the body is to "train," and the object of "training" is to "make medicine," to experience immediately a direct perception of a certain order of facts which serve to confirm one's potentials, one's particular slice of the Universe's energies, one's areas of specialization in life. "Making medicine" equates with what have been called "vision" or "power quests."

In training and in making medicine, exoteric techniques and esoteric experience are interdependent, balanced. To an extent, this is true in all situations and actions: "In the old days everything we did was a prayer. We are the praying people, that's who we are." However, training and medicine making comprise specific educational means, particular categories of action. Because training for medicine making always demands stringent austerity—including continence—young men and women are urged to start out as early as they can, before they get too interested in sex. Most training is an individual matter, involving student and teacher only, although there was once a ceremonial society, a kind of study-club of "helpers" through which young men and women trained, under a priest, towards participation in the Jump Dance, a major religous event.

Most available descriptions of training and of medicine making and of their equivalents in other Indian cultures have stressed the "supernatural" aspects of such undertakings. These are, indeed, present—but so are other, purely pragmatic elements. Of particular interest here is the role of perception, of "defining the facts," in these undertakings. An old man told me about training for "making ocean medicine" by swimming far out into the sea during a storm on a winter's night:

"I was afraid of the ocean. I was born that way I guess. When I was about eleven, my uncle made me go sit on a big drift-log that stuck in the beach and hung far out over the surf. I wanted to come in right away, but he made me stay. I sat there all night. Slowly, I began to see the water, to see what the important things about it were. And when I saw this, I started to see the facts about my fear of it. After I came in, for two or three years, I studied the water, and I studied my fear, and I swam a great deal. I defined all of these things for myself. Finally, I was ready to make my medicine. I didn't try to do it; I just did it. Actually, I'd made my medicine while I was training, before I made the swim. If I hadn't, my uncle wouldn't have let me do it. The swim itself, going out to that rock at night, swimming around it three times, slapping it—that wasn't the medicine. It was just demonstrating it, a way of making it public, and of recognizing what I'd become; showing that I could do it any time, on purpose. I was in control of my fear and of the sea before I started. If I hadn't been, I would have drowned, and people would have laughed at me for thinking that I was a Man."

In Yurok, one doesn't speak of "power." One speaks only of "doing," and of "control." Power, as this man's ocean-power, is there, always. But there is no specific Yurok word for it because it is irrelevant without an individual's ability to control it, to *do* with it.

An important part of doing is, then, "doing your thinking," perceiving non-material aspects of situations as objects, facts which may be defined and, hence, controlled. There is truth, and that truth is factual, independent of personal desire; one thus learns, with the teacher's help, to discriminate between "hallucination"—a fantasy, the product of wishful thinking— and "vision," and objective seeing of spiritual facts manifested in the physical.

All learning is experiential. It follows clearly from the Yurok theory of individuality that knowledge is an object of perceptual experience, and only an individual is capable of experiencing for himself. Here, we find what seems extreme subjectivity being interpreted as pure objectivity. What is thought by a person and what is experienced by him as true are two different things and, in the Yurok view, the difference is immediately obvious to the skilled observer, the teacher who has himself experienced the truth at hand. If this teacher does not see for himself the evidence of his student's having experienced, seen, the facts of a matter, the student's solution to the problem at hand is not accepted by the teacher. "Belief," obviously, has no part in the system; an individual either knows the facts, or he is ignorant of them.

The Yurok do, however, have a culture. This is to say that there exist myriad ways of directing the individual towards certain experiences, perceptions of specified truths or facts. There is, after all, a correct way to build a canoe, to make a bow, to become brave, to know the world. Individuals must, in a sense, reinvent the culture for themselves; but they must reinvent the culture that has been reinvented by individuals before them, the culture that will work because it is based in a finite series of facts.

Among the modes of directing experience towards specified knowledge is, as in most cultures, verbal instruction. Among the Yurok, all such discourse must start and end with the individual who wishes to learn. It is the student who defines, through "doing his thinking," what is worth knowing. It is the student who asks the questions, not the teacher, and if no questions are asked, no possible clues to answers are offered. When the questions stop, so does education.

Questions may be answered in a variety of ways, none of which seem direct. Perhaps the most common answering device, once, was the exhortatory recitation of myths, historical narratives, and set prayers in which, the teacher felt, were embedded the facts necessary for the student's correct approach to the problem at hand, there for him to see if he chose to and was capable of it. Even answers to questions on simple techniques are often fielded in this apparently obscure way. "I can't learn *for* you, can I?" asks a teacher. Thus, rare attempts at giving straight instructions usually come out as relatively oblique suggestions: "Well, in the old days, if a fella wanted to do that, maybe he'd get up before dawn and . . . ."

An interesting variation on the use of narratives and formulas in answering questions is the use of personal songs as *koan*-like problems, sometimes posed by a teacher or counselor in answer to the question of a student or client, and sometimes proposed by the student to his teacher in answer to his own question after he'd contemplated further. A modern example, made in English:

> The fawn lies quiet in the grass
> The lily does not sing[1]

(We note, in this example, the tendency to "think in pairs"; it is understood that the adequate "answer" reveals their "balance.")

Having been given such a song by a teacher it is up to the student to show the teacher that he knows what it means; that he is capable of perceiving, of experiencing the facts referred to. Here, the comparison with Zen *koan* rests on more than form or relative obscurity.

While these songs are of great interest, their use has apparently never been particularly common. Far more common, along with the recitation of myths and other narratives, is the simple technique of returning the question to the student, from a different perspective and, usually, at a higher level.

Back to the bow. If a young man wants to learn, he asks his teacher why he uses wood from the side of the tree that he does. "Use wood from the side that the moon never shines on," the teacher might answer, or "from the side that's away from the water," adding, in either case, "why's that?" (There are two sides, of course, to a correct answer in this case, a physical and a spiritual one.) The young man goes off and "does his homework," as people put it nowadays. When he's answered, proven that he's seen, defined the facts of the matter, he may ask another question and gets it also thrown back at him.

Each step is marked by a clear perception of what is construed to be purely objective, facts as concrete as the manifest world. Teachers tend to be extremely demanding in precisely this regard, and the educational process is accompanied by a good deal of frustration, anxiety, and impatience on the student's part. As Raymond White pointed out to be the case among the Luiseño, far to the south of the Yurok, "No one is permitted information beyond his *demonstrated* capabilities."[2] The only acceptable demonstration is that of having experienced the truth of the matter. "I think that probably . . ." will not suffice. Until the student comes up with something better, *sees* something through and through, he simply hasn't "done his thinking"; having experienced nothing for himself, he has done nothing at all.

From such experience, in the native theory, come self-confidence and freedom from doubt as surely as these things come from a ritual swim in the stormy ocean at night.

As the Yurok *teno·wok* has learned to see two sides to everything while seeing the whole as well, so we must see two sides to the Yurok mode of education. The collective, mystical, "supernatural" and "power-oriented" aspects of indigenous American educational systems have become familiar and popular fare during the past two decades. I have stressed a second side, an objective, pragmatic, and individualistic one that reveals a consistent and satisfying logic. It is but one of two sides that have always been intrinsically interrelated, blended into a single cultural mode that might be characterized as pragmatic mysticism.

"To make deer-hunting medicine, first you learn to see the bush that's in front of you, then the bush behind that bush, then the deer behind the bush behind the bush that's in front of you, then the spirit of that deer. Now you can call the deer, his spirit, and he'll walk up to you. The people with the strongest medicine learn to fly out, their spirits, and find the deer that way."

Gluskabe and
the Four Wishes

Abenaki: Retold by Joseph Bruchac

Now that Gluskabe had done so many things to make the world a better place for his children and his children's children, he decided it was time for him to rest. He and Grandmother Woodchuck went down to the big water. Gluskabe and his Grandmother climbed into his stone canoe and sailed away to an island. Some say that island is in the great lake the people call Petonbowk, others say that Gluskabe went far to the east, beyond the coast of Maine. They say that the fog which rises out there is actually the smoke from Gluskabe's pipe. But wherever it is that Gluskabe and Grandmother Woodchuck went to, it is said that for a time Gluskabe let it be known to the world that anyone who came to him would be granted one wish.

Once there were four Abenaki men who decided to make the journey to visit Gluskabe. One of them was a man who had almost no possessions. His wish was that Gluskabe would make it so that he owned many fine things. The second man was a man who was very vain. He was already quite tall, but he wore his hair piled up high on his head and stuffed moss in his moccasins so that he would be even greater in height. His wish was to be taller than all men. A third man was very afraid of dying. His wish was that he would live longer than any man. The fourth man was a man who spent much time hunting to provide food for his family and his village. But he was not a very good hunter, even though he tried very hard. His wish was that he would become a good enough hunter to always give his people enough to eat.

The four of them set out in a canoe to find the island of Gluskabe. Their trip was not an easy one. The currents were strong and they had to paddle hard against them. The man who owned nothing knew a song to calm the waters and when he sang it the currents ceased and they were able to go on their way. Now a wind began to blow very hard, pushing them back towards shore. But the second man took out some tobacco and offered it to the wind and it became calm enough for them to continue on their way. Soon great whales began to come up near the boat and it seemed as if they would tip the boat over. But the man who was afraid of dying had brought with him a small stone figure shaped like a whale. He dropped it into the water as an offering and the whales dove beneath the surface and were gone. Now the island of Gluskabe was very close, but they could not see it because a fog came up over the ocean and covered everything. The fourth man, who wanted to be a good hunter, took out his pipe and began to smoke it, making an offering of his smoke so that Gluskabe would stop smoking his own pipe and let the fog lift. Soon the fog rolled away and they saw the Island of Gluskabe was there before them.

They left their boat on the shore and made their way to the place where Gluskabe sat.

"Kuai!" Gluskabe said. "You have had to work hard to come here to see me. You have earned the right to each make one wish."

"I wish to own many fine possessions," said the first man.

"My wish is to be taller than any other man," said the second.

"I want to live longer than any man," said the third.

"My desire is not so much for myself," said the fourth man. "I want to be a good enough hunter to provide food for my family and my people."

Gluskabe looked at the fourth man and smiled. Then he took out four pouches and gave one to each of them. "In these you will find what you want. But do not open them before you get home and in your own lodge."

The men all agreed and went back to their canoe. They crossed the waters and reached the land. Then each of them started on his own way home. The first man, who wanted many possessions, took the canoe which had belonged to the one who wanted to live longer than any man.

"Take this to go home in," said the man who wanted to live long. "I am going to live forever, so it will be easy for me to get another canoe."

As the man who wanted many possessions paddled along he thought about all that he would have. He would have fine clothing of buckskin, he would have ornaments made of shells and bright stones, he would have stone axes and finely made weapons, he would have a beautiful lodge to live in. As he thought of all the things he would have he grew more and more anxious to see them. Finally, he could wait no longer.

"It will not hurt anything if I just peek inside this pouch," he said. Then he opened it just a crack to look inside. As soon as he did so all kinds of things began to pour out of the pouch. Moccasins and shirts, necklaces and wampum belts, axes and spears and bows and arrows. The man tried to close the pouch but he could not do so. The things came pouring out and filled the canoe, covering the man. They were so heavy that the canoe sank and the man, tangled in all his possessions, sank with them and drowned.

The second man, who wanted to be taller than all others, had walked along for only a short time before he, too, became curious. He stopped on top of a high ridge and took out the pouch. "How can this make me taller?" he said. "Perhaps there is some kind of magic ointment in here that I can rub on myself to make me grow. There would be nothing wrong with trying out just a little of it before I get home." Then he opened the pouch. As soon as he did so he was transformed into a pine, the tallest of the trees. To this day the pines stand taller than all others, growing on the high ridges, and in the wind you may hear them whispering, bragging about their height, taller than all men.

The third man, too, did not go far before he became curious. "If I am going to live forever," he said, "then nothing will be able to hurt me. Thus there is no reason why I should not open this pouch." He opened it up. As soon as he did so he turned into a great boulder, one which would stand unchanged for thousands of seasons, longer than the life of any man.

The fourth man, though, did not think of himself as he travelled home. He had further to go than the others, but he did not stop. "Soon," he said to himself, "I will be able to feed my people." He went straight to his lodge and when he got inside he opened the pouch. But there was nothing inside it. Yet as he sat there, holding the open pouch, there came into his mind a great understanding. He realized the ways he must proceed to hunt animals. He began to understand how to prepare himself for a hunt and how to show the animals respect so that they would always allow him to hunt. It seemed he could hear someone speaking to him, more than one person. Then he realized what he was hearing. He was hearing the voices of the animals themselves, telling him about their ways. From that day on he was the best hunter among the people. He never took more game than was needed, yet he always provided enough to feed his people. His was truly the best of the gifts given by Gluskabe.

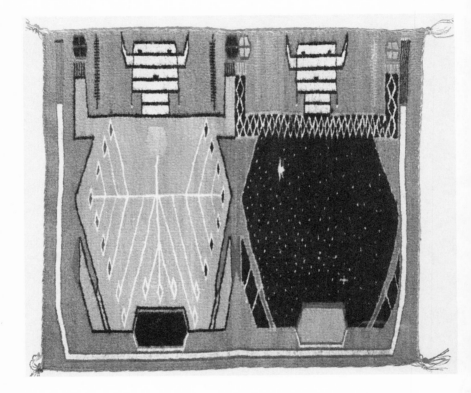

Mother Earth and Father Sky, 1968 BETTY BIA

The Demands of Harmony

Barre Toelken

*L*iterary critics are fond of observing that each work of great literature treats at least one of three relationships: Man and other Men, Man and Nature, Man and God. And students are fond of asking, "What else *is* there to talk about, after all?" While the students are accurate in pointing out the obviousness of these sets, we may still use them profitably as coordinates of our own cultural way of abstracting things: we recognize these as separate kinds of relationships which will bear scrutiny, which will allow for recognition and response.

These categories are especially helpful, I think, in providing us with a temporary "place to stand" when we inquire into the nature of important relationships in other cultures. The concept of *relation* itself is of course very broad until it is focused by some particularized inquiry. In the case of the Navajo, what relationships are considered central in these arenas of Man and Man, Man and Nature, Man and God? The answers—even those which can be brought forth in so superficial an essay—are illuminating. Of course, I suspect the matriarchal Navajo might like first of all to rephrase the sets as: Woman to Woman, Woman to Nature, and Woman to Holy Spirits. But in practice they would be sexually more fair; at the same time, they would reveal a basic set of Navajo relationships: The People, The People's relations among themselves; The People and Nature; The People and the Holy People. In this hypothetical renaming of the categories we begin to see our own familiar designations crumble, but in the erosion itself we begin to see more clearly those details of culture-specific attitude which characterize a people's way of looking at the world and which often set them sharply apart from other peoples—in spite of the well-intentioned liberal view that after all "we are all alike under the skin." The tripartite framework of these relationships, that favorite device of Western logic and conversation, will also begin to disappear; for the time being, however, precisely because it is a meaningful frame for our own perceptions, we may as well keep it artificially patched together.

My first direct experience with the formalities of Navajo interpersonal relations came in the mid-1950s when I had to cope with learning Navajo names. I found out through making a number of mistakes that each person had several names, some more important than others. First of all, each person had a "war name," which was known only to close members of the immediate family and was not to be divulged to others. This was thought of as a person's real name, but it was never used in direct address, nor was it used among friends in reference to the person in his absence. For purposes of conversation about others, each person had what I would call a "descriptive name" which called attention to some feature of his past history, or his looks, or his situation in life, or his geographical region. The old man who eventually adopted me was called by other Navajos (but never to his face) Little Wagon. In the Navajo, Wagon translates literally "a piece of wood rolling, wheel-like," and the adjective "little," placed after the noun, can mean small or it can mean offspring of. I was never able to determine if this old man was the son of someone called Wagon, but I could see that he was rather small in stature, and I had heard reference to the fact that when wagons first became available in that area, he had bought one of the smaller models. I found it was not an uncommon custom for Navajos to apply descriptive names to people that might have a number of possible meanings. Such names could be humorous as well as serious delineations; names ranged from Son of the Late Singer Blind in One Eye, to names like Old Man by Chinle Wash Where the Goats Sleep on the Rocks, to a name for a local woman of prodigious sexual appetites: Woman Whose Genitals Are Always Hungry. These names were used only by others, and were never used in direct address to the persons so described.

For direct conversation to take place in Navajo, some kind of relationship must be established which becomes the basis for personal terms used. One refers to his mother as *shima*, literally "my mother," and to all other people directly addressed the speaker must use the formula *shi-X*. Thus one can refer to another as "my friend," "my maternal grandfather," "my little mother" (the word usually employed for maternal aunt), "my older sister," "my granddaughter," "my close companion" (*shil-na'ash*, literally "my one who travels with me").

This is certainly as much a matter of Navajo grammar as it is custom, but in daily practice it insures that conversations seldom take place unless there is first some kind of amiable relationship established. These relationships are almost invariably matters of family alignment or of function, and they testify to the basic assumption of the Navajo that conversation itself is an enactment of relationships existing between people. In other words, conversation is not seen simply as a matter of passing information objectively between total strangers, but it is seen as a form of close relational intercourse in and of itself.

In addition to a "war name," a "descriptive name" and constantly shifting terms of personal address, most Navajos have an "Anglo" name which relates them to the non-Navajo world. Someone whose father was called "John" by the Anglos becomes John Begay (John's son); the schoolteacher or government employee takes Begay to be the "last name" and sets it down so; since there are twenty or so John Begays in the vicinity each is awarded, gratis, a middle initial (John A. Begay, John B. Begay and so on) or number (John Six Begay). Far from protesting, the Navajos find this a useful custom, for their formal relations with the Anglos require them to have a name; they cannot say their war name, usually will not say their descriptive name, and have no reason to use a relational appellation. Of course the local whites think that the Begays and Bennallys (grandson of) are huge families.

The family relationship for a Navajo is more extensive than the recognition of immediate relationships with parents and siblings. First, each Navajo belongs to two clans; primarily, he or she belongs to the mother's clan, but one is described as being born "for" the father's clan. His relationships with anyone in the clan of his mother are viewed as if they are the relationships of an immediate family: a young man from the Bitter Water clan, for example, cannot marry—or for that matter engage in any amorous actions—with a young woman of that same clan, even if they live miles apart, have never seen each other before, and even if their actual genetic ties are distant. At government boarding schools, it is common for young people attending a dance to ask a stranger initially what clan he or she belongs to before engaging in a public embrace on the dance floor which would be interpretable as incest. Family relationships are thus ritualized, and each Navajo's attention to these details helps to underscore and maintain the deep personal involvement with relational matters in everyday life which may extend far beyond the individual; these responsibilities are thought of not simply as onerous obligations, but as positive aspects of belonging to a large and strong group. On the reservation, this set of relationships has much to do with the maintenance of personal stability.

One of the harshest things I ever heard said of another person while I lived among the Navajos was "he acts like he doesn't have a family." This accusation, heard a number of times, seemed to be the epitome of personal degradation and lack of responsibility. For a person to act as if he had only himself or herself to care for or be concerned about was tantamount to an admission of interest in, or practice of, witchcraft. This brief essay does not allow an excursion into that fascinating and frightening subject, but it should be at least mentioned here as an adjunct to the topic. If close family and clan relationships are basic to a sense of normality in life, if one's reciprocal relationships with others are thought of as a basic premise on which stability stands, then the lack of those relationships is seen as essentially evil. Those who are thought to be witches are usually characterized by selfishness, acquisitiveness, lack of concern for other family members and for clan relationships. This would seem to be another vivid example of the Navajo insistence on one's attention to the details of relation with other People. It is interesting to note in this regard that many Navajos do not consider the same relationship a necessity with non-Navajos. For example, one friend of mine who makes mocassins in the traditional way uses only "sacred deerskin" when he makes mocassins for his family (sacred deerskin is obtained by a special manner of hunting, a special ritual skinning of the deer, and a ritual disposal of the carcass); on the other hand, he feels that mocassins made for sale to tourists do not need to be made of sacred deerskin because "whites don't care about that kind of thing." In this we see a distinct difference from the ordinances carried out by various of the Pueblo tribes for the benefit of all of mankind. The Navajo concern for relationship tends to be directed inward among The People themselves, rather than outward towards the whole world. Nonetheless, as I found out in my own experience there, the Navajos find it rather easy to accept an outsider who is willing to move in with them and live life on their terms. So it is not that they do not care about other people, but that one must move into and within their system for the relationship to "work."

An example of this is the customary way of receiving visitors at a Navajo hogan. If the members of the family are outside, they all run in and shut the door; and each takes his right place in the circle and starts doing whatever is appropriate there. Everyone is occupied. The visitors sit outside for a while, perhaps ten or fifteen minutes, as if to say "we're here"; then one of them knocks, or pushes on the door and if it opens he goes in. Someone inside may call out a Navajo word that means "Straight ahead" or "Come in," and the guest enters and makes the circle sunwise, from left to right, shaking hands quietly with each person. Nowadays there is a good deal of variation, but the old custom was that the women sat on the south—the first person to the left of the door, which is on the east, being the mother or owner of the hogan. This is because the south, represented by the color green of the turquoise, stands for fertility and the female generative power. So the first person to be greeted is the owner, and then the other women, and then the men who generally are on the west. The other visitors come in, one or two at a time, and shake hands around the circle, and each one squats or sits down without talking, or with very few words. It is a very delicate way of sharing the living space. The coming together is quiet and low-key, not joyous or noisy; there is a lot of smiling but not much eye-contact. It may be half an hour before a conversation begins to take place, but somehow in the middle of all this a communication is established about the visitors' needs and whether they will stay to eat or sleep. The guests are absorbed into the family circle without disturbing or interrupting it, in the gentlest way possible.

In discussing Navajo attitudes toward relationships with what Westerners call Nature, we find rapidly that the category is inadequate. First of all, Navajos tend to group and categorize things in Nature according to various kinds of ritual usage as well as in terms of shape and movement. For this reason, the word Nature is not as usable for us here as are some clear subdivisions. For example, there is a large frame of reference among the Navajo for what might be called sacred geography and geology. There are the four sacred mountains which relate to the cardinal directions; Navajos feel most stable and secure when they are living within the precincts suggested by these ritual points. Indeed, many Navajo families of my acquaintance carry along with them in their suitcase of ritual materials and items four bags of soil wrapped in sacred deerskin, one from the top of each sacred mountain. In this way each family has its own particular physical reference point to those geographical places which bound the Navajo world. One could also mention the volcanic plug called Shiprock which some Navajos believe represents the spot where mankind first entered into this present world. As well, there are many other areas of geologic importance which may be referred to as mythic monuments for the Navajos. Their shape, their form, their structure, their color, all lead to certain details in Navajo mythology in such a specific way that the places themselves are not seen primarily as objects or results of natural phenomena but holy spots bearing continual testimony to the validity of Navajo myth, ritual, and religion.

Indeed, the terrain of the Navajo world is actually viewed as the latest scene in the development of mankind and as such is directly related to those other worlds inside this one through which people and animals passed in order to come here. To put it more simply, this world is a visual confirmation of the previous world, seen in ritual terms, and it physically relates us to the mythic past, not to geological "fact."

Another aspect of Nature as it is registered by the Navajos could be called sacred astronomy. Again, rather than the sky being seen as the arena of free flowing natural phenomena, it is referred to as a compendium of patterns which relate directly to mythic and ritual events. A good number of star constellations appear in the sand paintings which are made to cure people of various sicknesses, and several of the more complex string figures done as "games" during the winter are representations of ritually important constellations.

Relationships with animals are in many ways central to Navajo thought, but the relationships differ according to whether the animal is wild or domesticated. For example, relationships with the coyote, the bear, and the spider are all ritualized and heavily ordered by myths and tales. One is not supposed to mention the word for bear, especially while traveling alone in the mountains or forest, for surely it will bring forth a bear on the spot. Coyote tales are not told except in the wintertime. String figures are to be done only in the wintertime, otherwise Spider Woman will become annoyed and will perhaps capture young people in her snare. Whatever one makes of these beliefs, it is clear that they represent among other things a subordination of human activity, even in areas such as storytelling and game playing, to religious assumptions about the proprieties of actions during certain times of the year. These concepts bear witness to the fact that nature is not seen as something outside the people which must be related to in any kind of practical approach to survival within it, but, rather, it represents a ritual circumstance in which man moves as carefully as in any other ritual occurrence. The principal parts are always related to each other.

The Navajo's connection with sheep, although it is historically quite recent, is perhaps their best known feature to outsiders. How the Navajos turned from nomadic hunters and raiders into such avid herders of sheep may never fully be appreciated; certainly it is due in large part to the "encouragement" of the U.S. Government, but the sheep have assumed such an important position in Navajo life that there must be other philosophical and cultural reasons beyond the economic and political dilemmas of the 1860s. The sheep do not show up prominently in any particular ritual that I know of, but they have become basic to the Navajo concept of relationship between people and fertility of the land. The woman of any family, since she is not only the matriarch but because it is from women that fertility proceeds, is usually the owner of the family's flocks. Thus women and sheep are central images in today's Navajo concept of stability and process in Nature. If something goes wrong with the grass or the rainfall, if sheep are getting sick, it is blamed on something unnatural and infertile in the world (in most conversations I heard, the blame was usually laid on the proximity of white people or attributed to intrusions of the U.S. Government). So central are sheep to the Navajos' relationship with the occurrences of everyday life that when anthropologist John Adair and filmmaker Sol Worth wanted to do some research on Navajo filmmaking, they were asked by a local medicine man if the filming would hurt the sheep. When they replied in the negative, they were asked if the filming would *help* the sheep. When they were forced to admit that filmmaking would not help the sheep either, they were asked by singer Sam Yazzie, "Then why make films?" When I showed my adopted Navajo father a news photo of the Empire State Building, his first question was, "How many sheep will it hold?" I first took his query to be related to the perception of space, then I assumed it was sarcastic in nature, and finally I realized that what it meant was "what is that thing good for, in terms of anything that relates to my way of life?"—obviously a complex cultural question to ask, and askable only in terms of those relationships which the asker recognized as valid.

Other ritual categories cause items from different parts of nature (as the Western eye would see them) to be grouped together; for example, in one category of medicine we will see stone arrowheads, corn pollen, lizards, and lightning, all in the same category because they are all used medicinally in a particular curing ritual. Even though these items come from "different" parts of nature, and would therefore be discussed under different headings by a scientific-minded person in Western culture, a Navajo would assert that just as naturally they go in the *same* category because they are ritually connected. It is for reasons like this that the consideration of the relationship between "Man and Nature" must be re-examined, at least from the Navajo point of view. As one sees these various natural phenomena appearing in Navajo conversation and custom, one realizes that they actually fall into our third category, relationships that exist between People and the Sacred; indeed, there seems to be no Navajo basis for separating these sets of relationships from each other to begin with. If it has been worthwhile for me to do so here, it is primarily because it has led to a demonstration of the culture-specific basis for the category itself.

The *yei* are hard to define using English words. They are very much in the nature of *kachinas*, the sacred embodiments of cosmic forces made manifest in physical form when humans dedicated to the task assume their clothing and song for the purpose of ritual. The *yei* whose figures appear on the floor of a hogan in the complex sand paintings used for healing are no less real than the *yei* whose figures appear in the dances using a human being for locomotion. Dealing with the *yei*, in other words, is not a matter of make-believe; rather, it is an attempt to align The People with the actual forces which surround them by making manifest the close relationship, practically the identity, between the two spheres of interest. During a healing ritual, for example, the patient is caused to walk around on the delicate sand painting of the *yei*, and through ritual is closely identified with each one and with the world of reality they live in. Psychologically, the patient is taken from his own context, the interior of his own hogan usually, and is described as standing on patterns, ledges, floating through the air with jewels, and other kinds of suggestive actions which bring the person simultaneously into two dimensions: this world and the "other world" interpenetrate and reciprocate at the point of the ritual. The patient is made whole, it is hoped, partly by the application of medicines, and partly by the forced realization of a deeper relationship between the person and sacred forces than might be evident in everyday life.

On another level, relationships play an equally important role in healing ceremonies (perhaps it is well to mention in passing that *all* Navajo ceremonies have to do with healing). In addition to the ritual itself, which relates the patient to the *yei*, there is the gathering of relatives and friends who share in the healing ceremony and who usually are administered the same medicines taken by the patient. It is as if one's relations are potentially ill, or perhaps likely to become ill, if one among them is sick. In any case, the participants in the healing ceremony are not present in the role of onlookers, but as actively involved components of the ceremony: they may sing and chant along with the singer when requested to do so, they spend a good deal of time concentrating on the health of the patient (especially the restoring of stability and health to particular affected parts of his or her body), and in sharing the medicine with the patient they proclaim a close relational tie both with his sickness and his cure.

It would be possible, on the basis of such sketchy evidence, to make one of those grand, romantic summations showing that for the Navajos all parts of nature are related; animals, plants, and people exist as brothers and sisters in a stable world; mankind has close relatives in the other world with whom he may share his sicknesses and woes and from whom he may expect succor. But I think the evidence does not allow us to entertain such dreamy conclusions. It is indeed true that the Navajo home life, in the immediate family, is extremely warm and supportive. There, relationships are at their most informal and deep interactions are expressed with an emotional power that would surprise most outsiders. However, beyond the immediate family, it seems to be that the relational ideas are applied as ritual metaphors, not as loving extensions of the family circle. At least I have never heard a Navajo speak of being a brother to his sheep, a sister to the *yei*, a cousin of the bear. Rather, the relationships seem to be part of the tremendously complex system of ritual enactments the aim of which is to maintain stability in a world which inclines toward instability. Most of the serious relationships are invoked at times of ritual enactments, when the illness of a patient is central to everyone's concern. It is an extension of the belief that one can always call upon relatives to help out in a dilemma, and it is based on the assumption that relatives must help if they are indeed part of the system. But it is ritual enactment and mythic system and religious belief which compel the relationships to work beyond the immediate family. These are obligations a Navajo feels as he moves through a world which is ordered more by ritual order and by its opposite—the disorder of sickness—than by broad natural forces.

The system is impressive to us because of its assumption that all phenomena are integrated and interdependent, not extractable and abstractable from each other. Similarly, individuals are integrated and interdependent with other individuals in the culture, and are not encouraged or expected to be totally independent agents. While individuality is allowed, and expected, it is always tailored to the larger ritual expectations of the group. Rather than viewing the Navajos as some kind of primitive desert "flower children," moving easily through a harmonious world because of their recognition of the relationship among all things in nature, we need to recognize that the Navajos are participants in an extremely rigorous philosophical and ritual system which places demands on individuals that most non-Navajos would find it difficult to cope with.

One can only begin to imagine the terrible impact on the Navajo and on other tribes of a system in which realities are always separable, discussable, abstractable; in which people are expected to be in competition with each other in order to be thought of as healthy individuals; in which animals are objects of scrutiny or quarries in the hunt rather than ritual counterparts in a complex and delicate environment; in which the stars are in random order and the gods are not partly ourselves; in which all multiform and delicate relationships necessary for stability in the world can be subdivided into three main parts and discussed in an essay.

The Coming of the Light

Cherokee

There was no light anywhere, and the animal people stumbled around in the darkness. Whenever one bumped into another, he would say, "What we need in the world is light." And the other would reply, "Yes, indeed, light is what we badly need."

At last, the animals called a meeting, and gathered together as well as they could in the dark. The red-headed woodpecker said, "I have heard that over on the other side of the world there are people who have light."

"Good, good!" said everyone.

"Perhaps if we go over there, they will give us some light," the woodpecker suggested.

"If they have all the light there is," the fox said, "they must be greedy people, who would not want to give any of it up. Maybe we should just go over there and take the light from them."

"Who shall go?" cried everyone, and the animals all began talking at once, arguing about who was strongest and ran fastest, who was best able to go and get the light.

Finally the 'possum said, "I can try. I have a fine big bushy tail, and I can hide the light inside my fur."

"Good! Good!" said all the others, and the 'possum set out.

As he traveled eastward, the light began to grow and grow, until it dazzled his eyes, and the 'possum screwed up his eyes to keep out the bright light. Even today, if you notice, you will see that the 'possum's eyes are almost shut, and that he comes out of his house only at night.

All the same, the 'possum kept going, clear to the other side of the world, and there he found the sun. He snatched a little piece of it and hid it in the fur of his fine bushy tail, but the sun was so hot it burned off all the fur, and by the time the 'possum got home his tail was as bare as it is today.

"Oh dear!" everyone said. "Our brother has lost his fine bushy tail, and still we have no light."

"I'll go," said the buzzard. "I have better sense than to put the sun on my tail. I'll put it on my head."

So the buzzard traveled eastward till he came to the place where the sun was. And because the buzzard flies so high, the sun-keeping people did not see him, although now they were watching out for thieves. The buzzard dived straight down out of the sky, the way he does today, and caught a piece of the sun in his claws. He set the sun on his head and started for home, but the sun was so hot that it burned off all his head feathers, and that is why the buzzard's head is bald today.

Now the people were in despair. "What shall we do? What shall we do?" they cried. "Our brothers have tried hard; they have done their best, everything a man can do. What else shall we do so we can have light?"

"They have done the best man can do," said a little voice from the grass, "but perhaps this is something a woman can do better than a man."

"Who are you?" everyone asked. "Who is that speaking in a tiny voice and hidden in the grass?"

"I am your Grandmother Spider," she replied. "Perhaps I was

put in the world to bring you light. Who knows? At least I can try, and if I am burned up it will still not be as if you had lost one of your great warriors."

Then Grandmother Spider felt around her in the darkness until she found some damp clay. She rolled it in her hands, and molded a little clay bowl. She started eastward, carrying her bowl and spinning a thread behind her so she could find her way back.

When Grandmother Spider came to the place of the sun people, she was so little and so quiet no one noticed her. She reached out gently, gently, and took a tiny bit of the sun, and placed it in her clay bowl. Then she went back along the thread that she had spun, with the sun's light growing and spreading before her, as she moved from east to west. And if you will notice, even today a spider's web is shaped like the sun's disk and its rays, and the spider will always spin her web in the morning, very early, before the sun is fully up.

"Thank you, Grandmother," the people said when she returned. "We will always honor you and we will always remember you."

And from then on pottery making became woman's work, and all pottery must be dried slowly in the shade before it is put in the heat of the firing oven, just as Grandmother Spider's bowl dried in her hand, slowly, in the darkness, as she traveled toward the land of the sun.

"It's Where You Put Your Eyes"

Sam Gill

Attention to the world's art historians!" was the message sent forth in 1885 by the Army physician Washington Matthews upon observing that Navajos routinely destroy their own sand paintings.[1] He was deeply impressed with the beauty and elaboration of these paintings in sand, but that only heightened the shock of the feature he was calling to the attention of the world. A number of people work to make a sand painting; on the same day they willfully destroy it. Matthews declared these paintings to be the most transient works of art in the world. We know that such short-lived works are not unique to the Navajo, but I don't think that Matthews' cry has been seriously considered. Perhaps that is because it would raise grave questions about the way we see and understand the nature of Native American art. Now, over a century later, I would like to consider some of the questions which echo from Matthews' message.

A description of Navajo sand painting will give us a place to begin. It is a ritual procedure in Navajo culture which is part of certain religious ceremonials performed to cure an ailing person. The sand painting is constructed on the floor of a ceremonial hogan and depicts mythic persons who have a connection with the cause of the illness being treated. It must be carefully replicated according to the memory of the officiating singer or medicine man. No visual record is kept by the Navajo people, but hundreds of different patterns are known to exist. The finished picture, like a costume and mask, provides a physical form in which the spiritual beings may manifest their presence. When cornmeal is sprinkled by the singer on the painting and the person for whom the ceremony is being performed, the holy people are present in the sand painting. The rite identifies the ailing person, who walks onto and sits in the middle of the painting, with each of the holy people present in it. The identification is physically accomplished by a transfer of sands on the medicine-moistened hands of the singer, taken from the feet, legs, body, and head of each of the sand-painted figures and pressed on the corresponding body parts of the person sitting on the painting. When this identification is complete the sand painting, badly defaced during the rite, is completely destroyed by the singer, who scratches through it with a plumed wand. The mixed sands are removed and return to nature.

In the study of Navajo religion, I have attempted to understand the significance of sand painting from the Navajo perspective. Each pattern is appropriate to only certain ones of the many Navajo ritual ways. Each has its own story of origin which in turn is framed by the whole Navajo tradition of creation. I have found that no Navajo sand painting can be understood very well without placing it in these contexts. Every ritual performance is uniquely appropriate to the specific motivating circumstances which emphasize certain features of a given painting. While attempting to understand any sand painting is a highly complex affair, I want to present a generalized interpretation.[2]

In the ceremonials in which sand painting rites play a major role, the cause of the illness being treated is attributed to impaired relationships with specific life-giving forces in the Navajo cosmos. These life-giving forces are associated with certain holy people whose powers have become directed against the life forces of the ailing person. In the ceremonial cure, rites are enacted to appease the holy people and persuade them to remove their life-threatening influence. But this in itself does not constitute a cure, for the person must be placed again in a state of order modeled upon the creation of the Navajo world. The sand painting rite is therefore a rite of re-creation in which the person is remade in a way corresponding to the conditions of his or her ailment. In this rite of re-creation, the sand painting is the essential vehicle.

The perspective of the person being re-created is based on his position in the center of the sand painting facing east, the direction of the road of life. This visual perspective on the painting is unique and cannot be shared by anyone. It is a view of the sand painting from within it, being surrounded by it. Only portions of the sand painting may be seen at any one time, and these only from the center outward. To sit upon the sand painting and to be identified with the many holy people and cosmic dimensions which are alive in it is to experience the complexity and diversity, the dynamics and the tensions, represented in the surrounding painting; but it is also to experience the one point common to all, and therefore to see and to feel the diversity and tensions.

The illness suffered is an experience of the world at odds with itself, but this experience is cosmicized when the person finds that this is but an incident in the whole drama of the universe. The illness is overcome when the person realizes (in the largest sense of that term) that in some places these tensions and oppositions can be balanced in a unity that signifies good health and beauty.

But how do we understand the destruction of the painting? We must see that it is not the materials of the sand painting, nor really even the design it takes, that is at the core of its meaning and power. Rather it is the process and use that is made of it that is important. It is a cosmic map. It is a vehicle by which re-creation, health, and beauty in life and the world are achieved. The sufferer finds his or her way to health from within the sand painting, and by becoming a part of it, it disappears and becomes a part of him or her. The picture disappears in the process of a person coming to know the fullness and unity of the reality it represents. The destruction of the picture corresponds to the dissolution of the tensions and imbalances which have given rise to the suffering.

We are now quite used to seeing Navajo sand paintings reproduced in books and articles on varying subjects. The circle inscribed by a cross is a widely known design, but its universal significance seems somehow shallow to me once I have considered Navajo sand painting, especially when I find that a fully closed border is rare and has very special significance and that double symmetry divided by a cross is but one of many general patterns.

The concerns I have are deepened as I begin to compare how we, as outsiders, view sand paintings with how Navajos view them, even from a physical perspective. Let me list several points of comparison. We have only representations of sand paintings drawn or painted on paper or canvas, which we enjoy as objects of art. Navajos strictly forbid making representations of sand paintings and they are never kept as aesthetic objects. Even the use of sand painting figures in the sand-glue craft has not met with the approval of most Navajo singers. Sand paintings must be destroyed by sundown on the day they are made. They are not aesthetic objects; they are instruments of a ritual process.

In terms of visual perspective we always view sand paintings from a position which would be directly above and at such a distance that the whole painting is immediately graspable, with each side equidistant from our eyes. This is completely impossible for Navajos. I got a laugh when I asked some Navajos if anyone ever climbed on the roof of a hogan to look at a sand painting through the smoke hole. When a painting six feet, or even larger, in diameter is constructed on the floor of a hogan only twenty feet in diameter, the perspective from the periphery is always at an acute angle to the surface. A sand painting cannot be easily seen as a whole. The most important point of view is that of the person being cured, and this person sees the painting from the inside out because he or she sits in the middle of it. These differences are basic and cannot be dismissed. The Navajo view is inseparable from the significance which sand painting has for them.

I think that we can say that for the Navajo the sand painting is not the intended product of the creative process in which it is constructed. The product is a healthy human being or the re-creation of a well-ordered world. The sand painting is but an instrument for this creative act, and perhaps it is the wisdom of the Navajo that it be destroyed in its use so that the obvious aesthetic value of the instrument does not supplant the human and cosmic concern. The confinement of our attention to the reproductions of sand paintings is somewhat analogous to hanging paint-covered artists' palettes on the wall to admire, not acknowledging that these pigment covered boards are not paintings but the means to create them. There is a certain aesthetic value in artists' palettes, I suppose, but surely most would think of this action as foolishly missing the point.

While I am delighted at the increased interest in viewing artifacts from Native American cultures as objects of art, I cannot dismiss the implications which arise from this Navajo example. Our view of Native American artifacts as art objects is a perspective the people themselves do not hold and sometimes explicitly reject. Our usual way of looking at these objects is stripped of the complex cultural views unique to the tribe which frame the significance of the artifacts. We often don't even know the physical perspective from which the object was intended to be seen. As a result the significance these objects have for us surely has little to do with their meaning for the people who created them.

If this were only a problem with Navajo sand painting it might ease my concern, but I think it is in a significant measure correct for any artifact not made for sale outside the culture. Some other examples will illustrate the point further.

Ted Brasser, of the Museum of Man in Ontario, studied the self-directed aspect of many Native American objects in the regions east of the Rocky Mountains.[3] He found that such things as moccasins, birchbark dishes, wooden bowls, effigy pipes, drums, woven bags, snowshoes, breechclouts, and pipe bags were commonly designed to be viewed from the perspective of the wearer or user. Moccasins, for example, have the design on the toe oriented to be seen by the wearer, not by those looking at moccasins worn by others. Craftspersons confirmed the intentionality of a self-directed orientation for many objects.

Brasser found that effigy pipes were used by the Iroquoian and Algonkian peoples as aides in the concentration of thought; that is, they were instruments of meditation. The pipe bowl bore the effigy of the guardian spirit or the familiar spirit of a shaman. It was so placed on the bowl that only when the smoker put the stem in his mouth did he come face to face with the representation of the spirit. Hence through smoking the pipe, drawing the tobacco smoke through the stem while concentrating on the effigy, the smoker gained power from his guardian spirit. Among the Sioux peoples, Brasser found self-directed effigy pipes of a bear facing the smoker, which were used by shamans whose power to cure and benefit war parties was attributed to the spirit of the bear. In their ritual performances these shamans personified bears, wearing fur costumes and moccasins with bear paws attached.

Examples from Brasser's research throughout the whole area east of the Rocky Mountains could be multiplied, but my point is that there is ample evidence indicating that the meaning of the effigy pipe is inseparable from the act of smoking the pipe, from the relationship the smoker has with the spirit represented on the pipe. It is inseparable from what occurs during the hours of concentrated smoking of strong tobacco. The visual perspective is dictated by the use for which the pipe is intended. When not in use the pipes are not placed on display for aesthetic pleasures but carefully wrapped in their bags.

To cite another example, I have long been dissatisfied with our whole framework for attempting to understand Native American ritual drama. I am uneasy especially with our views of masked performances. Our words *mask* and *impersonate* suggest that these ritual processes are somehow artificial, illusions, enactments of something else which is being imitated or represented. I have been little comforted that these performances are described as re-enactments of the events of the gods in the primal eras. I feel strongly that, rather than re-enactments or dramatic performances, they are the actual creation of reality. I have been concerned with some aspects of this process in terms of rites of initiation. I would like to consider another aspect of this related to masks. In initiation ritual it is fairly common to have initiates look through the eyeholes of masks. I think we usually interpret this as a means of demonstrating to the initiates the unreality of the mask; that is, we consider it as showing that what the uninitiated think is a real being is actually only a personification. But I think we may be wrong here. Again it is a matter of perspective. I would like to suggest that the perspective from which one gains the fullest meaning of a mask is not finally by looking at it at all, although this is certainly an essential stage in the process. The full meaning is gained by looking through the eyeholes of the mask and seeing the effect it has on the world. That is why it is a privileged view of the initiated.

A couple of Hopi examples give this some support. The Hopi Don Talayesva tells of a time when he portrayed a Giant Kachina in the Soyoko ritual proceedings, which are aimed at disciplining uninitiated children. These monstrous-appearing figures come to houses of misbehaving children and demand that the children be given them to eat. This forces the parents to bargain with the kachinas in order to save their children. The children's bad behavior costs the family a great deal in the physical goods they must provide to temporarily satisfy the awesome visitors, and this, along with the fear aroused by the kachinas, serves to encourage proper behavior in the children. Talayesva describes a time when he wore the mask of the Giant Kachina and enacted this ritual process. He played his part very well, with great effect on the children. That night Talayesva had a dream, which he describes:

> I was tired and restless, and dreamed that I was still a Giant Kachina arguing for the children. I reached out my hand to grab a child and touched him. [Touching a child is strictly warned against for fear of frightening a child to death.] The little one held up his hands to me, crying and begging to be set free. Filled with pity, I urged him to be a good child in order to free himself from the Giant Spirit. I awoke worried, with a lump in my throat, and bells ringing in my ears. Then I spat four times and decided that if I were ever the Giant again I would have a better-looking mask and speak in a softer voice.[4]

By looking through the mask from the inside out, its reality was reflected in the faces of the children.

The other example is a comment made by Emory Sekaquaptewa regarding the experience of performing as a kachina:

> I am certain that the use of the mask in the kachina ceremony has more than just an aesthetic purpose. I feel that what happens to a man when he is a performer is that if he understands the essence of the kachina, when he dons the mask he loses his identity and actually becomes what he is representing . . . . The spiritual fulfillment of a man depends on how he is able to project himself into the spiritual world as he performs. He really doesn't perform for the third parties who form the audience. Rather the audience becomes his personal self. He tries to express to himself his own conceptions about the spiritual ideals that he sees in the kachina. He is able to do so behind the mask because he has lost his personal identity.[5]

In this description of the experience Sekaquaptewa expresses the paradox of how one is at once enacting an impersonation and also transformed into what one is impersonating. It is described in terms of perspective. One best "sees" the reality one is oneself manifesting by wearing the mask; while looking through its eyeholes one paradoxically gains a view from the vantage of the audience so as to be able to know the reality it presents.

There is an inevitable conclusion which must be drawn from these examples. We can never appreciate some Native American objects we consider art without also appreciating the contexts in which they are produced. When our understanding of art is so heavily focused on objects, we tend to look in the wrong place for art. We find only the leavings or by-products of a creative process, never even realizing what is transparent to our view. We fail to grasp the inseparability of art and religion. I am reminded here of an essay by Amiri Imamu Baraka, formerly known as LeRoi Jones, entitled "Hunting is Not Those Heads on the Wall."[6] In it he criticizes the aspect of Western art which he identifies as a worship of art objects. He feels that the price paid for this is the failure to appreciate the creative processes of art. In his view art objects are what is left over from the art process, and they have no more to do with art than hunting trophies have to do with the hunt.

The Native American examples I have given are related to this idea, but the case is even stronger because the aesthetic values cannot be separated from religious processes. A point of view commonly found in Native American cultures holds that reverence for objects which we might judge as being of artistic or religious value can become a kind of tyranny which stifles the full expression of ideas and the proper performance of religious acts. These acts themselves are creative in a primary sense: they define and shape reality; they literally make life possible. In light of this we should dissociate ourselves from the notion that for Native Americans art is a noun. We might prefer to adopt the term *arting* coined by Baraka, so that we can think of the art of Native Americans as a process of creating and maintaining life-giving relationships.[7]

Each year we are dazzled by the publication of beautiful books on Native American art and by stunning museum exhibits. I read the captions to the plates: "Painted Hide, Sioux, Lent by . . . ," "Mask, Tlingit, from the collection of . . . ." The more elaborate identifications give a few descriptive notes, but since they are frequently drawn from publications of collectors who have little knowledge of the ethnography, they are often in error or severely inadequate.

When I find a plate depicting an object which is from a cultural context I know something about, I close my eyes and try to picture it in its living setting. Opening my eyes and focusing again on the object propped up with plexiglass or pinned against a completely blank background, I can't help feeling a little sick. While it is true that increasing interest in the aesthetics of what we call "primitive art" has provided an increasing interest in Native American artifacts as objects of art, I think we have done just about everything possible to remove the aesthetic and meaningful elements which they bore in the setting of their creation. And having done this, we find it impossible to appreciate them except in a relatively superficial way.

A few—all too few—publications about the art of Native Americans overcome the sterilization process which strips the cultural contexts from the objects. Outstanding among them is Edmund Carpenter's *Eskimo Realities*. The objects which we consider as art pieces are placed in the milieu of Eskimo world view not simply through verbal description but through the visual effects achieved by this beautifully crafted book (regrettably no longer in print) which leads to the conclusion:

> The concept "art" is alien to the Eskimo, but the thing itself, the act of art, is certainly there, carefully implemented as a dimension of culture. It is not, however, always easy to recognize. The Eskimo don't put art into their environment: they treat the environment itself as art form.
>
> Such art is invisible: it belongs to that all-pervasive environment that eludes perception. It serves as a means of training his perception upon the environment.[8]

Carpenter's book helps demonstrate this lesson of perspective I have been talking about. The shape of our own reality may blind us to the perspectives of others. Dominant objects from our perspective may, to the makers of those objects, be the leavings of a creative process completely invisible from where we look. What appears to us as an uninteresting background

Spirit Mask, 1988 EDNA JACKSON

may be to others the ground against which reality gains orientation and human meaning. What we must first realize is that there are many ways of looking; then, that understanding is shaped by where you put your eyes.[9]

Why Ant Has
a Small Waist

Warm Springs: Retold by Terry Tafoya

Long ago when the world was new, when mountains were the size of salmon eggs, all the people were animals. But they didn't look or act like the animals we have today . . . they were more like human people, and they spoke in one language, as we do now.

In those days there was no light, only darkness. There were some people who were always getting lost when they went hunting, unable to find their way home in the darkness. Their people would mourn them, but an even greater tragedy would be when the people would hear the pounding footsteps of a terrible monster coming closer and closer. This monster would snatch their babies, digging into their homes, swallowing their children, and then disappearing again into the dark.

There lived in those days a very wise woman, Klawisa, one of the ant people. Klawisa thought and thought about what she could do to help her relatives and friends. She thought of light. Now this was a brilliant thing to think of . . . she was the first one to think of light. She decided to go with some of her relatives on a great journey to the House of the Creator, and beg light from him.

And so it was she began that long journey in the company of her relatives, not knowing that the monster, Grizzly Bear, followed them. When she neared the Creator, she called out to Him, "I ask for light, so my people will always be able to see and work, be able to find their way home, and keep watch for the monster that swallows our children."

Before the Creator could speak, Bear appeared behind Ant, and in his dark voice shouted, "Don't give her what she wants! I want it always to be night, so it will be cool, and I can sleep."

The Creator said, "There will be a contest. It will be a Dance Contest, and the winner will have what he or she wishes." Now, whenever there are contests among our Indian people, there is always feasting. All different sorts of the Animal people came for the contest, and all sorts of Indian food were spread out for the feast.

Bear began to stuff himself, chewing and swallowing with great noise and pleasure. Little Ant chose not to eat, but began to fast. For many of our Indian people, fasting is a form of prayer, a way of cleansing and purifying the body. Instead of eating, she prayed for her people, begging light from the Creator.

When the dancing began, Klawisa, the Ant woman, sprang up. She pulled her belt tight. It held in her stomach so she felt no hunger. Her dance was fast. The Drum was a heart beat. She leapt to the music, her song, "I am Ant. I Dance for Light." She finished and sat down. She prayed again. She took no food.

Bear rose slowly like the moon would soon rise, crumbs still clinging to his heavy lips. "I am Bear, I Dance for Night," and so he did; his dance slow and ponderous, each footstep matching the drum like a tired canoe paddle. He finished his dance and immediately began to eat again.

Each time Ant would jump up. She pulled her belt tighter. She danced, swift, sharp movements. Quick as close echoes. "I am Ant, I Dance for Light." She continued her fasting and prayer.

Now every time Bear would begin to dance, his movements were slower and slower, as he grew sleepy and sluggish from all the food he was eating. "I am Bear," and then he yawned, his thick body stretching like an old alder tree, " . . . I Dance for Night." Slower and slower were his movements, and lower and lower was his song. Then he would return to his place at the feast, stumbling to the food to eat once more.

For what we would now call seven days and seven nights they danced and sang in this fashion. Finally, Bear staggered out to dance, his enormous stomach like a huge boulder in front of him, weighing him down. The floor shook with the massiveness of his faltering dance. He yawned, his mouth creaking open like a hidden cave, smacking his lips on a discovered bit of bitter-root. He yawned, and nearly fell over. "I . . . (yawn) . . . am . . . (Yawn) . . . Bear . . . (YAWN)." He stretched and slowed even more, no longer listening for the beat of the drum. "I . . . I . . . ZZZZZZZ." Then he began to snore, falling asleep right in the middle of his dance.

The Creator told the people, "You, Ant, have won this contest, but you and the Bear are both my children, and I love you both. For that reason I will give you both what you wish. I will create both Night and Day, so the Ant and her people will have time to work and can find their way around without getting lost, and the Bear will have time for peace and quiet."

Klawisa, the little Ant woman, was pleased. She had pulled her belt so tight that that is why Ant has a small waist, even today. She danced with her cousins, like Atneewah, the wasp, and that is why they also have small waists. It is because of Ant that we have daylight, even today. Ant's relatives still keep their watch in these times, fearing the approach of giants like the bear who raid their nests for their dinner.

Now the old people say that the Ant and Bear did not dance alone. Other animal people danced for their wishes as well. Rabbit danced for spring so he would always have tender young shoots to eat. When you hear the rabbit thump his foot in the woods, you know he practices for the next contest. These other animals had lost to Ant, and grew jealous of poor Klawisa.

With fear, tiny Ant and her cousins looked about them, into the angry black eyes of the other people. Wise Ant began to search her mind for an answer.

"There will be a new dance," she called out, "a laughing dance." She taught the people that while this laughing song was sung, everyone was to be very solemn. There should be no smiles, no signs of joy. But when the song stopped, groups of dancers were to break off from their circle dance, and run to an elder in the crowd. They would point to that person and laugh at them. It didn't have to be a regular laugh. It could be the high, light squeak of Grandmother Mouse, or the heavy, rough laughter of Bear.

When the people began to dance, they would do this, waiting for the stops in the song—then running out, pointing to elders, and laughing at the tops of their many voices. When the song would begin again, they would return to their circle dancing, trying to look solemn, but each of their faces would break into a smile. Just so, Klawisa had brought about her wishes once again.

And this is the way of it, that at the end of our dance contests, we sometimes end with the laughing song, so all will go home without jealous or angry hearts. It is the only time in our life we can make fun of old people, and even then, only in the short space between the dancing. The old people think it's the funniest of all.

Dancing with Dash-Kayah

Terry Tafoya

She is tall . . . bigger than Sasquatch, and her body is covered with long, black, greasy hair. Her eyes are large like an owl's, and her fingers are tipped with sharp claws. Her lips are formed in the eternal pucker of an eerie whistle, and children are told if they don't listen to their elders, she will come to them at night and suck their brains out of their ears. She is called Dash-Kayah, At'at'lia, Tsonoquah, and names whispered when the time is right, and not for publication.

Long time ago, long before the world turned upside down, there was a young boy who woke and went down to the river to bathe. The sun began to rise, and the boy enjoyed the warmth of the sun on the side of his face. He sang a song to greet the sun.

When he had finished he went fishing for salmon for his family, but he had gone so far out he knew he would not be able to return home before the sun set. So he decided to camp out where he was.

It was late at night. . . now White people say there is a Man in the Moon, but our Old people tell us it is a frog, and this frog was looking down at the little boy. Clouds came up and covered the moon, when all of a sudden the boy woke up, hearing the sound of heavy footsteps getting closer . . . and closer. Then he heard

the weird whistling as the clouds blew away, revealing the huge
dark shape of Dash-Kayah.

She called to him, "Don't be afraid; all those stories you hear
about me are just stories to scare little children. I'm really a very
nice person; in fact, I have some plump, juicy huckleberries for
you." And she held out her clawed hand, filled wiht berries.
When the boy reached for them, she took her other hand from
behind her back, which held sticky sap from the trees, and
slapped the boy across his eyes. Now his eyes were stuck
together as though with glue. Then she grabbed him and threw
him in the enormous basket she carried on her back. She ran
through the woods where she dumped him on the ground. She
had built a great fire and had placed other children she had stolen
in a circle around this fire, because she was going to roast them,
just as our people roast salmon. She began singing and dancing
around the fire, proud of the fine meal she would have of the
children. She sang:

Oh, Oh, Oh Oh La, Oh, Oh, Oh Ay,
Oh, Oh, Oh Oh, La, Oh, Oh, Oh Ay . . .

Now the little boy wished the whole day could start over
again, and he recalled how it had started, with him bathing in
the river, and the sun coming up. He leaned closer to the fire,
and it reminded him of the warmth of the sun. He leaned
closer—it felt so good—and suddenly, the heat of the fire started
melting the sap that held his eyes together, just as fire will melt a
candle's wax. Soon he could see a little out of one eye, and he
watched Dash-Kayah dancing around the fire. He thought of a
plan and whispered this idea to the little girl sitting next to him,
who told the little boy sitting next to her, until the plan went all
around the circle of the children.

Finally, Dash-Kayah had finished dancing, and she was so
tired she could hardly stand. That's when the little boy shouted,

"Now!" and all the children jumped up and pushed her into the fire. She began to burn, but not like ordinary things burn . . . she burned the way cedar throws up its sparks into the night; like sparklers and fireworks on the Fourth of July. And as the children watched these sparks rise into the air . . . the sparks turned into mosquitoes. And that's why mosquitoes bite . . . they still live off the blood of young children. Now that was the end of Dash-Kayah, but she had four sisters . . . .

I don't like to tell what legends "mean." Part of what the legend teaches, Bruno Bettelheim might suggest, is that no matter how great and dangerous a threat might be, if a child is clever enough, if a child acts in a proper way, he or she can be victorious. Dash-Kayah is not killed outright, but transformed from a huge monster to a small nuisance even the youngest child can handle with a slap.

However, this legend of my coastal relatives also carries an additional message, and to understand it we must look at the pervasive theme of the Cannibal Woman throughout the Pacific Northwest. Under her many different tribal names, she is depicted on totem poles, feast bowls, carving tools, and so, frequently, in masks.

She is related to power and status among Indian people to whom those things are most meaningful. In a common totem pole stance she displays the "copper," a coastal artifact that in many ways resembles a modern credit card in the sense that it represents a much greater value than its actual worth. The family that owns the right to use the Cannibal Woman as a symbol of its wealth and power is a family whose ancestors have faced Dash-Kayah and not only survived, but prospered.

She is shown in the act of whistling, and throughout the northwest we tell our Indian children not to whistle at night, for

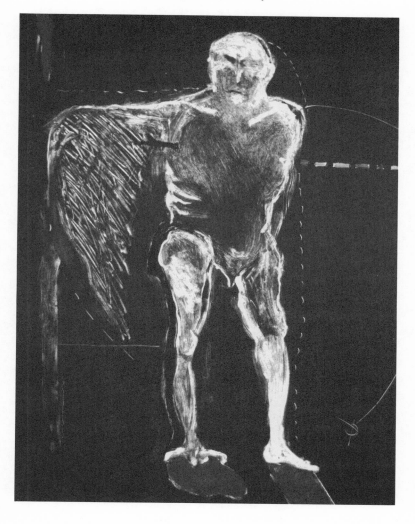

Owl and Man Talking, 1987 RICK BARTOW

you might call this type of spirit person to you . . . at great personal risk. The spirit people of the Southwest Indian people, the Pueblo, the Hopi, and the Navajo, are often portrayed with a tubular mouth, for their language is a sacred language that must be different from the profane tongue of the secular man, and this can be represented by whistling.

And like the other spirit people of distant tribes, Dash-Kayah's power has a dark and dangerous side, as well as a positive, protective one. Joseph Campbell suggests that there is a duality that exists between "cold hard fact," and the awareness of a sacred presence:

> Hence the guardian figures that stand at either side of the entrances to holy places: lions, bulls, or fearsome warriors with uplifted weapons. They are there to keep out the "spoilsports," the advocates of Aristotelean logic, for whom A can never be B; for whom the actor is never to be lost in the part; for whom the mask, the image, the consecrated host, tree, or animal cannot become God, but only a reference. Such heavy thinkers are to remain without. For the whole purpose of entering a sanctuary or participating in a festival is that one should be overtaken by the state known in India as "the other mind" (Sanskrit, *anya-manas:* absent-mindedness, possession by a spirit), where one is "beside oneself," spellbound, set apart from one's logic of self-possession and overpowered by the force of a logic of "indissociation"—wherein A is B, and C also is B.[1]

This then, is one of the functions of the Dash-Kayah figure: to frighten away those who are not pure enough in heart to survive being consumed by a spirit being. It is only by being eaten that one becomes incorporated into the spirit so that one takes on the power of that being . . . the complement of the Christian concept, where the deity is devoured by the worshipers.

When one dances with Power, one transubstantiates oneself. This is the central idea of what some have called "The Guardian-Spirit Complex," so common among many American and Canadian Indian tribes. The beautiful and frightening masks of the Cannibal Woman are most common among the more northern of the Pacific Coastal people, but it must be understood that with the exception of specific masks of the Sxwaixwe and a few other family-owned masks, the tribes of the southern areas of the coast use paint—red or black—for the same purpose as the mask. The various designs painted on with powdered devil's club or ochre represent whatever spirit is the Power of the dancer, and like the more northern masks, these designs are not always immediately recognizable to the outsider.

Throughout the Pacific Northwest, the theme of transformation is found over and over again. The Wild Man of the Woods, the Cannibal Woman's consort, has a mask among the Kwakiutl that flashes open to reveal a human-like face inside it . . . a marvelous irony when one considers that yet a third, and again, human face, lies behind the exposed human-faced carving. Time is measured by those things that happened before the Change . . . before the coming of the One called The Changer, or Transformer. There are other stories that occur during the Change, when the world began to take its present form as a result of the interactions between the Changer and those changed; and then finally there is Historical Time, that we live in even now. The Northwest designs are strange and difficult to comprehend to the first-time viewer because they can represent beings caught, frozen in the process of transformation; beings who have not quite taken on the shapes that they are forced to wear today.

The transformation of self—involving all the common dualities: of unknown to knowing, uninitiated to initiated, power-

less to power-possessed, child to adult—is reflected in the use
of mask and paint, making concrete the abstraction of change.
One's brother is no longer only a brother, but brother and Power.
And for those who listen to their elders, there is also a realization
that we are all born with a song that under the right training and
conditions manifests itself, so we learn of our potential. Thus
our brother has always been brother and Power, or perhaps,
brother and Power Immanent . . . hence yet another understanding of the Monster-faced mask with the human face
within.

To dance, either painted or masked, is never to be taken
lightly. The Salish say: "The paint doesn't wash off." One who
sups with Gods has permanent dinner partners. The realization
of one's potential is part of growing up, and the adult does not
transform him/herself back into a child . . . this is the one
transformation not permitted. During the initiation of the Coast
Salish, the one undergoing the rite is called a "Baby," for he or
she is learning to lead a new, and more fulfilled, life. After the
initiation, and the cross-bonding with a spirit Power, one grows
into true adulthood, regardless of one's chronological age.

Several years ago my relatives were attending a presentation
where a family who had been adopted by a Kwakiutl family were
displaying their adopted family songs and dances, along with the
use of masks. A young girl had been masked by this displaying
family, and been told to dance. When she had finished, she
could not remove the mask. My relatives worked over her,
singing their own Power songs until the girl was freed. One told
the Head of the displaying family, "You have acted irresponsi-
bly. You did not prepare this child to wear the mask." The man
defended himself by saying that the child did not wear the mask
with the proper attitude. He was told that this was not the point.
To wear a mask one must be prepared, and a young child should
not wear a mask if not properly trained by its owners.

Before the masks are donned, there are cleansing songs that must be sung, for these songs establish harmony between the dancer and his or her environment. The physical aspects of the masks and dance outfits are constant, concrete reminders to the dancers of their relationships to the World. The wood of the masks reminds the dancer of his/her relationship with the plants; the abalone insets and shell decorations remind the dancer of his/ her relationship with the people of the waters; the feathers, often eagle feathers, remind the dancer of his/her relationship with the people of the air, and so on, with the various meanings of colors and specific designs. The masks and paint assist the dancers in a mental and spiritual merging with the world, which can be seen as a multiplex manifestation of the Creator. As Joseph Epes Brown has stated:

> This sense of relationship pertained not only to members of a nuclear family, band, or clan. It also extended ever outwards to include all beings of the specific environment, the elements and the winds, whether these beings, forms, or powers are what we would call animate or inanimate. In native thought no such hard dichotomies exist. All such forms under creation were understood to be mysteriously interrelated. Everything was as a relative to every other being or "thing." Thus nothing existed in isolation. The intricately interrelated threading of the spider's web was referred to depict the world . . . . This is a profound "symbol," when it is understood. The people obviously observed that the threads of the web were drawn out from within the spider's very being.[2]

The masks and paint can be viewed as a "reference," to use Campbell's term, or a "symbol," but it is this and more. If one observes a beaded medallion so common among Indian people (or if one wishes to remain within a strict, traditional, coastal paradigm, consider the coiled basket) it consists of concentric circles whose relationships make up the intricate designs. But the most important bead is the center bead, for this represents the individual. We are the center of our own universe. Thus we are never lost, if we realize our center. It is not that the masks and paint only represent the outer world . . . they are representations of ourselves, and we are our own worlds. We are as much a manifestation of the Creator as anything else, thus the common Native contention that everything is sacred.

To dance, masked or painted, is to come to know sacredness with more than just eyes or ears, but with all senses of the body and mind operating at the same time. This I cannot tell you on paper alone. If you want to know the meaning of a mask, you must become masked yourself. It is not our way to sum up things in neat packages complete in themselves. A Keres Pueblo, Larry Bird, has said, "You don't ask questions when you grow up. You watch and listen and wait, and the answer will come to you. It's *yours* then, not like learning in school."[3]

Those who write and speak have no monopoly on the Truth, for Truth changes subtly as we change our perspective. There are many masks because there are many ways of understanding the world. It is only to those who are prepared to accept that their own view may not be the total Truth that the Monster face will open to reveal the human face inside.

How Gluskabe Stole Tobacco

Abenaki: Retold by Joseph Bruchac

*L*ong ago, Gluskabe and his Grandmother, Woodchuck, lived alone in a small lodge near the water. One day his Grandmother said to him, "My Grandchild, it is sad that we have no tobacco."

"What is tobacco, Grandmother?" Gluskabe said.

"Ah, Grandson, tobacco is a great gift from Tabaldak, Our Maker. If you are sick, you need only take tobacco out into the woods, and you will find the medicine plants. Then, when you place some tobacco on the earth, you can pluck those plants from the root and use them. Tobacco is a great comfort to the old. They can smoke it in their pipes and see all the happy days of their lives in the smoke as it lifts up. When you pray and burn tobacco, that smoke carries your prayers straight up to Our Maker. Tobacco is a very good thing indeed, when it is used as Tabaldak intended."

"Then we should have tobacco," Gluskabe said. "Where can I find it, Grandmother?"

"Ah, Grandson," Grandmother Woodchuck said, "it is not easy to get tobacco. It is on a big island far out in the water. A person with great magic lives there. He raises the tobacco and will not share it because of selfishness. He is very dangerous. Those who go to steal tobacco never return."

"Hunh!" Gluskabe said. "I will go and get tobacco, and I will share it with everyone."

Then Gluskabe went to the edge of the water. There was a hollow log there, and Gluskabe shaped it into a canoe. He put it into the water.

"Now," he said, "let me see if this canoe will go."

He pushed it with his foot, and the hollow log canoe shot out across the water. It went one whole look, as far as a person can see.

"This canoe is not fast enough," Gluskabe said.

Then Gluskabe took a big white birch tree. He stripped off the bark and fashioned it into a canoe and put it into the water.

"Now," he said, "let me see if this canoe will go."

He pushed it with his foot, and the birch bark canoe went very swiftly over the water. It went two looks, but Gluskabe was not satisfied.

"This canoe is not fast enough," he said.

Then Gluskabe fashioned a boat with ribs of cedar and the skin of a moose. He put it into the water and pushed it out and it went three looks. But Gluskabe was not happy with the moose hide canoe.

"This canoe," he said, "is not fast enough."

Gluskabe looked around. There at the edge of the water was a great white boulder. Gluskabe picked it up and turned it over. He shaped it into a canoe and put it into the water.

"Now," he said, "let me see if this canoe will go."

He pushed it with his foot, and it shot out across the water with Gluskabe inside. It went four looks almost as quickly as one could think, leaving a great white wave behind it. Gluskabe was very pleased.

"Now I can go and get tobacco."

He went back to the lodge. "Grandmother," he said, "I am going now to steal tobacco. But first you must tell me the name of my enemy, the magician who will not share the tobacco."

Grandmother Woodchuck shook her head. "Who will hunt for me and bring me wood for my fire and water for cooking if Grasshopper kills you? No, Gluskabe, I cannot tell you his name."

Gluskabe laughed. "Oleohneh, Grandmother," he said. "When I return, you will be the first one to smoke tobacco in your pipe."

Then Gluskabe climbed into his white stone canoe. He pushed off from the shore, and the canoe shot over the waves towards the island of the magician, Grasshopper. As the canoe sped along, Gluskabe sang:

> Grasshopper, you are going to travel,
> Grasshopper, you are going to travel,
> You must leave your home now,
> Grasshopper, you are going to travel.

He sang his song four times. By the time he finished, he had reached the island. Sure enough, just as he had wished in his song, Grasshopper was not there. The cooking pot was still on the fire, and a beautiful clay pipe decorated with bright stones was beside the fire, with smoke still rising from its bowl, but the magician was nowhere to be seen. Gluskabe picked up the pipe.

"Grasshopper," he said, "you are not going to need this anymore." Then he placed the pipe in his own pouch. Inside the lodge on many racks, tobacco bundles were drying. Gluskabe took them all and placed them in his canoe. All around the lodge were big tobacco fields. Gluskabe pulled up all of the plants and placed them in his canoe. He took all of the tobacco and did not leave a single seed. All around the fields were the bones of those who had come to steal tobacco and were killed by Grasshopper. Gluskabe gathered all of the bones together and then shouted.

"Get up!" Gluskabe yelled. "Your enemy is coming back." Then all of the bones came back together, and all of the people came back to life. They were very happy, even though some of them had been in such a hurry to return to life that they had gotten the wrong bones. Some of them had legs or arms that were too short or too long. The old people say that is why there are crippled people today. Gluskabe shared the tobacco among them. He mended their boats, which had been broken by Grasshopper, and sent them back to their homes.

"Tobacco is for everyone," he said. "You must always share it and give it freely or it will not do you good."

Then Gluskabe climbed back into his white stone canoe. He pushed it with his foot, and it flew back across the waves to the place where his Grandmother Woodchuck waited.

"Grandmother," he said, "I have brought tobacco. Never again will it be scarce."

Grandmother Woodchuck was very happy. She filled her pipe with the tobacco and smoked it and gave thanks to Tabaldak. She began to sing a song in praise of her Grandson, Gluskabe. But as she sang, the magician, Grasshopper, came. He came across the sky in a magical canoe.

"YOU!" he shouted in a loud and terrible voice. "You have stolen my tobacco!"

But Gluskabe was not frightened. He reached up with one hand and grabbed Grasshopper from his flying canoe.

"That is so," Gluskabe said. "It was not right for you to keep it all to yourself. Now my children and my children's children will have tobacco to enjoy." Then he rubbed Grasshopper between his hands, and Grasshopper became very small.

"Please," Grasshopper said in a small voice, "give me seeds so I can grow tobacco for myself."

But Gluskabe shook his head. "No longer can you be trusted to grow tobacco. That will be the job of my children and my children's children. But since you were the first to grow tobacco, I will give you enough to enjoy in your lifetime. Open your mouth."

Grasshopper opened his mouth and Gluskabe filled it with tobacco. Grasshopper was pleased, but he spoke again. "Give me back my canoe so that I can fly across the sky."

But Gluskabe shook his head. "It is not right for you to have such a magical canoe. I will split the back of your coat and give you wings. Now you will be able to fly on your own, but you will no longer be able to frighten the people."

So it is that to this day tobacco is used by the children of Gluskabe and their children's children, and when they use it as Tabaldak intended, always giving it freely to others, it does them no harm. As for Grasshopper, he flies about with the wings Gluskabe gave him and chews his mouthful of tobacco which will last all his life. And he remembers the lesson taught to him by Gluskabe. If you ever pick up any grasshopper it will immediately spit out its tobacco as if to say, "See, I am willing to share."

Disenchantment

Sam Gill

*F*or modern man in his complex secular world, religion has faded as an integral element of everyday life. Removed to the fringes of life, religion is allowed to play a central role only in time of crisis—a grave illness or death. But throughout history, religion has celebrated the tasks of a working day, the seasonal unfolding of the year, and the plateaus of personal development. When it marks these day-to-day experiences, religion pervades life and gives it meaning, but when the mundane events of human existence are no longer celebrated through regular and formal ritual, much of the power of religion is lost.

A vital religious life commonly begins with a formal rite of initiation. This rite is crucial, for it awakens in the individual the special character of religious life and spurs him to involvement in activities which nurture continual religious development. Rituals of initiation generally follow a pattern of symbolic death and rebirth, as Arnold van Gennep and Mircea Eliade have shown. Childhood and all its associations die for the initiate, and he is reborn into his adulthood having to accept both the privileges and responsibilities of this new life. In these rites the initiate is transformed into a new person—from a child into an adult, from a novice into an adept. Moreover, Eliade has demonstrated that the fundamental purpose of the religious initiation—the revelation of the sacred—is accomplished through this initiatic pattern. The special knowledge of the sacred is what distinguishes the initiated.

But occasionally these rites, which should germinate relationships with the holy, focus upon the intentional destruction or defamation of sacred objects in the presence of the initiates. It would seem in these cases that the symbolic blow of death is dealt to the gods or the sacred rather than to the initiates. How can an initiation be meaningful if its ritual process desecrates or defames the objects that reveal the sacred? The enigma is darkened by the fact that the adepts of the society often go to great lengths to deceive the initiates, to set them up for the disillusionment they will suffer. Occasionally these acts of chicanery are carried out with such hilarity that the success of the deception is threatened. The whole business of religious initiation, when conducted in this way, takes on the appearance of little more than a cruel joke, a miserable hoax. Such patent deception seems to negate the essential task of the rite: instead of revealing to the initiate a compelling sacred reality, the revered objects are defamed in his presence. Since the dire religious implications of such a conclusion are abhorrent to me, I am faced with the task of uncovering what must be going on beneath this perplexing surface. Upon examining several examples of this process, from widely diverse regions of the world, we may be able to see something of how these rude surface phenomena play an essential and profound role in initiation.

A striking example of the defamation of sacred objects in the initiatory process occurs in the rites of initiation into one of the healing cults of the Ndembu of Africa. As we would expect, the revelation of the nature of *Kavula*, the spirit of the healing cult, is an essential part of the initiation. But the process by which the initiates learn of *Kavula* is startling. The adepts prepare a frame made of sticks covered with a white blanket to represent the divinity. It is called *isoli*. One of the initiated hides beneath the blanket to play the part of *Kavula*. The initiates are chased by the adepts, caught, interrogated with unanswerable questions, taunted for being unable to supply appropriate answers, and eventually led to the *isoli*. The initiates are instructed regarding the formal procedure of greeting *Kavula*. When they address the spirit in the *isoli*, its voice returns their greeting. The initiates approach the structure, and when instructed to kill *Kavula*, they beat the object with the butts of their rattles. With each blow, *"Kavula"* shakes convulsively, as if dying. The initiates are then led back to the village. When they enter it an adept takes a firebrand, strikes it violently on the ground and cries out, "He is dead!" And after a brief closing oration the initiation is concluded.

Victor Turner, who reported these events, elicited comment on the "killing of *Kavula*" from the Ndembu people. Muchona, a very knowledgeable old man, said, *"Kavula* is killed to frighten the candidate. For he believes he is really killing *Kavula*. He has been instructed by the adepts that 'If you see the spirit of *Kavula*, you must consider this is a spirit which helps people. . . .' The adepts are just deceiving the candidates at *isoli*." One of the female initiates told Turner that it was *"Kavula's* back that we saw in *isoli*. When *Kavula* was killed the spirit flew away into the sky, not to *Nzambi* (the High God), but 'into the wind.' It could come again."

In this initiation rite, the adepts use techniques of deception to build an illusion, a fictitious conception of reality, for the initiates. Bringing the initiates into *Kavula's* sacred presence, they confuse them with unanswerable questions, tell them to kill the very spirit that is to be revealed to them, and assure them at the conclusion of the rite that "he is dead." Once the rites are over, the initiates are even shown the construction of the *isoli*. The illusion is disclosed; the enchantment with *isoli* broken. *Kavula*, as presented to them, is shown to be nothing but a blanket-covered framework of sticks. Remarkably, however, the initiate demonstrates in her comments on the event that she discovered in it something of the mysterious nature of *Kavula*. She has come to realize that *Kavula* is not limited to his appearance in the *isoli*, but is something more. Somehow in the process she gained the knowledge that *Kavula* is a spirit that flew "into the wind" and can come back, or perhaps as Muchona told Turner, "*Kavula* takes all powers." It is through the creation of an illusion that is subsequently shattered by a dramatic and powerful act of disenchantment that the revelation of the spiritual nature of the sacred is effected.[1]

In a comparable fashion, Hopi children are initiated into the *kachina* cult which signals the start of their formal participation in religious activities. Prior to the age of initiation, the children are very carefully protected from seeing *kachina* figures without their masks or seeing the masks when not being worn. The children are led to believe that the *kachinas* visit the village at certain intervals through the year, and they come to expect gifts from them. During the *kachina* cult initiation rites the children are frightened by the ogre *kachinas;* they are entertained by numerous *kachina* dances; they come into close contact with a great many *kachinas;* they may even be whipped by the *kachinas;* and they are told secret stories about the origin of the *kachinas*. But the most lasting impression comes during the last night of the ceremony. The children are taken into a *kiva* to await a *kachina* dance—a now familiar event. They hear the *kachinas* calling as they approach the *kiva*. They witness the invitation extended from within the *kiva* for the dancing gods to enter. But to the children's amazement, the *kachinas* enter without masks, and for the first time in their lives, the initiates discover that the *kachinas* are actually members of their own village impersonating the gods.

Dorothy Eggan found that this revelation distresses the children and that most Hopi recall it as a traumatic and disorienting experience. She selected the following comment as representative:

> I cried and cried into my sheepskin that night, feeling I had been made a fool of. How could I ever watch the Kachinas dance again? I hated my parents and thought I could never believe the old folks again, wondering if Gods had ever danced for the Hopi as they said and if people really lived after death. I hated to see the other children fooled and felt mad when they said I was a big girl now and should act like one. But I was afraid to tell the others the truth for they might whip me to death. I know now it was best and the only way to teach the children, but it took me a long time to know that.[2]

The Hopi children, unlike the Ndembu initiates, are not a party to a ritual killing of the gods, but the effect is much the same. For observing the unmasked *kachinas* produces within the children the sense that the *kachinas*, as they had so fondly known them, are dead. Once disenchanted with the masked figures, the children can never feel the same about the *kachina* figures or the things they had been taught about them. Yet it is clear there is more to the initiation than revealing to the children that "the *kachinas* are not real gods, but merely masked impersonations of them," as the rite has commonly been interpreted, for Eggan's informant indicated that she realized the value of the technique in teaching children, and surely she means more than simply disclosing the masked nature of the *kachinas.*

This initiatory process begins with the careful nurturing of a naively realistic perspective in the children. They are encouraged to be enchanted by surface appearances. They are led to believe that the *kachinas* are nothing more or less than what they appear in material form to be. This "education" into a simplistic, one-dimensional world view sets them up for the shock of disenchantment which is experienced at the conclusion of the rites. It cultivates their childish outlook into a ripe fruit ready for plucking.

With the unmasking of the *kachinas* the naiveté of the children is shattered all at once and forever. The existence of the *kachinas*, the nature of one's own destiny, the trust in parents and elders, and the very shape of reality itself are all, in a flash, brought into radical question. The children can either accept the world as bereft of meaning, with Hopi religion a sham, or find some deeper sense in the ceremonies and objects which had come to mean so much to them. Necessarily, they begin their religious life in a state of serious reflection and in quest of an understanding of the sacred profound enough to sustain their new life. There is tremendous incentive for the children to listen even more carefully to the stories of the old people and to participate in the ceremonies with a new seriousness.

Once again the process of disenchantment can be seen at work in the initiation rites of the Wiradthuri tribes of Australia. The occasion is the initiation of boys into manhood. The rites are loaded with chicanery. The boys are frequently commanded to walk with their eyes fixed on their feet so that they may not observe the staging of the trickery. A principal focus of the several rites rests upon the revelation of the nature of the spirit *Dhuramoolan*. Frequently the boys are told that *Dhuramoolan* is coming near and are advised to listen for his approaching voice. They hear a whirring noise that grows louder and louder, but they do not know that the sound is being made by men whirling bullroarers. At a critical juncture in the rites, the boys are covered with blankets and told that *Dhuramoolan* is coming and that he may eat them. With bullroarers roaring close by, the elders reach under each blanket and with hammer and chisel they knock out an incisor tooth of each boy. The boys think the spirit is taking their teeth, while sparing their lives.

Again an illusion of the nature of the sacred is prepared, and it is fully accepted by the initiates. And once again the initiation culminates in disenchantment. On the last day the boys are covered with blankets and a crackling fire is built. The bullroarers are whirled nearby, and the boys are told that *Dhuramoolan* is going to burn them. When the boys appear sufficiently frightened, the blankets are removed from their heads, and they see for the first time the men whirling the bullroarers and learn that this artificial noisemaking is what they've taken to be the voice of *Dhuramoolan*. Pointing to these men, the head man says, "There he is! That is *Dhuramoolan*," and he explains to the boys how the noise is made by whirling flat pieces of wood on strings. Then the boys are given the bullroarers to examine; they may even try whirling them. They are forbidden to tell the uninitiated about them or ever to make a bullroarer except during the initiation rites. Then the adepts destroy the bullroarers by splitting them into pieces and driving them into the ground, or sometimes by burning them. There is little information about how the boys respond to this revelation, but clearly they can never be terrified as they once were by the voice of the bullroarers. Nor can they retain the naive knowledge of *Dhuramoolan's* nature engendered in them during the initiation rites. They too have learned that the sacred is more than it appears to be, that it can never be identified wholly with one mode of revelation. The medium of epiphany is shown to be something trivial and powerless in itself.[3]

In these examples, the whole process of initiation builds to a climax in the shock of disenchantment. The sacred objects are destroyed in the eyes of the initiates. But despite this, the initiations evidently succeed, although the revelation of the sacred occurs more as a result of the initiatic process than as a part of it.

When the dynamic of disenchantment is the driving power in an initiation rite, the first and essential ingredient is encouraging identification of the sacred with the cult object. The uninitiated must come to believe that the objects and the sacred are exactly identical. The white blanket in the framework of sticks *is Kavula;* the masked dancers *are* Hopi gods; and the roar of the noisemakers *is Dhuramoolan* shouting. Ingenious techniques of secrecy and deception have been devised to nurture a perspective of naive realism, and the effectiveness of the initiation depends on how firmly this viewpoint is established.

The whole initiatic process reinforces this sense that the fullness of the sacred is invested in the cult objects. Then in the concluding moments, upon the threshold of a new life, the illusion is dissolved and the shock of disenchantment shatters all that went before. The experience makes a return to the previous state of life impossible. The naive realism of the uninitiated perspective has been exploded. The rites have demonstrated irreversibly that things are not simply what they appear to be, that one-dimensional literalism is a childish faith that one has to grow beyond or else despair of a life rich in meaning and worth.

Coyote's Journey, 1985 RICK BARTOW

Surely, being thus forced to abandon one's ingrained notion of reality is to experience a true death of the former self. And this loss of self constitutes the concrete transformation signified by the symbolic dying experienced in the rites.

The purpose of initiation—revealing the nature of the sacred reality—is, of course, one with the nature of religion itself. For religion springs from the unique human capacity to grasp a reality which is infinite and "wholly other," to use Rudolf Otto's phrase. This is possible only because of our gift for symbolization, in which, as Goethe said, "the particular represents the general, not as a dream or a shadow, but as a living and momentous revelation of the inexplorable." It is through the dynamics of symbolization that the sacred is manifest in ordinary, mundane objects. In religion, symbols mediate the infinite through the finite, the general through the particular. The challenge of initiation is to begin with the cult object, which is finite and particular, and to reveal in it the infinite fullness of the sacred. The rites of initiation have to show that the symbols are only a form or a representation of the sacred; and at the same time, they must demonstrate that the transcendent is really embodied in them. The initiate must be simultaneously convinced that the divinity is independent of its finite manifestation and that the contingent symbols are vital to the revelation of the sacred.

Through initiation culminating in disenchantment, the novice enters religious life in a state of crisis, disappointment, or perplexity about the nature of the sacred. The only thing he knows is that he has been fooled and his sense of what is real and what is not is confounded. His options seem clear. He may see the sacred objects as meaningless—childhood toys to be put away with the onset of maturity—in which case a life centered in these symbols is likewise pointless and empty. Or he may undertake a quest for a fuller, adult understanding of the higher reality that has been revealed and regard the symbols as pointers to an encompassing mystery that is inexhaustible. The newly initiated are invited and expected to participate in the religious activities. Through such participation, they begin gradually to grasp the full scope of the higher reality revealed in the symbols. With this expanding awareness, meaning is conferred on the sacred objects in an enhanced and maturing way. For it is only when the fullness of religious meaning is grasped that the symbols genuinely mediate the sacred.

The profound wisdom of the method of initiation by disenchantment lies in its capacity to bring the initiate through succeeding stages of perception to an encounter with the full reality of the sacred. The rites necessarily must end on the threshold of revelation, for it is only through the living of the religious way that the sacred becomes fully known.

Victor Turner has discerned a similarity between the symbolic structures of the "killing of *Kavula*" and the Gospel story of the Empty Tomb. The death and resurrection motif also involves the enchantment-disenchantment process at work in the initiation of the first Christians as a religious tradition.

The Gospels recount the life and teachings of Jesus as the story of the incarnate revelation of God. The episode of the Empty Tomb concludes the books of Matthew, Mark, and Luke, and in John only one chapter follows it. It comes directly after the account of the Crucifixion, and for those destined to be members of the first Christian community, this death caused fear, despondency, and consternation. This is especially clear in the conclusion of the last chapter in Mark:

> And very early in the morning the first day of the week, they came unto the sepulchre at the rising of the sun. And

they said among themselves, Who shall roll us away the stone from the door of the sepulchre? And when they looked, they saw that the stone was rolled away: for it was very great. And entering into the sepulchre, they saw a young man sitting on the right side, clothed in a long white garment; and they were affrighted. And he saith unto them, Be not affrighted: Ye seek Jesus of Nazareth, which was crucified: he is risen; he is not here: behold the place where they laid him. But go your way, tell his disciples and Peter that he goeth before you into Galilee: there shall ye see him, as he said unto you. And they went out quickly, and fled from the sepulchre; for they trembled and were amazed: neither said they any thing to any man; for they were afraid.

Considering this as the concluding event in the initiation of the first Christians, several elements are remarkably similar to the rites of initiation described above. As the Ndembu experienced the death of *Kavula*, the Hopi the unmasking of the *kachina* figures, the Wiradthuri the destruction of the bull-roarers, so the followers of Jesus were forced to witness his death. They had come to know him well and had accepted him as their Lord. Yet, they saw him captured, tortured, and crucified. They saw that he was a man who felt pain, suffered, and died. He, like any man, was placed in a tomb. The followers of Jesus had embraced a naive view of his reality—that Jesus the man and Jesus the Christ were simply identical. But going to the tomb, they found that he was not there. The Ndembu who examined the *isoli* found only a framework of sticks—*Kavula* was not there. The Hopi found only their own relatives under the masks—the *Kachina* gods were not there. The Wirandthuri coming from under their blankets found only old men whirling bullroarers—*Dhuramoolan* was not there.

The story of the Empty Tomb in Christianity follows a pattern akin to the process of disenchantment. Christianity as a religion begins with the Empty Tomb which is received not with joy and comfort, but with trembling, astonishment, and fear. That which had appeared to be so real, the man Jesus, had ceased to be and not even his body remained as an object to care for and reverence. It has been in the face of the fear and astonishment at the loss of Jesus, the man, that Christians throughout the Christian era have been led to grasp the reality of Jesus, the Christ, who was resurrected from the tomb, and hence the reality of God Himself. It must follow that only with that revelation could it be clearly recognized that it is the life and teachings of Jesus that are the "living and the momentous revelation of the inexplorable" God.

An event occurring at the initiation of a Zen monk into his order is again comparable to what has been discussed. A statue of the Buddha is placed before the initiate, whereupon it is broken and cast aside. The initiate is told, "We are throwing the Buddha to the dogs." It is, of course, the object of Zen to come to know the wisdom of the Buddha directly and not through doctrine or teachings, and this act of disenchantment with the image of the Buddha serves to shock the initiate into grasping the higher reality of the Buddha-nature. Zen methods are well known for their use of shock and illusion to lead the followers toward the experience of *satori*—the grasping of and union with the higher reality. The initiatory process of disillusionment is uniquely reflected in an ancient Zen saying, "To begin with, everyone sees mountains as mountains and trees as trees; then when one seeks to come to terms with them, mountains no longer appear as mountains, nor trees as trees; but finally when enlightenment is attained, mountains are again seen as mountains and trees as trees."

In these few examples from a broad spectrum of religious contexts, there appears the common structure of a technique of disenchantment used to initiate the mature religious perspective and to promote authentic apprehension of the sacred. The apparent effect of disenchantment is itself illusory. Acts which seem to spell the end of religion have been found to be techniques that thrust the initiate into the arena of adult religious life with incentive to plumb its full depths. They lay bare the limitations of naive views of reality so that through deepened participation in a religious community and celebration of the day-to-day events of life in religious ritual, the individual may increasingly experience the mysterious fullness of the sacred, sustaining realm. And a mature sense emerges that the sacred symbols can reveal the sacred without ever exhausting its reality.

The Elk Skull

Winnebago

One day, as Trickster was wandering around in the world, he came to a valley where he heard someone beating a drum. Along with the drumming, he heard many war whoops: so loud was the noise it seemed to reach the skies.

"What is all this drumming?" said Trickster to himself. "Someone is having a lot of fun. I wonder what he is up to? I guess I will go and see for myself: I haven't had any fun in a long time. If there is going to be dancing, I shall surely join in, for I was a fine dancer in my day."

Thus spoke Trickster to himself, and he hurried across the valley to get to where the drumming was. With every step the drumming and the war whoops got louder and louder, so he knew he was getting nearer. Everyone was shouting for joy. What a glorious noise there was! It was just the sort of thing that Trickster longed for. Now the drumming was so loud, it seemed the heavens would burst. The shouting was so close that Trickster felt sure that the people who were making it must be somewhere in sight. Yet wherever he looked, he could see no one, and still louder he heard the drumming and the shouting.

"Now," thought Trickster, "I must be right in the midst of that war-party." He looked and looked, yet he could see no one.

There were, however, a lot of bones lying about, the bones of an animal, and a little further on, he saw an elk skull, with many-branched horns. The drumming and shouting seemed to be coming from the vicinity of the skull, so Trickster sat down and began to watch it very carefully, looking all about him from time to time to see if he could catch a glimpse of the drummer and the dancers. Presently he became aware that all the noise was coming from the skull itself, so he got up to take a closer look. Sure enough, the celebration was taking place inside the elk skull! The head was filled with thousands of flies. The skull echoed with the sound of their wings, and as they rushed in and out of the openings, they all shouted for joy. Trickster sat down and watched them. He was very envious of all the fun they were having.

"Well," said Trickster after a while, "I see you are all having a lot of fun. You are all doing exactly what I have been wanting to do for a long time now. Little brothers, this is a very important thing you are doing. I would very much like to be doing this thing with you. How can I do it? Please show me so I can join you and be one of you."

"There is no difficulty," the flies answered Trickster. "If you want to be like one of us, all you have to do is enter through the neck just as you have seen us do." So Trickster picked himself up and tried to enter through the neck, but of course the opening was too small and he failed. Time and again he tried to put his head through the neck opening, but he was too big. Then the flies said to him, "Listen. If you really want to come in, say 'Neck, become large!' and when the opening is big enough, put your head in. That is the way we do it."

So Trickster sat down and said solemmly to the elk skull, "Neck, become large!" and sure enough, the hole grew big enough for him to put his head through. Ah, he was delighted!

He put his head in and entered the skull, all the way up to his neck. But then all the flies flew away, and the opening he had put his head into became small again, and he was held fast. He pulled and pulled with all his power, but to no avail. He could do absolutely nothing.

When he realized that he was caught, Trickster went down to the river. He looked in the water and saw that his head now had long branching horns. What was he to do? He walked along the river's edge and thought. Finally, he had an idea. This is what he did. All night long, he sat by the river. When morning came, he stretched himself out and covered himself with his racoon-skin blanket. Augh! What a terrifying thing he was to look at now! From the neck down, he was covered with fur, and from the neck up he had a long white face with many-forked antlers.

Soon the women came down to the river for water. They saw this strange figure and were terrified. They began to run away, but Trickster held up his hand. "Stop!" he said to one of the women. "Turn back. I have come to bless you!" The woman was nearly frightened out of her wits, but she stopped when she heard the voice from the elk skull. Now the voice said to her, "Go home. Get an axe and bring it here. Bring all the appropriate offerings too, while you are at it—your relations will tell you what to bring. When you have come and presented the offerings, strike the top of my head with the axe. Whatever you find inside you will be able to use as medicine and get whatever you wish. I am an elk spirit and have come from the waters of this river to bless your village."

The woman immediately went home and told her relations what had happened. "There is a great elk water-spirit by the river, and he has come to bless our village," she said. "He has a medicine box and he said that if we brought the right offerings and struck him on the head with an axe, we could use whatever we found inside for making various medicines." So the people of the village prepared all the offerings appropriate for elk water-spirits—red feathers, white deer skin, and red yarn-belts—and went to the river.

When they had presented all the offerings, they chose a man to wield the axe. Cautiously, the man came up and struck the elk skull and behold there was Trickster, laughing at them uproariously! "Such a fine head-dress I was wearing, and now you have spoiled it," he said between fits of laughter. "Now what will I wear?" When the people saw that it was Trickster and that they had been fooled, they were ashamed. However, Trickster spoke to them and said, "Inasmuch as you have made these offerings, they will not be lost. I have made a promise, and I will not go back on it. You split the elk skull and found me inside; however you wish to use me, therefore, your purpose will be accomplished."

That was how the great medicines came to those people—Trickster taught them everything he knew, and all that he taught them was efficacious. When Trickster had given the people all the medicines they needed, he left them and continued his wandering.

Boundaries of Belief

Barbara Tedlock

On July 20, 1969, when the lunar module of Apollo 11 landed and Neil Armstrong and Edwin Aldrin, Jr. stepped out on the surface of the moon before the television cameras, the Zuñis of New Mexico had to deal with a new threat to their religious beliefs. If what the television cameras recorded was true, and not merely a studio fiction, then the Moon Mother, who (along with the Sun Father) is the ultimate source of all light and life, had been violated by two white men in a metal space capsule. Not only did these white men not practice sexual abstinence and make offerings of cornmeal and prayersticks before they visited the Moon Mother, but they walked around on her body, left refuse on her, planted an American flag in her, and removed nearly fifty pounds of her sacred flesh without so much as a prayer.

Zuñis feared that these profane acts could spell the end of the Moon Mother's gifts to humankind. Perhaps she, like Salt Woman and Turquoise Man before her, who were defiled by ignorant Zuñis, might also move farther away, causing serious repercussions. In the myth "Salt Woman Migrates,"[1] Old Lady Salt is said to have lived close to Zuñi, at Black Rock Lake, but she became angry because young people who came to gather her precious flesh urinated and spat upon her. They wasted the salt they brought home, necessitating trip after trip to her. Likewise, the people found pretty turquoises, part of Turquoise Man's body, east of the salt lake, but they found so many that they wasted them, treating them as if they were a common thing. One day Salt Woman and Turquoise Man left Zuñi, migrating southward. After a bit Turquoise Man turned east alone and settled far away near Santa Fe, while Salt Woman settled down forty miles south of Zuñi. In this way, they removed their precious gifts from the reservation. Perhaps the Moon Mother, after suffering repeated indignities and being robbed of her flesh, would also move farther away; if so, she could cause totally black nights, droughts or floods, and massive human infertility. Many Zuñis called the space odyssey "white man's witchcraft," and some old men felt that perhaps this was another omen of the coming death of the world, when all man-made things would rise against us and a hot rain would fall. Younger Zuñis wondered aloud if the Moon Mother was really a deity. Perhaps the white man was right after all and she was only another object spinning around in space. Other youngsters pointed out that she had thrown stones at an earlier Apollo mission, causing it to turn back to earth.

Simply stated, the moon shots came as a profound religious shock to many Zuñis. One of their important deities—one they offer prayers to each month (when she is full) for health, wealth, and fertility—was being visited, photographed, and dug into with mechanical claws by white men who did not worship her. Even worse, this important deity had been defiled and her divine status brought unto question right before their eyes on national television. Zuñi religion had withstood more than three centuries of Spanish and American missionization, the latter aided by the "Religious Crimes Code" implemented by the Bureau of Indian Affairs during the 1920s, but perhaps no single white religious argument of the past had been quite so startling and direct in its impact as the simple fact of the moon landing. Could Zuñi religion, whose most basic obligation is monthly offerings to the Sun Father and Moon Mother, survive the unwanted group initiation of the majority of its membership, via mass communications, into the profane cult of space exploration?

During the space programs initiated in 1957 by Sputnik 1, the world's first artificial satellite, the Newekwe clowns, one of the fourteen organized curing societies at Zuñi, had added space burlesque to their repertoire of hilarious skits. In an early skit, performed during a kachina dance-drama (in which Zuñi ancestral gods are impersonated), a Newekwe clown with a cardboard box around his waist, shaped and painted to look like a spacecraft, went into orbit and circled the village several times before he crashed and rolled over dead before the line of singing dancers in the main plaza. In another skit, again during a kachina dance, one of these same clowns climbed up on the tallest building at Zuñi and made a round ball out of himself; a second man was hurled aloft by a whole group of clowns to visit the "Moon Mother." This "astronaut" clown then jumped off the roof and was immediately surrounded by other clowns bearing a stretcher, playing nurses and doctors. They examined the returned clown carefully with a stethoscope, gave him a series of shots with a giant hypodermic, and then asked him what it was like on the moon. The patient reported that there were people, animals, lakes, watermelons, and what-not up there—all to howls of laughter from the audience. A third popular skit involved a clown from Houston Control who telephoned the moon to talk (in English) with "The Man in the Moon." Here the astronaut "in" or "on" the Moon Mother was a deliciously bawdy joke for Zuñi audiences.

These popular skits were performed throughout the period of the most intensive Russian and American space exploration.

Over and over again clowns dressed as satellites, rockets, and astronauts ran madly around the village, threw one another into the air, and fell off roofs, all this in the sober context of kachina dances. Such antics were not for mere entertainment. Before each performance, clowns are reminded by their leaders "to make your mind blank" and "to go out there with a happy heart, a heart free from worry, to help the people." Their whole goal is to startle and even shock the audience in order to get a response, perhaps a sudden laugh, or at least a gasp of disapproval. In so doing, they "get to the people," they "open them," and release them from internal idle thoughts or worries. In the Zuñi view, worry lodges in the stomach and is a primary cause of illness in general. The space program was a source of general (and one might say visceral) worry at Zuñi, and so it was that for more than ten years the clowns trivialized, folklorized, and negated both its religious threat and its scientific seriousness. Throughout this period Zuñi audiences laughed and laughed at the absurdity of space exploration—it was a fiction, a lie, or a silly joke.

The Newekwe, who constitute a medicine society, were particularly well suited to produce these space skits, since they specialize in public burlesques of intrusive foreigners and in private shamanic journeys on the Milky Way. Membership comes when a person with a serious stomach ailment seeks help from the Newekwe; after recovery, initiation into the society is necessary for a permanent cure. Among the shamanic powers gained through membership is the ability to eat any kind or amount of food and garbage (including human excrement) and to engage in shocking sexual displays without feeling shame. The Newekwe are known as the wisest and most fearless people in the entire pueblo.

The altar which this society of clowns sets up for its initiation and monthly meetings includes a long wooden beam, stretching across the entire width of its meeting room, bearing iconic representations of cumulus clouds, the seven stars of Ursa Major, and two figures of Payatamu, the son of the Sun Father. The beam itself is painted in alternating squares of black and white which represent the Milky Way, called "Ash Way" in Zuñi, and in turquoise, the color of the Sun Father. Attached to the lower edge of the bar are twelve eagle feathers which both are, and flutter in, the sacred breath of the Sun Father and the Moon Mother. The clowning costume of members of this organization includes a feathered wooden baton or jester's bauble, sloppy street clothes, a black overcoat, and a tight-fitting cap painted white, with bunches of cornhusk strips fastened on either side and on top. Wide, alternating black-and-white horizontal stripes are painted on the skin, from head to toe.

The stripes of the clown represent the Ash (Milky) Way, the sacred path travelled through the sky by Payatamu, the son of the Sun Father and the founder and patron deity of the Newek-we. In the myth of Payatamu,[2] it was his job to bring out the sun each day. One day, on his way to perform this task, he met a woman who challenged him to a game of hide-and-seek with their lives at stake. When he lost, she cut off his head and buried his body. She returned to her sisters with his head and placed it in a water jar. As a result of this deed, the sun ceased to rise. Payatamu's relatives met as a medicine society, summoning various animals to help find him. Finally, the lowliest animal of all, the mole, succeeded, and the society members reunited Payatamu's head and body, together with the flowers that had sprouted from his spilt blood. They sang over him, and by the fourth song both he and the sun rose. But Payatamu had changed: his hair-knot was in front instead of in back, and when he spoke he said, "I'm not even tired." From then on he has said the opposite of what he means and has been known as Nepayatamu (*Ne*—from Newekwe, the clown society).

In the myth, Nepayatamu decides to take revenge. He blows
on his flute and out comes a Rocky Mountain swallowtail butterfly, which he sends to lure the murderess and her sisters out of
their house. The butterfly sprinkles them with its wing powder,
causing them to become sexually crazy, and then leads them to a
tree where the beasts who had been sent out to find Payatamu—
the mountain lion, bear, badger, coyote, and mole—have intercourse with the women. Next, Nepayatamu takes the women
home, where his sisters make them grind the corn that is too
hard to grind and mock them. Finally, he takes the women on a
journey to the east. When they become tired, he turns them into
moths and butterflies and sucks them into his flute. He joins his
Sun Father in the eastern ocean and rides with him across the
sky toward the west, returning to earth at a spring called Ash
Water. This becomes the shrine of Nepayatamu, founder and
patron of the Newekwe of today.

The medicine of the Newekwe includes the plant, as yet
unidentified, that sprouted from the spilt blood of its founder,
and it may also include *Datura inoxia*. This sacramental medicine enables the communicant to clown without shame, to eat
anything with impunity, and to travel on the Milky Way in
search of knowledge and guidance for the Zuñi people. The
shamanic dimension of Newekwe knowledge was not often
recognized by early ethnographers; their reports are largely
limited to sketchy and disapproving descriptions of clowning.
For example, in *The Urine Dance of the Zuñi Indians of New Mexico*,
published in 1881 by John G. Bourke — "strictly for private
circulation" and "not for general perusal" —he calls the ritual
gluttony of the Newekwe, including the drinking and eating of
human urine and excrement, "a disgusting rite . . . revolt-
ing . . . abominable dance . . . vile .ceremonial."[3] Twenty
years later Matilda Coxe Stevenson described similar practices:

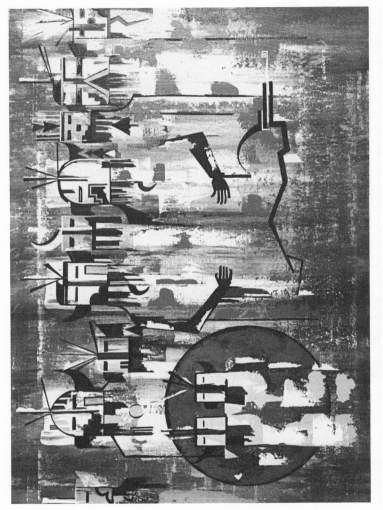

Blue Winter Kachinas, 1978 DAVID PALADIN

Each man endeavors to excel his fellows in buffoonery and in eating repulsive things, such as bits of old blankets or splinters of wood. They bite off the heads of living mice and chew them, tear dogs limb from limb, eat the intestines and fight over the liver like hungry wolves. It is a pleasure to state that the Ne'wekwe is the only fraternity that indulges in such practices.[4]

But Frank Hamilton Cushing, who lived at Zuñi for nearly six years during the 1880s and spoke the language, seems to have enjoyed the ritual gluttony:

I have seen one of them gather about him his melons, green and ripe, raw peppers, bits of stick and refuse, unmentionable water, live puppies—or dead, no matter,—peaches, stones and all, in fact everything soft enough or small enough to be forced down his gullet, including wood ashes and pebbles, and with the greatest apparent gusto, consume them all at a single sitting. Once after such a repast, two of these Ne'we . . . fixed their staring eyes on me, and motioned me to give them *something else to eat*! I ran home, caught up some crackers, threw them into a paper, and in order to make them relish them better, poured a pint or two of molasses over them. I wrapped an old woolen army jacket around this . . . hurried back (and) cast the bundle into the plaza. The pair immediately fell to fighting for its possession, consequently broke the paper, scattered some of the crackers about the ground and daubed the back of the coat thoroughly with the molasses. They gathered up the fragments of crackers and ate them, with their whole burden of adhesions, then fought over the paper and ate that, finally tore pieces out of the back of the coat with their teeth and ate them (though it nearly choked them to do so), after which the victor put the coat on and triumphantly wore it, his painted skin showing like white patches through the holes he had bitten in the back of the coat.[5]

Whatever they thought of gluttony, Matilda Coxe Stevenson and John Bourke did seem to rather enjoy Newekwe mockery of Roman Catholic ritual. Stevenson reported that one afternoon, during a kachina dance, a small clown was declared to be a *"Católico santo"*; larger clowns carried him around in procession until they came to the main plaza, where they seated him on a blanket spread on a ledge (representing an altar) and placed a torch on either side of him.[6] John Bourke vividly draws the picture of himself being taken for a saint by these same clowns:

> One was more grotesquely attired than the rest in a long India-rubber gossamer "overall" and a pair of goggles, painted white, over his eyes. His general "get up" was a spirited take-off upon a Mexican priest . . . I suppose that in the halo diffused by the feeble light and in my "stained-glass attitude" I must have borne some resemblance to the pictures of saints hanging upon the walls of old Mexican churches . . . The dancers suddenly wheeled in line, threw themselves on their knees before my table, and with extravagant beatings of breast began an outlandish but faithful mockery of a Mexican Catholic congregation at vespers. One bawled out a parody upon the Pater Noster, another mumbled along in the manner of an old man reciting the rosary, while the fellow with the India-rubber coat jumped up and began a passionate exhortation or sermon, which for mimetic fidelity was inimitable.[7]

More recently, however, the government agent stationed at Zuñi did not appreciate the clowns' mockery of the birth and death of Jesus Christ. This elaborate Newekwe skit of the 1930s was recently retold to me by a man who still savors it:

Once they had a king and queen, and they had angels, too. They made a cart, and they had two burrows pulling it. That king and queen rode in the cart, and they came to see Jesus. The guy who was Jesus had a real long beard, about this long [indicates two feet]. They nailed him up on one side of the plaza. The agent, Mr. Trotter, was there. I guess the governor had told him they were having a dance or something in the plaza, and he could go and see it. When he came they fined him right away. [Clowns "fine" outsiders who watch their antics, demanding $50, but all they want is a pack of cigarettes.] Later he left. I guess he didn't like the way they were nailing Jesus up—they had boards or something behind his hands to put the nails in, and that guy was really yelling and crying. They whipped him— you know how King Herod whipped Jesus. After a while he stopped crying and they said he was dead. They took him down and put him in a box, and he rose in three days—you know how Jesus rose from the dead in three days. They counted to three, and he popped out of the box.

The opening of this skit is ambiguous. Is this king one of the three wise men, so henpecked that he brings his wife along on his visit to the baby Jesus at Bethlehem? Or is this the poor carpenter Joseph, who led a burro to Bethlehem with his pregnant wife Mary seated upon it, transformed into a king who rides with his queen in a burro-drawn cart? Or perhaps both simultaneously. At any rate, for anyone to ride in such a cart is quite funny to a Zuñi audience, since burros were used as pack animals to haul firewood at Zuñi and never to draw carts with people in them.

The skit then moves on, leaving out the entire life and teaching of Christ, and picks up at his crucifixion. Although no whipping of Jesus by King Herod took place in the Bible, Jesus was blindfolded, beaten, and mocked by the captains of the temple before his crucifixion. Portraying Jesus as "really yelling and crying" while being nailed to the cross—instead of calmly saying "Father, forgive them; for they know not what they do"—changes Jesus into a common man with common emotions. It strips him of his divine imperviousness to his own human suffering, so masterfully portrayed in Luke 23:46, where, at the moment of his own death, like a priest at the deathbed of another, he calmly hands himself over to God by saying in a loud voice, "Father, into thy hands I commend my spirit," the placement of Christ in a box, from which he suddenly pops up on the count of three, reminds one simultaneously of a child's delight with a Jack-in-the-box and of a boxing match, where a man still down after the count of ten would be out.

As in the space burlesques, religious and secular ideas and beliefs alien to Zuñi culture are brought into the sacred context of a kachina dance. Here the clowns share the plaza with men who have ritually purified themselves and have observed sexual continence before putting on the masks of ancestors. In contrast, the Newekwe members are not impersonating the dead, their face paint is not an ancestral mask, and they have neither fasted nor observed sexual continence. Instead of taking the part of the dead, they are very much alive; as medicine society members they ritually died during their initiation, but they were reborn with a new heart. The kachina maskers, under the guidance of well-known ritual forms, face the old dangers of close association with the dead, whereas the clowns are always facing new dangers, whether sent by Madrid or Washington, by Rome or by Houston Control. Eventually, in 1972, there did come a kachina song that alluded, through the indirect means provided by allegory, to the moon landings, but this happened only after the clowns had been dealing directly with such events for some years.

It is the clowns, and not the kachinas, who step so far beyond the boundaries of ancient tradition as to put on a religious performance specifically for the benefit of the newly-elected officials of the Zuñi secular government. This government, instituted long ago by the Spanish, is still thought of as a foreign imposition, a necessary evil for dealing with the political aspect of the white world. In 1965, the theme of the Newekwe performance for the officers of this government was the intertribal pow-wow then being proposed for the Zuñi Tribal Fair.

The hour-long clowning opened when a clown marched into the plaza carrying a sign reading "Oklahoma Indians" on the front and "Zuñi ceremonial 1965" on the back, the choice of the word "ceremonial" being an allusion to the white-run Gallup Ceremonial. Six other clowns followed, with their usual feathered wands, skull caps, and black-and-white striped face paint, but now sporting the fringed breech clouts and vests of Plains Indian pow-wow performers. The lead man wore a Plains war bonnet and plastic glasses, with both bonnet and frames in dayglow colors, and the drummer wore a buffalo fur cap and half-moon sunglasses. Another clown was dressed as a woman, with fringed white buckskin jacket and skirt, beaded collar and headband, a necklace of luminous plastic beads that looked more like Christmas-tree ornaments than proper silver jewelry, a single eagle feather that jutted out ridiculously from the back of the head, and a feather fan. Four more clowns wore large half-circles of feathers attached in the back at their waists, hanging down over their rears. These feathers were all dyed in loud primary colors, a Plains preference which Zuñis always avoid in their own costumes, even for pow-wows.

The assembled clowns performed several dances to Plains music, provided by a Victrola in the window of a house near the plaza. The dancing emphasized such Plains characteristics as a lack of organized formation, crouched posture, vigorous steps, and much up-and-down tossing of the head. During one song the dancers assumed a push-up posture and wiggled their hips in time to the music; at the point where they were supposed to leap to their feet and pivot around 360 degrees with one hand still on the ground, one of them fell down instead and did the entire pivot flat on the ground, to howls of laughter. At another point two dancers collided heavily with each other and responded with a comic-book "Oof!" The lines of dialogue between dances included these: "We from Oklahoma—that's a long ways from here," "When are we gonna get the money from the white men?" and "We'll put the white men in jail," this last a reversal of the situation when pow-wows are held in white towns. One clown suddenly asked, with great urgency, "Where's the Zuñi restroom?" and then went over to the wall of the kiva and thrust his hand beneath his breech clout, relieving himself on the wall of that sacred edifice. When a clown began to sing "Oklahoma!" (with an interminable "O"), another interrupted him with a classic hillbilly song, "You're in the Jail House Now." The woman clown, clutching a mock microphone and smiling broadly, sang a song of the "Indian Love Call" genre, in cracking falsetto.

At this point the lead clown, announcing himself as the Governor of Zuñi and calling attention to the star-shaped badge he was wearing, laid out a large piece of canvas and two Navajo rugs on the bench outside the main kiva and seated the seven newly-elected members of the Zuñi Tribal Council. The seven clowns then shook hands with the officials and gave each of them a sacred ear of corn (one with every kernel perfect and in place, even at the tip); to the top-ranking councilmen—the Governor, Lieutenant Governor, and First Teniente—they gave a feather as well. Now the clowns played especially for them. The impersonated woman sang again in falsetto, repeatedly breaking into a piercing screech. The council members seemed slightly embarrassed by some of the more ridiculous parts of the skit, and one of them even shrank back and held one hand before his face at several points. At the end, the clowns stood in an east-west row along the northern side of the plaza, facing south. The councilmen rose and stood in a group near the clown leader, at the east end of the row, and prayed. But even while the prayers were being said the vocalist clowned by herself, fanning herself and then making the head feather of the clown next to her wiggle in the draft she created with her fan. The councilmen ritually thanked the clowns by sprinkling them with cornmeal. When the woman was sprinkled, she said, in an insipidly sweet English falsetto, "Oh, *thank* you!" Finally the clowns were given change by the councilmen. The woman clown, while looking on and waiting her turn, said in a sharp voice, "I want some *money!*" When the councilmen had finished and left the plaza, all seven clowns suddenly broke ranks and, with shouts and war whoops, danced wildly for a few more minutes.

This side-splitting, hour-long clowning episode, which had attracted an enormous audience, brought out all the worrisome implications of staging an intertribal pow-wow within the Zuñi Reservation. The clowns made an exploratory crossing of the boundary between Zuñi and pan-Indian culture, bringing their findings right into the middle of the sacred dance plaza. At a level beyond that of pow-wows, their lampoon served as a reminder to the civil officials that even when they went on junkets to Washington, they would still be Zuñis with Zuñi traditions, symbolized here by the gifts of perfect ears of corn and natural feathers, and not pan-Indians with fancy dancing, dyed feathers, and a preference for English.

Newekwe dramas, as exemplified by the ritual gluttony, space burlesque, Passion Play, and pan-Indian pow-wow described here, take place on or beyond the boundaries of the religious forms and civil decorum observed by ordinary Zuñis. More subtly, such dramas might be said to constitute a continuing discovery, or re-discovery, of just what those boundaries are. The behavior of the clowns provides an anti-creed for a religion which lacks any formal creed or codified body of doctrine. A believer in the Zuñi religion does not say, "I believe in the Moon Mother," but the space skit provides an anti-statement of this belief. The clowns' portrayal of the materialist exploration of space as (in part) a literal search for signs of biological life beyond the earth contrasts with the implicit Zuñi religious belief that the "life" of the Moon Mother, like that of Salt Woman, Turquoise Man, rainstorms, and the ancestors, is of a kind that transcends biological definitions.

Beyond creeds and anti-creeds, the clowns, by their ability not only to conceive but to carry out their burlesques, display their own ultimate detachment from the particulars of religious beliefs of all kinds. Even Zuñi beliefs come under direct inspection: when the woman from Oklahoma said, "Oh, *thank* you" to a sprinkling of cornmeal, the humor cut both ways. In ritual gluttony, the clowns even violate the boundaries of their biological being: not satisfied with saying the unsayable, they eat the inedible. Their path is finally that of the Milky Way (or Ash Way), which arches over the entire human and biological world. From such a perspective, these doctor clowns see boundaries as easy hurdles rather than as walls. That is why they never laugh at their own jokes. But by causing others to laugh at the leaping of a boundary, they share a moment of shamanic detachment with the uninitiated.

Blue Jay

Salish

Yes, this here Blue Jay and his brother-in-law Wolf, that's what I'm going to tell. This here Wolf was married to the oldest one. And he was their leader. There is also another tribe, and the chief's daughter, and the chief's law relations. And long time ago they didn't know what money was, they put the providers above everything else. Yes, those who get grub, that's who they put above everything else. They are the highest.

And so that's when Wolf proposed to the chief for his daughter, and he consented because Wolf is smart in getting things to eat, deer. And the chief told him: "All right." And so they married, he and his daughter. And when they go hunting they put Wolf on the head.

And at that time the people didn't stay alone but in a group. Yes, they stick together in winter time; they call it wintering. They don't have buckskin tipis. They use all kinds of things to cover their houses, this here tules; they use this here tree bark; or just anything, boughs, these here cedar boughs.

Well, Blue Jay got to them. Well, he proposed to the chief. The youngest one had grown up too. They say in Indian she was a maiden. She wants a man. Well Blue Jay started to flirt. Blue Jay got stuck on her and she told her father: "You better consent." Her father tried to tell her: "But we don't know him. We don't know in what things he's smart, in getting things to eat, maybe you will suffer from it. It might not be long and you'll throw him away if he's good for nothing. Get the one that'll do us good, take that one for your man." But no, his daughter. "He's going to be *my* husband, not your husband. Even if I got hard up, it's me who gets hard up." He told her: "Well, all right, if that's how you feel."

That was that, and they gave Blue Jay his answer. Well, he got married. And Blue Jay went on a honeymoon. And they were all together, Wolf and his woman, and this here Blue Jay and his wife, and his law relations, the regal couple, the chief and his mate. There are all together there in one house, I don't know how many tipis put together, maybe four, maybe three, because there are three couples. Well, all Blue Jay does is play with his wife. He sleeps till noon, then he wakes up, he gets up with his wife, because they're on their honeymoon. Everybody is gone by that time.

They hunt, get things to eat, and Wolf is their leader because he sure is smart in getting things to eat. He knows where the wintering places for deer are, and he is very good on snow shoes. When they make a drive for the deer Wolf chases them. The deer don't go far and then he catches up with them and then he slaughters them. Then he overtakes his relations, and the other people, and he gives the deer to the others. And then they drag them home, they don't even have to shoot and then they get meat. That's when he gives it to them to eat, Wolf. Because he is great, smart in hunting. That's why he is their leader.

Well, his oldest daughter started eating her feelings, getting cross, Wolf's wife. She is always watching her brother-in-law. She hates her brother-in-law. She even said to her younger sister: "What's the matter with you? It's been many days, and you two

are still honeymooning. You should already be getting tired of
one another. And he should be getting things to eat, your husband. And all you do is play. But no. You know that your brother-
in-law sure gets tired that all you do is play. Even if he doesn't
shoot, just so he goes along. And his brother-in-law would feel
good. I guess he has all kinds of different thoughts."

Well, she kept nagging at her younger sister. First she tried to
take up for her husband; finally she believed, she understood.
"That's true, my older sister is telling the truth." The parents
never say anything. They tried to stop their oldest daughter
when she hates her brother-in-law and she backbites him. Well,
the younger daughter told her Blue Jay: "Listen here. It has
been too many days, and we are still on our honeymoon. Listen,
think about getting some grub. We have sponged on them too
much. Maybe they are getting tired of us. Look at your sister-in-
law. They hate us very much. And they are your law relations.
They tried to take up for you. They tried to stop their daughter,
the oldest one. They said to her: 'Just leave your brother-in-law
alone.' " He said to his wife: "Give me a piece of skin, since you
complain with me. I haven't got any snow shoes, nor have I got
any bow and arrow. I am going to prepare myself."

Well, he got a bow, Blue Jay. Well, the bow he made, it wasn't
even that, it was awful. It wasn't any good. And the arrows he
got, they are just the same. And even when he put the feathers
on those arrows, he just stuck them on. And the arrows weren't
good enough. He doesn't make things well enough; his snow
shoes, no, they are bad, and they were weak. It was just new
shoots that he made the frame with. Well it's not even fit.

Well she finally asked her mother some skin for weaving
thread. She said to her: "What's that for?" She said, "Your son-
in-law, the one I'm married to, well, he's going with the hunters
and he has no snow shoes, and now he's got sticks ready, and he's

made frames but he has nothing to lace them in. That's what he told me, and I interpret him to you, maybe you got some hide." She told her: "Well, yes. I keep some in stock. I will give you some." So she started cutting it.

Blue Jay then started stringing the shoes. Well, it took him one whole day to fix his bow and arrow and his snow shoes. And those that are used to fixing them it takes them a good many days to finish shoe-work or arrow-work. But he, in one day and already he had finished his arrow and his snow shoes. Surely, they're not good enough. They took pains, the ones that know how to fix them. The sticks for the arrows have to be dry, and then they straighten them. Then they fix the feathers on the arrow and the bow the same way. They dry the sticks; when they get dry they whittle them, and they wipe them. Then they use something . . . I don't know the word . . . to make it shine in the center of the bow. And then they wrap it with a string, with sinew, and they pitch it. And it doesn't come loose, it's solid. Then it's good and strong. And maybe Blue Jay has got weak arms, because what he made is no good.

The next day it was still dark, and Wolf hollered: "Daylight will overtake us, we will be too late, we're going far. Get up!" Goodness, the people got up, the young folks. They ate, they drinked, they were all ready. He hollered, Wolf was hollering: "All right, we're going." All the young folks started coming out. Blue Jay is there too. He came out.

Blue Jay was still inside, and he coaxed his wife to put his snow shoes on him because he doesn't even know how to tie his shoes. Well, this woman put his snow shoes on him right from inside. My, and how they made fun of him. They laughed at him because he put his snow shoes on from inside. He just takes one step and he hooks on something, Blue Jay. He has to protect himself with his hands. It must be from the snow, and his hands get really cold. I don't suppose he had gloves on and he started sucking his fingers because they're cold.

Then the young ones said: "No, maybe he'll just get out of sight and then he'll go back home because he's way behind. He'll give up, take his head and hang it down, and he'll go back. He's just making us lose time." They walked away. This here Wolf is way ahead. He is making the trail, he fixes the trail for his friends. They go, then they find tracks, and then they scatter. Wolf'll point where to go. This here Wolf is the leader, he is the smartest of all. He goes where the deer goes. Because he is smart and strong. He can go fast.

They were going, and then they see the tracks. Lots of deer where they were feeding. They scattered. There were lots of deer. He stopped. There is a hollow place, it's a big place. The deer must be there. "We didn't scared them. Here are their tracks, they might be still eating." It was broad daylight then. They stopped and he told them: "Are you all here?" They said: "Yes, we are here. Just your brother-in-law Blue Jay, he hasn't come in sight yet. Just as we left, he was falling around because he doesn't know anything about snow shoes, he might have turned back. Let's not wait for him. We're wasting time." Wolf said: "Well, that's right, we saw these tracks, deer tracks, fresh tracks. I don't think they went anywhere. Maybe they are in that hollow, in them slate rocks. We'll scatter. Just when you get to the top there's a saddle. That's where we'll all get back together. If they've already gone over that, then we'll think more how we're going to scatter again."

Blue Jay has been watching for them. He saw his friends all scatter. And he must have good hearing, he heard every word of it. Blue Jay was just putting on, and that's why he fell deep in the snow as if he didn't know his snow shoes. Blue Jay just rised up, kicked the trees. The wind started blowing. The snow on the trees came down to the ground. The snow was floating around the earth. They ran up the hill, these here deer. The same thing happened with the air, they done their best to get where they could get shelter, to a place for shelter where there's no air, and where the snow and wind didn't reach, and where it's still. Blue Jay went up the hill. He went. He got there to the top of the mountain where that low place is. The deer had already gone over. His brother-in-law, he's already went over behind. He started following and he was right in the tracks of his brother-in-law.

Wolf hadn't gone very far, and he heard something. He got the chills. He looked behind him, well, he was being overtaken by his brother-in-law Blue Jay. Then he runs, he's doing his very best. He thought: "Ah, and we thought he couldn't make it, and here I am, the best in hunting, and he overtakes me. It won't be far now, he'll give out." Until he overtakes the deer that's when he'll turn back this here Wolf.

Well, then Wolf run down the hill. His snow shoes go dust, dust, dust, dust; with the corner of his eyes he saw his brother-in-law. His snow shoes too go dust, dust, dust, dust. He had got used to his snow shoes. Wolf didn't get to the bottom and he got give out. Wolf just tried, couldn't make it and turned around. He was too tired. He told his brother-in-law: "Go ahead, maybe you're a little better off than I am. I'm plum to the end, I'm done tired. Maybe you are stronger," he said. Wolf gave him the way, he stepped aside. Blue Jay made another jump. Just like Wolf never made a move. He started to go. Just like that Blue Jay was out of sight.

Wolf tried his best and finally got to the bottom, because he always tracks the deer. Blue Jay's tracks are right along. It got dark, and it was dusk when he got to the bottom. Deers laying all over. Well, Blue Jay was busy doing something. That was the last deer. And Blue Jay had got done taking the guts out. And that's when he overtook him. He's got them all killed, the deer. Wolf thought: "From the time I was born, from the time I got my senses nobody could step in front of me. And now this here brother-in-law of mine stepped in front of me. I'm not going to believe it. Maybe I'm just dreaming."

Blue Jay told him: "Well, now let's turn back. We might be too late. Our women are still far away yet, and so is our staying place." Wolf thought, and he figured it's all uphill, and then to the top, then it's all downhill to their houses, and he said: "No, I fear it. I have no more breath from fatigue. All I could do was catch up with you. I can't make it to go up the hill. I'm going to camp here."

Blue Jay had already figured out what to do. The biggest, the leader of the deer that he killed, it had a lot of fat inside of it, he thought. Well he had buried the deer-gift down—that is, deer he gave to the other guy. He broke up the stitches, because he had stitched up the deer. He told his brother-in-law: "You go in here, in this here deer." He told him. "And then you'll live. Well, look how clear it is, it'll be very cold. You'll freeze. What can you do to make fire? What can you do to get wood? Look at all this snow. What can you do to get fir boughs, in the dark, and you're tired besides. That's the only way you can save your life. Don't refuse. If you refuse, you'll die. Don't you get stingy of your wife? You want to stay alive!"

He coaxed his brother-in-law. Then Wolf believed him. He thought: "I'm all in from tired. What he told me is true." He said: "Yes, I'll take your advice." He told him: "Well, get in."

Well he went into the deer, because it was big and he stitched the deer back, and he put snow back on the deer. Well after he got snow on top, Wolf got warmed up because he still wasn't too cold. He got very hot, sweated; he hadn't got too chilled before.

He really liked how he was getting warm. It was really warm. But he's very hungry. He felt something, the fat. He cut some off, and then he ate. That was delicious. He cleaned all the inside of his gift deer. In a little while since it's fresh deer, he got diarrhea. There's no way of him getting out, because he's sewed up there. Right then Wolf shat himself, he that used to be the boss.

Blue Jay run up the hill, got to the top he run down the hill. He got half way; he got closer to home. Then he hollered and hollered, because that's the way the hunters go when they get late, because their relatives don't go to sleep. They always wait up for them.

They heard. He was hollering. They answered him. They thought: "This is Wolf." This here Wolf's wife pushed her younger sister. She said: "Hah, hurry, fix the fire! Stir it for him! That might be your man that's hollering. Put the coffee on! He must be awful hungry." She's making fun of her younger sister.

Well they heard him, because the snow shoes are loud, because it's frozen. Puckh, puckh, puckh, puckh. That's snow shoes. The sound is good not as if tired. Well, he came in. He raised the curtain. He came in. He still had snow shoes on. And he sat down.

His wife rushed to him. She put her arm around his neck, and kissed him. She told him: "I bet you're tired." He said: "Yes, yes, I am tired. I've traveled around far. I was all in when I got back. Take my snow shoes off." She took his snow shoes off, and he said: "And my moccasins too, because my feet are wet." Because he had moccasins on. "I got wet when I covered the deer with snow." Well she took his moccasins off. She set dishes for him, a whole pot of food.

Blue Jay was just about to eat and he pulled something from his vest. And he throwed it at his father-in-law. He said: "Take it, look at this. Then you'll know what this is, you'll wonder what it is." His father-in-law took it. He started to unwrap it. "What part of the deer?" He laid it down, he done like that, and shook it, and put it down; he can't figure out what it is. It doesn't come out right.

The old man went out, because he's the boss, and yelled. He told them: "Come on in. My son-in-law Blue Jay came back. And he gave me this, it was tied up. And I can't get them together, and I can't get it right. I want you to figure it for me, that's why I am asking you." My, the people run over there because that's surprising news. Well, they all come in the chief's tipi. And it was a full house, the young folks. And the chief gave it to them. They tried to figure it out. No, they couldn't figure out this here ear. They know it's a deer's ear; but it wouldn't match. They even laid it down. One half doesn't fit the other half. Well no, it didn't match.

Then they asked Blue Jay. They told him: "We are puzzled. What is wrong with this ear, and it won't match?" Blue Jay just laughed and laughed at them, and he told them: "You got no sense. You know it won't match. And each one has one ear. And I marked all of them, just one ear on one side. And if it comes out right, then it will be easy to count." That's when they all agreed. They understood, and they knowed about the ears. They counted them. There was lots of deer if there is that many ears.

The oldest one, his sister-in-law, asked him, "What became of your brother-in-law? Didn't you see him?" He said: "Yes, we scared a bunch of deer. I just went ahead of him. I left him. The deer had just got down to the bottom and I overtook them. I killed them, finished them all. As many as there are ears. I just got done gutting them, I was going to bury them, when my brother-in-law overtook me. He's just played out with tiredness, he's just walking. And he told me: 'Well, with me, I got tired. I got give out. And I can't make it, I'm discouraged to go back. And I'll just camp here with them deer.' I told him: 'No. You'll freeze to death. I'll put you away in here in the biggest of the deer, because they're all open. I'll put you in here and you won't freeze to death.' I put him there, and sewed him up. I twisted a stick. I sewed the deer up. I tromped the snow. It made a hole there. I stuck him in there, and I buried it with snow. And then I stepped away."

Then he told the chief. He told his father-in-law. Blue Jay told them: "All of you that are related will get up early, the women folks too. We're going after the dead deer. Because it's far." They said: "OK." They never went to sleep, the folks. The morning come, and they woke up, they started hollering.

They went. And they got a leader, Blue Jay. Blue Jay is really smart on snow shoes. He didn't used to know how. And they made fun of him. Blue Jay's wife had also gone along. And his sister-in-law was right behind too, also his mother-in-law and father-in-law, they're behind. And then the rest of the folks, they string along. They went there in a big valley, and at the end there's a little mountain, that's where the low place is. They went right over that hill. Then they went down the hill. They got to the bottom. He told them: "It's right here."

There is lumps all over where the deer is buried. He told his father-in-law: "You are the boss, my father-in-law. You give the meat away. The whole deer." The father-in-law said: "No, even if I'm the chief, you're the one that killed it, you are the one that worked hard. You pass it around. And here I was just setting down, laying on my back; pulling my whiskers with tweezers. And for me to take the lead to pass it around . . . You do it!" He said: "OK."

He passed it around. He knows where he put Wolf in the deer. He told his sister-in-law: "That's what I'm going to give you this lump. You dig that out, do what you please, drag it home or skin it, pack it back, do anything. Whatever you think." My, this sister-in-law was glad; I suppose she kissed Blue Jay, his sister-in-law was so tickled. She used to hate him, his sister-in-law, because he was good for nothing. She started digging that deer up. When she got all the snow off, she got to the deer. It was sewed up with the sprig he had twisted. She undid them stitches. She done like that, she opened it where it was cut opened and sewed up. She opened it. And all of a sudden out came her man. He's nothing but shit. Goodness, the stink hit the woman in the nose. It really stunk, her husband. She tried to fix things. She's going to try to skin it. She couldn't stand it. This here deer is nothing but shit.

The woman just stood there frowning. She got after her husband. She said: "You've done something too awful. Why, that was our eats, and you messed it up." "Ha," he told his wife: "You talk pitiful. I didn't mean it. I got give out; I was tired. If I hadn't slept inside that deer . . . He done my thinking, my brother-in-law. I'd been froze to death. He left me. In a little while I got rested, that's when I felt hungry. And I ate the fat. That's what done me bad and I got diarrhea. There is no way of me getting out. That's when I done that pitiful thing inside there, I didn't do it on purpose."

They started packing the deer. And Blue Jay got to be boss. They got all the dead deer back home. They got to drying meat, the men folks to roasting. And the women cutting it open, they started drying it over the fire. Lots of deer meat, each one gets a whole deer. And this here Wolf's woman, I don't think she'll throw it away, whatever she did with it. Maybe she washed the deer. She aired it out till it smelled no more, and then she roasted it.

And because it's just fairy tales, I say: The sun is coming up high, it's late, and I'm going to end, like they say in Moses language. With us, we say: "It's the end of the story."

One More Smile for a Hopi Clown

Emory Sekaquaptewa

*T*he heart of the Hopi concept of clowning is that we are all clowns. This was established at the very beginning when people first emerged from the lower world. In spite of the belief that this was a new world in which no corruption and immorality would be present, the people nevertheless took as their own all things that they saw in the new world. Seeing that the people still carried with them many of the ways of the corrupted under-world, the Spirit Being divided them into groups and laid out a life-pattern for each of them, so that each would follow its own life-way.

Before the Hopi people left from the emergence place, one man chosen by them as their leader went up on a hill. I can just imagine the throng of his people around him who were excited and eager in getting ready to be led out to the adventures of a new world. The leader gets up on this hill and calls out, "yaahahay!" four times. Thus gaining their attention he says, "Now you heard me cry out to you in this way. You will hear me cry in this way when we have reached the end of our life-way. It will be a sign that we have reached the end of the world. We will know then whether we have fulfilled our destiny. If we have not we will see how it is to be done."

The leader who was a visionary man chose this way of reminding his people that they have only their worldly ambition and aspirations by which to gain a spiritual world of eternity. He was showing them that we cannot be perfect in this world after all and if we are reminded that we are clowns, maybe we can have, from time to time, introspection as a guide to lead us right. From this beginning when we have been resembled to clowns we know that this is to be a trying life and that we will try to fulfill our destiny by mimicry, by mockery, by copying, by whatever.

This whole idea of clowning is re-enacted at the time of the *katsina* dances. When they are dancing in the plaza the *katsinas* represent the spiritual life toward which Hopi destiny is bent. The *katsinas* dance in the plaza at intervals throughout the day and sometimes for two days. When the clowns come they represent man today who is trying to reach this place of paradise. That is why the clowns always arrive at the plaza from the rooftops of the houses facing the plaza where the *katsinas* are dancing. The rooftops signify that even though we have reached the end, we are not necessarily ready to walk easily into the spiritual world. The difficulties by which clowns gain the place of the *katsinas* make for fun and laughter, but also show that we may not all be able to make it from the rooftop because it is too difficult. We are going to clown our way through life making believe that we know everything and when the time comes, possibly no one will be prepared after all to enter the next world. We will still find the way difficult with obstacles in front of us. Maybe some of us won't make it.

The clowns come to the edge of the housetops around noon and they announce themselves with the cry "yaahahay!" four times. This announces as foretold at emergence the arrival at the end of the life-way journey. And then they make their way into the plaza with all sorts of antics and buffoonery representing the Hopi life quest. In their actions they reveal that we haven't yet fulfilled our destiny after all. By arriving at the late hour, noon, they show that we are lagging behind because we think we have many things to do.

Once in the plaza they act just as people did when they emerged in this world. They presume that they are in a new world, clean and pure. They are where they can finally have eternal life like the *katsinas*; indeed, this is the day all Hopi look forward to. But as they are remarking on the beauty of this place filled with plants and good things they hear the *katsina* songs. They grope around the plaza looking for someone. They pretend they cannot see them because they are spirits. Finally, one of the clowns touches a *katsina* and upon his discovery of these beautiful beings, the clowns immediately try to take possession of them. "This is mine!" "This is mine!" They even fight each other over the possession of the *katsinas* and over the food and things they find.

The remainder of the afternoon is filled with all sorts of clown performances, many of which are planned in advance. Others just happen. These are satires focused on almost anything whether it be in the Hopi world or in the non-Hopi world. Clowns make fun of life and thereby cause people to look at themselves.

Imagination is important to the clown. There are good clowns and not so good clowns when it comes to being funny and witty. But all clowns perform for the smiles and laughter they hope to inspire in the people. When the clowns leave the kiva on the way to the plaza the last request by each is a prayer something to the effect, "If it be so, may I gain at least one smile."

The clown skits and satiric performances done throughout the afternoon are reminiscent of the corruption that we experienced in the underworld, where we presumably had Conscience as a guide. We chose not to follow the Conscience and it comes

Longhair Kachina, 1987 DAN NAMINGHA

into play during the clown performances in the form of *katsinas* that visit the plaza. The Owl *katsina* on his first visit comes with a handful of pebbles, carrying a switch. He appears at each corner of the plaza presumably unseen by the clowns and throws little pebbles at the clowns, occasionally hitting them. These pangs of Conscience are felt but not heeded by the clowns. Owl *katsina* returns to the plaza later accompanied by several threatening *katsinas* carrying whips. And this time, instead of pebbles, he may brush up against one of the clowns. He may even knock him down. Conscience keeps getting stronger and more demanding and insistent. On Owl's third visit, the clowns begin to realize that they may suffer consequences if they don't change their ways. Still, they try to buy their safety by offering Owl a bribe. On the sly, the head clown approaches Owl, presumably unseen by anyone, but, of course, they are in the middle of the plaza and are witnessed by all the spectators. Those two kneel together in an archaic conversation modeled upon an ancient meeting.

Owl finally accepts the bribe of a string of beads and thus leads the clown to believe that he has bought his safety. The head clown asks Owl to discipline the other clowns so as to get them back on the right road, but he thinks he will be safe.

With each of Owl's visits more and more *katsinas* accompany him. They do not come as one big group, but in groups of two or three. Throughout the afternoon the tension builds with the threatening presence of the whip-carrying *katsinas*. All of the spectators begin to identify with the plight of the clowns. You feel as if you are the one who is now being judged for all these things.

Owl's fourth visit may not come until the next day. On this visit he brings with him a whole lot of warrior *katsinas*. The atmosphere is one of impending catastrophe. They move closer and closer, finally attacking the clowns, who are stripped and whipped for all they have done. In this way they force the clowns to take responsibility for their actions. After they are whipped, water is poured on them and sprinkled about the audience to signify purification.

When it is all over the threatening *katsinas* come back to the plaza again, but this time they are friendly. They shake hands with the clowns signifying that they have been purified. Then they take each clown the length of the plaza and form a semi-circle around him. At this time the clowns make confessions, but even here they are clowns for their confessions are all made in jest. Having worked up satires for the occasion they jump and sing before the *katsinas*. Their confessions usually are focused on their clan, who, by way of being satirized, are actually honored.

I'll tell you one I heard not long ago. When it was time for this young clown man to make his confession he jumps up and down in front of the *katsina* and says, "ah ii geology, geology, ah ii!" Then he makes a beautiful little breakdown of this word so that it has Hopi meaning. "You probably think I am talking about this geology which is a white man's study about something or other. Well, that's not it," he says. "What it really is is that I have a grandmother, and you know she being poor and ugly, nobody would have anything to do with her. She is running around all summer long out in the fields doing a man's job. It breaks her down. She would go out there every day with no shoes and her feet are not very dainty and not very feminine. If you pick up her foot and look at her sole, it is all cracked and that's what I am talking about when I say geology." Every Hopi can put that together. *Tsiya* means "to crack" and *leetsi* means things placed "in a row," so these cracks are in a row on the bottom of the feet, geology. Things like that are what the confessions are like.

There is a story about the last wish of a Hopi man who died

many years ago that shows the character of clowning.

In those days the clown society was very much formalized. It was a practice for men who had great devotion for their ritual society to be buried in the full costume of their office. Of course, this was not seen by the general public since Hopi funerals are rather private affairs.

This story is about a man who had gained great respect for his resourcefulness and performance as a clown. Clowning had become a major part of his life and he was constantly attending to his work as a clown by thinking up new skits and perfecting his performance. As he reached old age he decided that clowning had made his place in this world and he wanted to be remembered as a clown. So he made a special request for what was to be done with him at his death as he realized his time was short. He made his request to his family very firmly.

When he died his nephews and sons began to carry out his request. In preparation for burial the body was dressed in his clown costume. Then the body was carried around to the west side of the plaza and taken up on a roof. While this was being done the town crier's voice rang out through the village calling all the people to the plaza. Everybody was prompt in gathering there. I can just see the women, as with any such occasion, grabbing their best shawls on their way to the plaza. It didn't matter whether they were dressed well underneath the shawl.

When the people arrived they saw this unusual sight on the roof of the house on the west side of the plaza, men standing around a person lying down. When all of the people had gathered, the attendants—pall-bearers I guess you could call them—simply, quietly, picked up the body and took it to the edge of the house near the plaza. They picked it up by the hands and legs and swung it out over the plaza as if to throw it and they hollered, "Yaahahay!" And they'd swing it back. Then they'd swing it once more. "Yaahahay!" Four times! On the fourth time they let the body go and it fell down, plop, in the plaza. As they threw the body the pallbearers hollered and laughed as they were supposed to. It took the people by surprise. But then everybody laughed.

How Salmon Got Greasy Eyes

Coos-Coquille: As told by Will Wasson

Old Mr. Coyote was up Big Creek, which is a creek that runs into Sunset Bay. Salmon was coming up the creek and oh there was all those pretty little Salmon girls. "Oh," he says, "come here let me pet you. Oh you're such pretty girls. Oh you've got such bright shiny eyes; oh come sit on my lap." They did; he was holding all them Salmon girls on his lap, and all those little Salmon girls got pregnant. Everybody was mad at him and they were chasing Old Man Coyote. He ran looking for a place to hide. About that time came a hailstorm. Hail pelts were hitting him, beating him. There was this big hollow tree standing there. He jumped in the tree and commanded the tree to grow closed 'round him, because the hailstones were still coming in. It went and closed up except for one little hole to breathe through. So while he was in there, why, people came looking for him telling everybody what he'd done—what a bad person he was. He commanded the tree to open up, but the tree knew what he'd done and the tree wouldn't do it; the tree wouldn't obey him. So there he was stuck in there, and he could just see out through that little hole, and oh he saw a woodpecker. He said, "Oh little woodpecker, come here, peck this hole a lot bigger so I can get out." She said, "Oh I don't know if I want to or not." "Oh please do, come on, come on." "All right." She came over and she started pecking on the hole, pecking it out bigger. "Oh," he said, "you're a pretty little bird. Oh you're so pretty. Come over here, let me feel your breasts." And he reached out and she jumped and flew away. "Oh-oh, I didn't mean anything, come back." No, she wouldn't come back. She stayed away; she wasn't going to have anything more to do with him.

There he was and he couldn't figure how to get out of that tree. Ah, he got an idea. He got his clamshell knife in his hair behind his ear. He got his clamshell knife and he started cutting himself up in little pieces, and poking the pieces out through the hole. While he was poking the pieces out, why Raven came flying by and oh he saw all those pieces down there and picked up one and flew off with it. When he got himself all poked out through the hole, why he put himself all back together.

Well it was in the spring and all the wild strawberries were growing. Oh he went along eating strawberries and eating strawberries. "Oh," he said, "what's the matter—I don't get full!" He looked around behind him and there was just a whole string of strawberries right behind him, because there was nothing to hold them in. His rectum was gone. "Oh what am I going to do?" He hunted around and found a spruce knot, and he put that up there and that was too rough and that hurt. Then he found a fir cone, and that was too rough and that hurt. Then he found a wild carrot, and oh he put it up there and that felt pretty good. It wasn't rough and it felt all right but it wouldn't stay in. He went around to the fir tree and he got some pitch. Then he took it and covered it all with pitch and then it stayed in. He went on eating strawberries and oh he got full of strawberries. He got down to Bassendork Beach, near Coos Bay. There was some Seagull boys down there playing on the beach and they had a fire and they were jumping over the fire. "Oh," they said, "mother's brother, uncle—come over and play with us." "Oh," he said, "what are you doing?" "Oh, we're jumping over this fire." "Oh," he says, "O.K." He ran and he jumped over and they said, "Oh no no no, not there, jump over here where it's high." So he did. He ran and he jumped over there and the pitch caught on fire and pop! went the carrot! and shit and strawberries all over the Seagull boys. The pitch was burning and he ran down; he was going to jump in the ocean. As he jumped, there was a whale came up. He opened his mouth and he jumped right inside the whale's mouth.

There he was down inside the whale, looking around in there. Something up there above him— he reached up and battered it a few times, and it flopped back and forth, and took out his clamshell knife and he cut it off. It was the whale's heart, and the whale died. There he was up inside that whale drifting and he could feel the waves getting shorter and shorter as he got in close to the beach and drifted up and up on the beach, and he feel it when it hit the sand. Well how was he going to get out of there? So he took his knife and he just cut his way right out through the side and crawled out through there and he got his eyes all full of blubber. Oh he was going around and he could hardly see. He was just feeling his way around. He got up and back to Big Creek again and oh he found the salmon there. He said, "Look at my beautiful eyes." He said, "Wouldn't you like to try eyes like this?" Oh the salmon didn't know if they wanted to try eyes like that or not. "Oh, try 'em and see! Let's trade eyes and you can see how good these eyes are." O.K., so they traded eyes. Ah! He went around and went away. And that's why to this day salmon's got greasy eyes and the coyote's got bright shiny eyes.

Our Other Selves

Arthur Amiotte

Black Elk told us:

> I was four years old then, and I think it must have been the
> next summer that I first heard the voices. It was a happy
> summer and nothing was afraid, because in the Moon
> When the Ponies Shed [May] word came from the Wasi-
> chus that there would be peace and that they would not use
> the road any more and that all the soldiers would go away.
> The soldiers did go away and their towns were torn down;
> and in the Moon of Falling Leaves [November], they made
> a treaty with Red Cloud that said our country would be ours
> as long as grass should grow and water flow. You can see that
> it is not the grass and the water that have forgotten.
>
> Maybe it was not this summer when I first heard the
> voices, but I think it was, because I know it was before I
> played with bows and arrows or rode a horse, and I was out
> playing alone when I heard them. It was like somebody
> calling me, and I thought it was my mother, but there was
> nobody there. This happened more than once, and always
> made me afraid, so that I ran home.
>
> It was when I was five years old that my Grandfather
> made me a bow and some arrows. The grass was young and
> I was horseback. A thunder storm was coming from where
> the sun goes down, and just as I was riding into the woods

along a creek, there was a kingbird sitting on a limb. This was not a dream, it happened. And I was going to shoot at the kingbird with the bow my Grandfather made, when the bird spoke and said: "The clouds all over are one-sided." Perhaps it meant that all the clouds were looking at me. And then it said: "Listen! A voice is calling you!" Then I looked up at the clouds, and two men were coming there, headfirst like arrows slanting down; and as they came, they sang a sacred song and the thunder was like drumming. I will sing it for you. The song and the drumming were like this:

> *Behold, a sacred voice is calling you;*
> *All over the sky a sacred voice is calling.*

I sat there gazing at them, and they were coming from the place where the giant lives [north]. But when they were very close to me, they wheeled about toward where the sun goes down, and suddenly they were geese. Then they were gone, and the rain came with a big wind and a roaring.

I did not tell this vision to any one. I liked to think about it, but I was afraid to tell it.[1]

Time and time again, in the literature and in the oral tradition of the Lakota, references are made to visions, ghosts, and dreams. Specific differences are also made between the common dream—what modern research calls REM dreams—and what the Lakota believe to be the capacity to pierce a barrier and participate in another realm which is considered sacred.

To grasp the significance to Native people of the dream experience, one must take into account the unique stance from which they describe the metaphysical underpinnings of person and personality, not only of the human being but of all creatures, plants, the world, and the universe.

Central to a host of beliefs connected with dreams and dreaming is the conviction of the transparency and mutability of all *things*. The mythologies of the tribes affirm for the Native the synchronous existence of various planes of reality in which both linear time and physical geography are only one level—one that consistently needs one's attention, for it appears to be incomplete and mutable, still in a process of ongoing creation. The other planes are the sacred counterparts of what we know to exist in the temporal world, but which are imbued with their own sacred power—often under the control of the gods, or operative because of their intervention.

Often, through the powerful language of metaphor, the sacred world is delineated and anthropomorphized, a process by which the various dimensions of the personality of the Wakan (Great Mystery or gods) are made comprehensible and visible to the mind of the Native. This capacity of the Native mind to sustain the mythological presence of the transparent world, to integrate sacred time and geography with ordinary time and space, gives rise to a unique view of self in relation to all things and to others, including those who dwell in the sacred or "spirit" world, or as the Australian Natives call it, the "dreaming."

Attempts to delve deeper into the nature of the spirit world give one the idea that perhaps it is not for everyone to know, and that many people—Native Americans as well as others—who have been touched too deeply by technological and scientific modes of living and thinking cannot again recapture the capacity to operate in it. "Wondering about it" and listening to the tribal wise men sometimes gives us clues about the potential that is inherent in this capacity to live in both worlds; and yet only through the unique experience of witnessing the transformation of the contemporary practicing shamans do we get a glimpse of its awesome reality. It seems that the shamans are now still the vital link between the contemporary student of the phenomenon on one hand and the spiritual efficacy for the Native worshipper on the other.

Within the context of a specific tribal group, the Lakota wise men tell that "All things in the world are sacred. All things in the world in their order of creation were given four spiritual counterparts besides the gross" or physical form which is the most obvious. All things were created first in the spirit world, and there they first learn and know that plane of existence, its language, and the gods who dwell there. Through a miraculous process of transubstantiation, often depending upon the co-operation of living, earthly people through the fulfillment of ritual acts, entrance into earthly life is given to the four spiritual counterparts of all things, or as they will be referred to from now on, the four souls.

The first one to be considered is the *Niya*, which is described as the *life-breath* of a being. The word itself is derived from the Lakota *woniya*, which means the capacity of a being to breathe or possess living breath. This soul is very much a part of the body, for it is this that gives life to the organism, that causes it to live and to have its limited movement in the life process; it cannot *move fully* unless the other souls are also in harmony, in "working order." This is the basis of the importance of ritual preparation of foods; proper care and nourishment of the body is "to strengthen and keep strong the *Niya*"; physical activity is to keep the body attuned as an instrument by which life tasks can be accomplished. Ritual cleansing in the sweat lodge is thought not only good for expelling toxic matter, the *miniwatutkala*, through the pores, but also for strengthening and purifying the *Niya* through ritualized union with the spirit world. This is accomplished within the lodge through song and communion utilizing the sacred pipe. The final act of the sweat lodge is the emergence from within to the outside—a ritual act of rebirth and rejuvenation witnessed by sighs of "How refreshing it was" or "Ah . . . I feel so light and good now." All rejoice and give thanks while sharing a ritual meal and feeling blessed to be able to breathe anew.

The ritual "doctoring" and healing processes, then, treat not only the body but also the *Niya*, a relation the modern world has begun to realize with the holistic approach to medicine. In this sense we see one dimension of the Lakota belief that dreams are explanations of medical realities. For if a person's *Niya* leaves his body, probably accompanied by the second soul or *Nagi*, and re-enters the spirit world, the body is quite without motion and the *Niya* must be retrieved and reintegrated with the body. While away, the *Niya* may once again dwell in the sacred world, dream-land, consorting with all kinds of other *Niya* and spirit-like beings. Following the regaining of this-world consciousness, a person who has been reintegrated has been known to report fantastic experiences to others who have kept a vigil near what to all appearances was a corpse, devoid of life-breath. It is this possibility of return and revival that gave rise to the Lakota tradition of above-ground burial and of keeping a vigil with ritual feedings for a minimum of four days and nights. There are many old stories of a moving camp of Lakota passing a scaffold burial and being surprised by the moving and thrashing about of the supposed dead body, returned to life and trying to release itself from the tightly bound burial wrappings. When freed by the passing party, such "born again" people were said to have reported many things about the spirit world, or about "being away as in a dream," including having seen spirits of people long passed away.

A similar situation in recorded history is the phenomenon of the Ghost Dance of the Lakota in the 1890s. Numerous ac-counts, written and oral, tell of dancers, after long and exhaust-ing periods of dancing, falling into a trance-like state, "like being dead." Upon their regaining consciousness, without the aid of a shaman (for "no one was to touch them"), they reported having seen their relatives and others who had died and a world full of peace and beauty, a restored world of primordial completeness.

The second soul, known as the *Nagi*, is closely akin to the stereotyped definition of ghosts as described in books, films, and oral tradition. Much more personal and individualistic than the *Niya*, the *Nagi* is much like a mirror image of the person's form, at once ephemeral when seen, transparent, and capable of easy transition to and from the spirit world. With its adeptness at mobility, the *Nagi* is thought to be capricious and a cause for concern when it is out of harmony with the form that it reflects. This can result in a type of soul loss or disequilibrium when it is absent from the body, but which is different from the loss of the *Niya*. If by chance the *Nagi* should leave and the *Niya* remain, the body would continue to function, but in a state of coma or in semiconsciousness. In such a state the person may appear to others as strange in his or her actions and attitudes.

In many cases the temporary absence of the *Nagi* is cause for illness or insanity. It is believed that the *Nagi* retains the idiosyncrasies of the this-worldly nature of the personality, and hence can be capricious and unpredictable, reliable or benevolent, depending on the nature of the person or the being. So it is that it may linger near the temporal world and be seen on occasion by those with the capacity to see it. Or it may migrate deeper into the spirit realm, where it may have to be retrieved through the shaman's art and his ability to make contact with it, or with his own intercessors who contact it and attempt to lure it back or to rejoin it with the body.

Among the Lakota there are those who at a very young age exhibit a pre-knowledge of the world and of customs or persons long passed away. Such a person is said to be the explicit and individual *Nagi* of one who has lived before, returning in another body to participate again in the earthly life. This is frequently believed of twins and of certain shamans with their sacred and often mysterious ability to comprehend what ordinarily appears illusive to others. Such people, when meeting for the first time, will often have feelings of inordinate familiarity with each other, as if recognizing their strange commonalty.

A case of which I was a witness took place several years ago at a Lakota Sun Dance in northern South Dakota. A middle-aged couple appeared in the camp of the head intercessor, who was exhausted and suffering from the rigors of the ceremony, asking him to come and see their daughter. I went with him and the parents to their camp. The daughter, who appeared to be ten or twelve years old, was dressed in conservative old-fashioned clothes more suitable to a grandmother than to a young girl of the present time. She talked to the shaman alone, with downcast eyes, in a polite and almost inaudible voice. Then she opened a small bundle and handed him water and food including a piece of melon, which is a preferred food after long periods of fasting and dancing in the heat of the Dakota sun.

Later the shaman explained that this girl was believed by her family to have lived before. On this day she had identified him with all his birthmarks, scars, and other physical characteristics as someone she recognized from her previous life. A year before, the shaman had had extensive surgery and bore a great scar on his abdomen. The girl explained to him that in her previous life, she and her husband had been through a terrible battle with enemies resulting in her husband's suffering similar if not identical scars and wounds from which he eventually died.

She had insisted that her parents bring her by car many miles to this Sun Dance because she had dreamed the night before that she saw her husband from her previous life dancing and suffering and in need of refreshment.

The shaman himself took all this matter-of-factly and treated

Untitled, 1984   JAUNE QUICK-TO-SEE SMITH

her with all the respect Lakota etiquette demands of the younger meeting the elderly, although at this point in time he himself
was the elder and could indeed have been her grandfather.

Arising from these beliefs are the rituals for putting the *Nagi*
in contact with the spirit world to gain insight, vision, and
strength. The Lakota still believe firmly in the efficacy of the
vision quest, a ritual fasting and sacrifice through which contact
is made with the dream world and the spirit-selves of the other
realm.

Since all creatures possess *Nagi*, they are able to commune
with the *Wica-nagi* or spirits of men and women in the one
language all *Nagi* learned in the spirit world. It is, therefore, not
uncommon that the spirit visitor to the man seeking a vision on
his isolated hilltop is that of any of the *Nagi* of people, animals, or
birds believed to possess special god-like powers originating in
the other world.

The term *Hanbleceya* is usually translated as "crying for a
dream." A deeper meaning hidden in the word's roots suggests a
standing and enduring. The *ceya*—crying or suffering—
indicates the need for sacrifice, which appears in the ritual of the
vision quest as the giving up of water, food, and protection from
the elements. In the process of sacrifice, *sacer facere*, to make
sacred, one is ritually denying the physical existence of the
mundane world in order to reach into or experience the sacred
world by numbing the senses required for ordinary life. For the
Lakota, to sacrifice is to ritually transform physical substance
into spiritual substance, and in doing so, to transcend the gross
in order to reach the greater reality of non-pain and the non-
suffering, non-physical parameters of being. In the spirit world
—dream time—all becomes possible. There, if the quester has
a good heart and a pure mind, the dream beings may reward him
or her with special powers which can be activated and translated

into means of attaining harmony and balance between the spiritual and the mundane.

This brings us to the third aspect of soul or manifestation of spiritlike principle. The wise men tell us again, "All things possess a special power of their own which can be added to, expanded, and utilized to help others and themselves." The *Sicun* is that mysterious spiritlike power which all things possess. For the plant it may be its lifegiving fruits, seeds, leaves, or roots or their chemical results as medicines. For animals it may be their unique traits, or the knowledge they have of plants or of celestial and earthly phenomena or behavior, that man desires for himself to help to survive. In some animals, it is their possession of the eternal and unfettered wisdom of the gods which man desires to know. This can only be communicated while in the state of *Nagi,* transported and placed over the ritually prepared sacred area where the suppliant stands, or in a magical flight from that place where the *Nagi* of the seeker enters upon a mystical journey to that other world and returns, as in a waking dream, to reinhabit his original body, now weak with hunger, thirst, and weariness.

While in the other realm, the encounter might have been a most dramatic affair endowed with all the trappings of a pageant, or as a solitary meeting with an old friend. Emerging nonetheless, whatever the form, the *Nagi* of the seeker is offered a portion of the *Sicun* of his spirit visitor, and instructed about its use and about the ritual songs, dances, or prayers to be utilized in activating it once he returns to the ordinary world.

It is just such *Sicun* that is contained in sacred bundles, stones, or animal parts worn or used by the shaman, warrior, or Native doctor in the ceremonies and rituals designed to make life efficacious.

As such, it can be said that some people possess more *Sicun* than others, or that some have fostered their *Sicun* well and have thus continued to insure its potency. While all things possess *Sicun*, those who have received more of it by crying for a dream are supposed to be particularly blessed, and hence responsible that it will always be used for the benefit it can bring to the people so that the proper relationship of all life will be maintained.

Relationship and harmony form the foundation upon which the fourth soul lives in all things. The Lakota conceive of *Taku Skan Skan*, or that which moves and causes all of life to move or to live, as though the entire universe were injected or infused with a common source and type of cosmic energy. This which causes all movement was the original source of all things at the beginning, says our mythology. From it came all of the energy of life, ranging from that of the stars, sun, and earth to that which causes the tiniest insect to move about and know its rhythm and part in the scheme of things. This *Taku Skan Skan* in all things is referred to as the *Nagila*, or *little ghost* that dwells in everything. Less personal and more magnanimous than the other souls, the *Nagila* is responsible for wholeness—much like the web or sacred cord that binds and holds together all components. It is a bit of the divine essence—the mysterious force that makes all things and beings relatives to each other and to their common ancestor.

The profundity of this realization is expressed in the shortest and most commonly expressed Lakota prayer as a total response in ritual situations or as an ending to a longer narrative prayer. That prayer is *mitakuye oyasin*, "all my relatives" or "I am related to all that is."

Realizing, then, that one is more than mere physical being, the possibility for interaction, transaction, and intercourse within other dimensions of time, place, and being is what the dream experience is to the Lakota: an alternative avenue to knowing.

When Black Elk and others tell us of their great visions and subsequent excursions into the sacred realms, we are compelled to believe that something greater happened than a "train of thoughts or images passing through the mind in sleep," as the dictionary tells us,[2] or " . . . expression during sleep of various aspects of the ego and superego typically withdrawn from consciousness but, when recorded and analyzed, having some value in the diagnosis, interpretation and treatment of certain maladjustments of the personality."

The importance of the Lakota belief about dreams is not just a memory contained in accounts by such men as Black Elk. Today and perhaps at this very moment, traditional activities are taking place on contemporary reservations. Legitimate shamans and healers regularly maintain a schedule of clients whose requests range from dream interpretation to the rectifying of personal disequilibrium to the ritual preparation and strengthening of soul for future participation in the spring and summer high ceremonies. These include the contemporary Sun Dance and Hanbleceya with all their attendant rites for encountering the sacred world, from which will come that "stuff" of ethnicity that causes the Lakota to persist as tribal people in a twentieth century society.

It is not uncommon for professionally educated and employed Lakota living in urban centers to travel great distances, leaving behind the ways of contemporary life to participate in the mysterious, in the tribally prescribed mode. Often this is because they are still beckoned by the dream encounter that moves them to do as the messenger instructs them.

This should give us insight into and respect for the diversity and uniqueness of humankind's ability to participate in and explore the inner and outer landscapes of mind and myth, where truth abideth in many guises.

The Blackfoot Genesis

Blackfoot

All animals of the Plains at one time heard and knew him, and all birds of the air heard and knew him. All things that he had made understood him, when he spoke to them—the birds, the animals, and the people.

Old Man was travelling about, south of here, making the people. He came from the south, travelling north, making animals and birds as he passed along. He made the mountains, prairies, timber, and brush first. So he went along, travelling northward, making things as he went, putting rivers here and there, and falls on them, putting red paint here and there in the ground—fixing up the world as we see it today.

Old Man covered the plains with grass for the animals to feed on. He marked off a piece of ground, and in it he made to grow all kinds of roots and berries—camas, wild carrots, wild turnips, sweet-root, bitter-root, sarvis berries, bull berries, cherries, plums, and rosebuds. He put trees in the ground. He put all kinds of animals on the ground. When he made the bighorn with its big head and horns, he made it out on the prairie. It did not seem to travel easily on the prairie; it was awkward and could not go fast. So he took it by one of its horns, and led it up into the mountains, and turned it loose; and it skipped about among the rocks, and went up fearful places with ease. So he said, "This is the place that suits you; this is what you are fitted for, the rocks and the mountains." While he was in the mountains, he made the antelope out of dirt, and turned it loose, to see how it would go. It ran so fast that it fell over some rocks and hurt itself. He saw that this would not do, and took the antelope down on the prairie, and turned it loose; and it ran away fast and gracefully, and he said, "This is what you are suited to."

One day Old Man determined that he would make a woman and a child; so he formed them both — the woman and the child, her son — of clay. After he had moulded the clay in human shape, he said to the clay, "You must be people," and then he covered it up and left it, and went away. The next morning he went to the place and took the covering off, and saw that the clay shapes had changed a little. The second morning there was still more change, and the third still more. The fourth morning he went to the place, took the covering off, looked at the images, and told them to rise and walk; and they did so. They walked down to the river with their Maker, and then he told them that his name was *Na'pi*, Old Man.

The first people were poor and naked, and did not know how to get a living. Old Man showed them the roots and berries, and told them that they could eat them; that in a certain month of the year they could peel the bark off some trees and eat it, that it was good. He told the people that the animals should be their food, and gave them to the people, saying, "These are your herds." He said: "All these little animals that live in the ground — rats, squirrels, skunks, beavers — are good to eat. You need not fear to eat of their flesh." He made all the birds that fly, and told the people that there was no harm in their flesh, that it could be eaten. The first people that he created he used to take about through the timber and swamps and over the prairies, and show them the different plants. Of a certain plant he would say, "The root of this plant, if gathered in a certain month of the year, is good for a certain sickness." So they learned the power of all herbs.

In those days there were buffalo. Now the people had no arms, but those black animals with long beards were armed; and once, as the people were moving about, the buffalo saw them, and ran after them, and hooked them, and killed and ate them. One day, as the Maker of the people was travelling over the country, he saw some of his children that he had made, lying dead, torn to pieces and partly eaten by the buffalo. When he saw this he was very sad. He said: "This will not do. I will change this. The people shall eat the buffalo."

He went to some of the people who were left, and said to them, "How is it that you people do nothing to these animals that are killing you?" The people said: "What can we do? We have no way to kill these animals, while they are armed and can kill us." Then said the Maker: "That is not hard. I will make you a weapon that will kill these animals." So he went out, and cut some sarvis berry shoots, and brought them in, and peeled the bark off them. He took a larger piece of wood, and flattened it, and tied a string to it, and made a bow. Now as he was the master of all birds and could do with them as he wished, he went out and caught one and took feathers from its wing, and split them, and tied them to the shaft of wood. He tied four feathers along the shaft, and tried the arrow at a mark, and found that it did not fly well. He took these feathers off, and put on three; and when he tried it again, he found that it was good. He went out and began to break sharp piece off the stones. He tried them, and found that the black flint stones made the best arrow points, and some white flints. Then he taught the people how to use these things.

Then he said: "The next time you go out, take these things

with you, and use them as I tell you, and do not run from these animals. When they run at you, as soon as they get pretty close, shoot the arrows at them, as I have taught you; and you will see that they will run from you or will run in a circle around you."

Also Old Man said to the people: "Now, if you are overcome, you may go and sleep, and get power. Something will come to you in your dream, that will help you. Whatever these animals tell you to do, you must obey them, as they appear to you in your sleep. Be guided by them. If anybody wants help, if you are alone and travelling, and cry aloud for help, your prayer will be answered. It may be by the eagles, perhaps by the buffalo, or by the bears. Whatever animal answers your prayer, you must listen to him."

The Bison and the Moth

Joseph Epes Brown

To man as a hunter, the divine became transparent above all in the animals.

—Ivar Paulson

An intense interaction necessarily takes place between the people of a nomadic hunting culture and the animals of their habitat. This is evidenced in a rich variety of cultural expressions, which projects what could be called the people's total world view. The Oglala Sioux of the North American Plains are a classic example of such a culture. In the words of one of them, Brave Buffalo of Standing Rock, "When I was ten years of age I looked at the land and the rivers, the sky above and the animals around me, and could not fail to realize that they were made by some great Power. I was so anxious to understand this Power that I questioned the trees and the bushes."[1]

What precisely is the Oglala's conception of "power" as manifested through the animals? What is the relationship between the multiplicity of such "powers" and a unitary concept of a "Supreme Being"? Who, or what, is the Indian's acquired "guardian spirit," and what is the relationship between this "spirit power" and the "master" of all the animals?

Basic to the Plains Indians culture was the vision quest, the search for the power and protection of a tutelary spirit. Among the Oglala, for whom it was termed "crying for a vision," the quest was participated in by virtually all the men and, although less frequently and in a somewhat less rigorous form, often also by women. "Every man can cry for a vision, or 'lament,' " Black Elk told me, "and in the old days we all—men and women—lamented all the time." Although the quest which resulted in the attainment of a vision need not necessarily involve formal acquisition of a "guardian-spirit," normally the successful encounter was with a bird or an animal. It was through this agency that the desired goal, or even quality of being, could be achieved if the seeker then carried out properly the specific instructions which were conveyed to him by his mentor.

For the Oglala it seems that distinguishing between dream and vision is of little or no concern, for many of the recorded encounters with animal spirits which took place in the dream state held the same "power" as if the experience had been a waking vision. I remember the emotion and intensity with which Black Elk described a dream to me one morning: "I was taken away from this world into a vast tipi, which seemed to be as large as the world itself, and painted on the inside were every kind of four-legged being, winged-being, and all the crawling peoples. The peoples that were there in that lodge, they talked to me, just as I am talking to you."

Evidently in both dream and vision there is an intensification of the interrelationships with animal forms, and these experiences go beyond and are deeper than the encounters which take place in the waking state. There is a shift to another level of cognition, on which the Oglala is no longer encountering the phenomenal animal, but rather archetypal "essences" appearing in animal forms. Although these could appear in almost any of the forms of the natural world, in an overwhelming majority of documented cases the vision encounter was with representatives of a wide range of animals and birds, any of which could become the seeker's "guardian spirit." After the quest, the "lamenter" returns to his sponsor who interprets the vision, and instructs the man as to actions which must be taken to "actualize" the power he has received.

The component elements of either the dream or vision in which the animals or birds appear may take a number of forms. Among the recurring patterns are association of the animal or bird "spirit-form" with the powers of the four directions, which appear in conjunction with manifestations of the terrifying aspects of these powers, notably the Thunder-Beings. (The vision quests normally take place between early spring and fall when thunderstorms are the most frequent and violent in the Plains.) Or men may turn into animals, and vice versa, or one species of animal may shift into another, or an animal may take on some plant form which is to become the sacred medicinal herb later identified and used in curing. Frequently it is the animal who finally disappears who becomes the seeker's guardian-spirit; or else, " . . . the animal that appeared . . . entered his body and became part of his *wakan* strength. He might fast many times and have many such tutelary spirits within his body."[2]

It is interesting to note that though all men were expected to seek through a vision a "tutelary spirit," certainly not all received such favor, and among those that did there were great variations in its quality. For some, experiences were of such an intense and recurring nature that the recipient might become one of a number of types of "medicine-men"; those who dreamed or had visions of the Thunder-Beings or of dogs were destined to become *hehoka*, or contraries. Although the Oglala rarely express it explicitly, and never systematically, there is a certain ranking of the animals, or of their underlying "spirit-power." Grizzly Bear, for example, was understood to be chief of the underground earth forces, conceived in a negative and terrifying aspect; the bison was chief, in an exclusively positive sense, over all animals of the surface of the earth, and the eagle was seen to have supremacy over all the flying beings. Some animals outranked others in terms of their "attracting" powers, and the spider outranked all in terms of cleverness. So it may be said that the Oglala's conception of his guardian-animal-spirits represents *qualitatively* different manifestations of power, which may be obtained by men under certain conditions.

Success in the vision quest brought with it certain obligations. Among other things (such as the making of a fetish or a medicine bundle) the one who had received a vision was normally obliged, especially in the case of a powerful experience, to extend and share it by enacting it in some way, sometimes by a dance ceremonial, or by singing the songs learned in the vision, or in some other form. By dynamically acting out or dancing the inner, subjective experience, a reintensification of it results, and the larger social group is able to participate. This helps to influence the young people toward this quality of experience and so to preserve the central values.

An excellent example of what is probably the most complex type of dance ceremonial in enactment of a vision is provided by Black Elk's account of his "Horse Dance." The ceremonial was preceded by fasting and the ritual sweat both for Black Elk himself and for the two medicine-men who were assisting. A tipi was set up in the middle of the camp circle on which were painted images representing aspects of the vision, white geese for the North, and also horses, elk, and bison. In this sacred enclosure an altar was established, and songs received in the vision were taught to the two medicine-men. Sixteen horses were secured, four of which were black for the West, four white for the North, four sorrels for the East, and four buckskins for the

South. A bay horse was provided for Black Elk similar to the one he had ridden in his vision. The horses were painted with lightning stripes and hail spots. The riders, too, were painted with lightning stripes on their limbs and breasts, and they wore white plumes on their heads to look like geese. On Black Elk's horse a spotted eagle was painted where he would sit, and Black Elk himself was painted red with black lightning, and he wore a black mask with a single eagle feather in his forehead. In the actual dance the vision songs were sung by the four teams of riders, so that the horses pranced to the rhythm as they moved to the four directions of space and circumambulated the camp, finally charging down on the central tipi. All the people in the camp danced along with the horses and all sang the sacred songs. So similar was this enactment to the original vision that Black Elk stated that the vision came to him again, for " . . . what we then were doing was like a shadow cast upon the earth from yonder vision in the heavens, so bright it was and clear. I knew the real was yonder and the darkened dream of it was here."

Evidence such as this indicates that the gradations of reality which the Oglala attribute to the components of this world represent a type of thinking, an attitude of mind, which is very different from that of the non-Indian. We find here an experienced world which sets less rigid limits than those obtaining for the non-Indian. There is a fluidity and transparency to their apperceptions of the phenomenal world which permits no absolute line to be drawn, for example, between the worlds of animals, men, or spirits. I could cite numerous parallels from Black Elk's own lips to this statement of his quoted by Neihardt: "Crazy Horse dreamed and went into the world where there is nothing but the spirits of all things. That is the real world that is behind this one, and everything we see here is something like a shadow from that world." Sword, another great Oglala medicine man, told James Walker that "the Four Winds is an immaterial god, whose substance is never visible . . . While he is one god, he is four individuals . . . The word *Wakan Tanka* means all the *wakan* beings because they are all as if one."[3]

To the non-Indian, the Oglala world structure, modes of classification, and associative processes often appear incomprehensible; but the world of the Lakota is neither unstructured nor chaotic, for underlying the fluidity of appearances there is the binding thread of the *wakan* concept, and an ultimate coalescence of the multiple into the unifying principle of *Wakan Tanka*, whose multiplicity of aspects does not compromise an essential unity. Such seemingly disparate companions as the bison, elk, bear, dragonfly, moth, cocoon, and spider have for the Oglala a perfectly "logical" connection. The connecting concept underlying these apparently ill-assorted associates is the wind, or Whirlwind. In Lakota mythology, the Whirlwind (*Umi* or *Yum*) is the little brother of the four winds, all five the sons of Tate, the Wind. Whirlwind was born prematurely and never grew up, but remained a playful child, sometimes naughty, but much loved, especially by the beautiful Wohpe, who married his brother the South Wind and who is associated with White Buffalo Woman, bringer of the sacred pipe to the Lakota.

It will be appropriate to begin to examine this strange chain of associations with the cocoon; for it is from the cocoon that there emerges, in a manner undoubtedly as mysterious to the non-Indian as to the Indian, the fluttering butterfly or moth. The moth is thus conceived as similar to the whirlwind due to the "logical" fact that the moth may be no more contained than may the wind. Further evidence of identity of this form with the "formless" wind are the fluttering, wind-producing actions of

Deer Rattle—Deer Dancer, 1981 FRANK LAPENA

the wings, a trait possessed by other winged forms, such as the dragonfly, which therefore must also have access to whirlwind power. The cocoon-encapsulated whirlwind power is of obvious value to a warrior; having such power, the man would be as difficult to hit as the butterfly or the dragonfly. Also the Whirl-wind's playful, twisting movements have power to produce con-fusion of the mind—according to Oglala patterns of thought, the minds of the enemy.

Another member to be added to this strange assembly of cocoon, moth, butterfly, and dragonfly is the bison, and even tangentially the bear, said by the Oglala to possess power to confuse the enemy. The buffalo is the chief of all the animals, and represents the earth, the totality of all that is. It is the feminine, creating earth principle which gives rise to all living forms. The bear represents knowledge and use of underground earth forces (roots and herbs) in a "terrifying" and strongly masculine manner. It has no fear of either man or animal, and Black Elk, who was both a medicine-man *(pejuta wicasa)* and a holy-man *(wicasa wakan)* explained that many of his powers to cure were received from the bear.

It has been observed that in winter, when a bison cow drops a calf, she is able to blow out from her nose and mouth a red filmy substance which envelops and protects the calf, just as the cocoon protects the developing moth. The imagination of the Oglala has also been stimulated by the trait of the bison bull, who "paws the earth, every now and then deftly scooping up the dust with his hoof and driving it straight up into the air . . . the buffalo is praying to the power of the whirlwind to give him power over his enemies."[4]

Graphic illustration of this affinity with whirlwind power has been noted on a Gros Ventre ornament where a line is seen connecting the horn of a bison to an insect, explanation being given that this represents "a rapport between the buffalo and the moth . . . these were two great powers . . . and they were in sympathy with each other."[5] A double function, from the Oglala's point of view, may be seen in this dust-throwing trait, for it may also be used to lure bison cows away from the herd during the rutting season; this attracting power quality is regarded as especially *wakan* since among bison it is normally the cow who acts as leader of herds. Similar power over women was sought after by young Oglala males.

The spider is associated with the other beings of our mixed assembly, again through association with the winds. One natural cause of this is the trait, which most certainly has been observed by the Oglala, of the young of certain spiders to send out long filaments which are caught by the wind and which carry them for long distances. Further concrete expression for the Oglala of this wind-relationship is found in the observed fact that at least certain types of spiders lay out their webs on the ground in rectangular shapes with the four corners extended towards the four directions of space. Within the larger context of Oglala mythological belief, the four directions of space are identified with the "homes" of the four winds, and these winds and their appointed directions are under the control of Thunder-Beings.

These conceptions are based on the fact that the spider's web cannot be destroyed by bullets or arrows, which pass through without leaving a hole, and further that as a "friend" of the Thunder, the spider or his web has power to protect from harm. The application of these principles is made specific in the Oglala custom of stringing up a web-like hammock between four trees upon which a young child is placed, which is thought to bring him good fortune. Also, since spider is seen as particularly cunning and industrious — the latter trait being especially desirable in women — and since his nets have the capacity to ensnare, it is conceived that this power may be drawn upon by the men for attracting women to them. It has been recorded that a "courting robe" of bison hide was painted with figures of the spider, along with the whirlwind and elk, and this robe was so manipulated that the desired girl would step upon the design and thereby be ensnared.

The final member to be treated in this assembly of unlikely associates is the elk. The elk plays a dominant role for the Plains peoples generally. There are explicit references to a "hypothetical," supernatural Elk—a "spirit" animal that lacks a heart, or rather, has a space where the heart should be, an animal without a heart being conceived as immortal and supernatural. Such a belief is undoubtedly associated with the rites of the Oglala Elk Festival, where an elk is painted over the door of the ceremonial tipi in such a manner that all who enter must pass through the very body of the animal.

The characteristics of the phenomenal elk are essentially based on the mysterious power of the bull to attract cows to him through his whistling call, or "bugle," which again represents control over the air or Wind principle. The bull elk is therefore considered to be the incarnation of power over the female, which is sought for by the men. The man's further identity with such power is achieved through the simulated call of the bull elk through the use of the flageolet, which is thought to draw irresistibly the young women of the camp to the man playing the instrument. Such Plains "love flutes" frequently have carved upon them the figure of the elk.

In all these interrelationships it is evident that the historical-cultural tradition plays an important role in determining the forms selected, their use, and the nature of the values attached to them. These values are expressed with an extraordinary aptness; the correspondence between levels of reality are as if one were the reflection of the other; they flow into each other in a manner that expresses a total, integrated environment.

Intercepting the horizontal dimension to the world of appearances, there is always, for the Oglala mind, the vertical dimension of the sacred, and in this sacredness there is the sense of "mystery." In sacramentalizing their world of experience, and in recognizing levels of abstraction within and transcendent to this world, the Oglala give place to all components within what for them must be an eminently coherent world view.

The Fox and the Buffalo

Pawnee: Retold by Brian Swann

A fox was walking about looking for food. He was very hungry. He was so hungry he was almost starving to death. Having been walking and looking for a long time, he was weak and tired. He could catch nothing, not even a beetle to gnaw on. He lay down.

Suddenly, a large shadow fell across him. Startled, he leaped to his feet. There stood a large buffalo, but the buffalo didn't seem to have noticed him. He was grasping the tufts of rich grama grass and tearing them up, chewing them between his large white teeth with great contentment. Slowly the fox walked right in front of the buffalo's head. Then he sat down, he was so weak. He watched the buffalo chewing, chewing, chewing. Oh, that grass looked so good! So juicy! And the buffalo looked so contented . . . .

The buffalo saw the fox, but paid no attention to him. He just went on eating that rich grama grass. In a while, the buffalo ate his way right over to where the fox was sitting, and looked straight down at him.

"Friend buffalo," said the fox in a thin voice, "I wish, I wish you would give me a blessing. As you can see, I am about to starve to death. I wish I was the same as you. I wish I could eat the delicious grass, just like you. Please make me the same as you. You have the power."

The buffalo looked at him.

"That's really very sad," he said. "Very sad indeed. But it's also too bad. I have no intentions of making you like me."

"Oh please, buffalo!" the fox cried. "Take pity on me! Look how my bones poke through!"

The buffalo stopped chewing the grass, and began to chew his cud.

"You know, fox, you are a born liar. You are not to be trusted. How do I know you're not up to one of your tricks? How do I know you're telling the truth?"

"How do you know! Why, just *look* at me. I'm all skin and bone. You can almost see through me. I swear I am telling the truth."

The buffalo stopped chewing his cud, and gave the fox a hard stare. Then he said: "Go and search for a place where a buffalo has rolled about. Go on! What are you waiting for? Are you afraid?"

Fox was weary, but he said: "I'm on my way." As he walked off, the buffalo called after him:

"You *are* telling the truth, aren't you? You're not lying?"

"I'm not, I swear," the fox replied.

"All right," said the buffalo. "Now listen. When you get to the buffalo wallow lie down in it. Then wait for me."

Fox walked slowly, footsore, but with his spirits a little higher now. Soon he found an area like a small dust bowl where a buffalo had rolled about. He looked back and saw the buffalo following him. He lay down. When the buffalo arrived, he said: "Now don't watch me. Close your eyes."

Fox did as he was told.

Then the buffalo lowered his head with its large in-curved horns, and waved it from side to side, readying for the charge.

Then he pawed the ground with his forefeet. He charged! But just when he started forward the fox leaped aside in fear. The buffalo pulled up, dust swirling all around him.

"That's it," he snorted. "Just as I thought. You're not serious. I asked you to close your eyes. You are not humble enough. You have no trust."

And he turned around, swishing his tail, to go back to where he had been eating the delicious grama grass.

But the fox ran after him, pleading. The buffalo stopped and looked at the fox. "I'll give you one more chance, and that's it."

So back they walked to the wallow, and again the buffalo gave his instructions and made his frightening preparations. He lowered his horns, waved his head from side to side, pawed at the earth—and charged. And all the while a terrified fox was thinking to himself: "I had better not jump aside this time, even it he kills me. I'll keep my eyes shut tight so I won't see a thing."

The buffalo came on with thundering hoofs, right at the fox where he had lain down, eyes shut tight, scared. And the buffalo ran smack into him.

Two buffalos ran away from that place.

The fox was able to eat his fill. He gulped down grass, and was soon stuffed to bursting. The real buffalo watched him. When the new buffalo had eaten so much that he had to lie down, groaning, the real buffalo said to him: "Now, everyone knows you are a born liar. So don't do anything that would get you into trouble. Remember you are not a real buffalo, though you look like one. And now I'm leaving you. Take care."

A long time passed. The new buffalo digested his meal, chewed his cud, and then started eating again. It seemed he would never get enough to fill him. As he ate, he walked, and in time he came to a new part of the prairie where the grass was just as good, if not better. A flicker of movement caught his eye. He looked up. There in front of him was a fox. The fox was sitting down, looking up at him. The new buffalo kept his eye on him, but continued grazing. The fox stood up.

"Friend buffalo," he said. "I wish I was the same as you."

The buffalo looked at him. "Do you really," he said.

The fox sat down again. "I really do. I mean it," he replied. "I am so hungry I am about to starve to death. You have all the food you can eat. I wish I was like you. Take pity on me. You have the power."

The buffalo gave a swish with his tail. "All right," he said, after a delay and some pretend reluctance. "If you say what you really want, and are not up to some trick. Foxes are such born liars."

"No, I really want it!" the fox exclaimed. "I swear I'm not lying. Just look at me!"

"Very well then," said the buffalo. "Do exactly as I say. Go and find a buffalo wallow and lie down in it. Whatever happens, don't open your eyes."

The fox trotted off, with the buffalo walking behind. When he found a buffalo wallow, the fox lay down in the dust, and closed his eyes. He could hear the buffalo snorting and tearing up the earth with his hoofs as he prepared to charge. The fox could barely control his terror. "He's going to kill me now," he said to himself, and when he heard the first few hoofbeats, the fox opened his eyes wide and shot out of that hole.

The buffalo came to a thunderous halt. "You'd better leave," he told the fox angrily. "You are not humble enough. You don't have enough trust. Just like a fox."

"Oh, friend," cried the fox. "Just one more chance! Please give me just one more chance. You did promise to give me a blessing." The buffalo pretended to be about to refuse. Then he said: "Go and lie down in that wallow again. And keep your eyes shut."

Trembling, the fox did as he was instructed. But he had a

hard time of it preventing his legs running off with the rest of him.

So again the buffalo readied for the charge, head swaying, hoofs pawing. And this time he charged with even more noise and force than before. He caught the fox on his in-curved horns, and tossed him high in the air.

And suddenly there were two foxes in that wallow, fighting and scratching and yelping and making just an awful racket.

Then the fox who had been a buffalo turned on the other and snarled: "*You!* You have ruined me! I should never have listened to you!"

And he ran off to find the first buffalo who had given him his blessing. When he found him, he said: "Friend buffalo, I am still starving to death."

The buffalo stopped grazing and raised his huge bearded head. "I know you," he said. "Aren't you the one I blessed already?"

"I am," said the fox quietly, reluctantly.

"Go and find a buffalo wallow, and do as you did before," the buffalo said.

"Here's one," he called out, excited.

"Lie down in it," the buffalo commanded.

Fox lay down.

"Now he is going to bless me again," he said to himself, and shut his eyes tight.

The buffalo charged. He impaled the fox and dashed him to pieces on the dusty earth of the buffalo wallow.

The Spiritual Landscape

Elaine Jahner

Wakan Tanka, the great spirit. This one word is known by innumerable persons who are not even aware that its tribal origin is Lakota. Although the word is widely known, its meaning, like that of *Yahweh* in the Old Testament, remains a mystery that reverent members of the Lakota tribe continue to meditate on. One Lakota asked older members of the tribe about the meaning and origin of the word. He received a story as his answer.

"Way back many years ago, two men went walking. It was on the prairies. As they walked, they decided, 'Let's go up the hill way towards the west; let's see what's over the hill.'

"So they walked and they came to the top of this hill and they looked west and it was the same. Same thing as they saw before; there was nothing. They just kept going like that, all day and it was the same. They came to a big hill and there was another big hill further back. Finally they stopped and they said, 'You know, this is Wakan Tanka.' "

This story needs to be situated within the context of the Lakota world view, but once it is, its nuances of meaning seem almost endless. In the years since I first heard it I have come to appreciate a few of its many dimensions and, for me, these revolve around three different features of the episode: 1) the searchers are exploring the *physical* universe when they sense the mysterious depth of the spiritual one; 2) the search is not an individual one — *two* people wander toward the west; 3) the searchers' response to their new insight is an awed response to mystery.

Anyone who has lived in the American plains region knows something about the way in which the landscape can shape modes of thinking and feeling. There are the extending lands where occasionally buttes rise from the level stretches and seem sharp, assertive definitions of form. Then there are the winds, those permanent presences that vary in intensity and direction but are always there. All combine to demand a response from inhabitants that requires them to go beyond the trivial. It takes time and courage for people to find themselves at home in such an environment and perhaps only the American Indians have succeeded not only in feeling at home but also in learning to see in it a set of symbols for a personal and cultural self-understanding that makes them genuinely present to the environment. By means of their basic cultural symbols and the corresponding social organization, the Lakota have taught that the physical world is spirit seen from without and that the spiritual world is the physical viewed from another dimension. During the two hundred years since the Lakota moved from the woodlands into the plains, they have found in the area's natural rhythms and demands an effective design for their own lives and movements. Their sensitive accommodation to the environment is an essential chapter in the story of human efforts to relate creatively to the rest of nature.

The Lakota world view facilitates presence to oneself, to nature and to the community; Lakota religious symbols represent ways of thinking that dramatize that mode of presence. To understand the basis of the imagery we have to turn to the ancient sacred stories — the myths. Fragments of the sacred story have been preserved in oral tradition and in the fieldwork notes of various scholars who sought to record Lakota traditions. J. R. Walker's manuscripts contain parts of a Lakota creation myth that show the intimate relation between the physical and the spiritual worlds. This powerfully moving story deserves extensive quotation. In this version, Creation begins with Inyan, the rock, an effective symbol of primal power in a plains setting.

Inyan (Rock) had no beginning for he was when there was no other. His spirit was Wakan Tanka (The Great Mystery), and he was the first of the superior gods. Then he was soft and shapeless like a cloud, but he had powers and was everywhere. Han was then, but she is not a being; she is only the black of darkness.

Inyan longed to exercise his powers, but could not do so for there was no other that he might use his powers upon. If there were to be another, he must create it of that which he must take from himself, and he must give to it a spirit and a portion of his blood. As much of his blood as would go from him, so much of his powers would go with it, for his powers were in his blood, and his blood was blue. He decided to create another as a part of himself so that he might keep control of all the powers.

To do this he took from himself that which he spread around himself in the shape of a great disk whose edge is where there can be no beyond. This disk he named Maka (earth). He gave to Maka a spirit that is Maka-akan (Earth-goddess). She is the second of the superior gods, but she is a part of Inyan.

To create Maka, Inyan took so much from himself that he opened his veins, and all his blood flowed from him so that he shrank and became hard and powerless. As his blood flowed from him, it became blue waters, which are the waters upon the earth. But the powers cannot abide in waters, and, when the blood of Inyan became the waters, the powers separated themselves from it and assumed another shape. This other being took the form of a great blue dome whose edge is at, but not upon, the edge of Maka.

Inyan, Maka, and the waters are material or that which can be held together, and they are the world; the blue dome above the world, which is Tanka (the Sky), is not material, but spirit. Nagi Tanka (Supreme-god or Sky-god) is the great Spirit who is all powerful and the source of all power, and his name is Skan (Almighty or Most Holy).

Thus in the beginning there were Inyan, Maka, and the waters, all of which are the world, and Nagi Tanka, named Skan, the blue dome which is the sky above the world. The world is matter and has no powers except those bestowed by Nagi Tanka.

When these powers assumed one shape, a voice spoke, saying,

"I am the source of energy, I am Skan."

This was the beginning of the third superior god, who is superior to all because he is spirit. This was the beginning before there was time. This was the beginning of the world and of the sky over the world.[1]

When we study this version of a creation myth, we see how it is that a journey of exploration into the physical world can be a meditation on the interdependence of consciousness and the environment, an interdependence that is manifested in the course of life itself. The myth defines the purpose of life as a progression from unity, through existential encounters with the meaning of diversity, toward renewed experience of unity. The physical universe flows from Inyan's need to exercise power, so Creation begins because the very nature of power requires relationship and sharing. The initial exercise of power reveals the contrast between materiality and spirituality and shows that power's mode of functioning is through reciprocity. Materiality is represented by the earth and spirituality by the Sky—one feminine and one masculine. Walker translates *Skan* as "Almighty or Most Holy." A far more accurate translation is "Movement." "I am the source of energy, I am Skan." Movement seen as creative power and its relationship to the Rock, an image of movement held in abeyance, is an important motif in the Lakota world view. When Ella Deloria tried to validate the Walker version of the myth by collecting other versions in oral tradition, she heard the following comment, "There is only one thing like that which I have heard; it runs thus: It is belief in the God of Movement. That thing, they say, is stone . . . And that Stone was all-powerful, like nothing else; so whenever the race had to pursue anything very difficult, then faith was placed on It in prayer."[2]

The dialectic between movement and rest is a major element of Sioux sacred story but it is not the only important cultural concept articulated in the myth. Light and Darkness (metaphorically related to knowledge and ignorance in Sioux ritual) are shown to be aspects of the same reality. "Skan divided Han (darkness) into two halves—one remained darkness . . . From the other Skan created the light (Anp)." The Lakota considered movement in nature and learned to see in it an imperative pattern for their social organization that derived its authority from the belief that it was basic to the nature and structure of the universe itself. It is in this context that we can see the importance of my concentration on the second aspect of the story that introduces this essay— the exploration of the universe is not an individual one; *two* people wander toward the west. The camp circle and the surrounding environment are not mere juxtaposed elements of space; they are co-ordinated patterns of life. The response to the movements of nature is to coordinate human movements so that they correspond to the universal pattern, and the effort to understand that pattern is a shared effort. The Walker version of the myth justifies the close link between social life and environment.

The gods in Lakota sacred story established their patterns of movement in specific spatial domains only gradually; and the story of the four winds establishing their directions constitutes a major part of the Walker collection of narratives. Tate, the wind, had five sons; Yata was the first-born, then came Eya, Yanpa, Okaga and Yum. The youngest did not grow strong and brave but remained like a child. All the sons lived with Tate, their father until Woope (later represented in Lakota story as White Buffalo Woman) came to them with a message from Wakan Tanka about their tasks. "His message is this. Now there is no direction in the world, and your four sons must each fix a direction, and establish it so that it will forever be known. When each one has fixed a direction, it shall be his living place. The directions must be on the edge of the world, and each an equal distance from the one next to it. They must divide the edge of the world into four equal parts, and one part shall belong to each of them. They must go around the world on its edge. From when they start on this journey to when they finish it will be the fourth time, the year."

The events that occur as the brothers establish the four directions and the fourth time are prototypes for Sioux ritual and for heroic action. The first part of their journey takes the brothers to the west where Wakinyan lives, the powerfully beneficent, winged god. Only Eya, the second born, dares to demand to look at Wakinyan, and the sight causes him to become a heyoka, a "contrary," who does and says everything in reverse, because this is the only way to approach the creative force. Thus Eya gains the right to establish himself in the first direction and Yata loses his birthright. Yata has to establish his place in the north from whence he continues to send his cold, sometimes cruel winds from his loveless home. The east is left to Yanpa and the south to the warm, generous Okaga, the one loved by Woope. In all Sioux ritual, the four directions are greeted with the usual order for the greeting being the same as the myth's order for the establishment of directions.

The positions of the four directions make the world a mandala and every place of ceremony a center of the world. This idea is visualized in the fundamental image of Sioux religion, the image of the crossroads within a circle, an image that still retains its expressive content and power because its immense structuring power has helped the Lakota people reorganize their lives in a reservation environment. The road from the south to the north is the red road of growth and advancement that the people try to follow while the road from west to east is the black road of change and disruption that inevitably crosses the red road at times. The circle that contains the crossroads has a wide range of cultural references and all other major symbols are related to the circle image.

Joseph Flying By, a Standing Rock Sioux, explained the image and its range of meaning in the following way: " . . . the sun from the east and the moon from the west are all symbolic of a circle. Likewise, our Lakota people are also symbolic of a strong circle. Whenever you see our people camp, it is always in a circle. When they sit and have a parley or in a council of many fires, the pattern of their sitting is always in a circle. From this circle of our Lakota people comes the extended family. Whether they are cousins, brothers, sisters, or distant cousins, they are still bound by love, honor, respect, and strong ties which symbolize a circle."

As a symbol of social unity, the circle receives consistent emphasis because its reference is extended to the way social organization is articulated. The circle refers to the organization of the camp and of the tipi. Within the tipi, all space and all positions were meaningful and it represented a plan of order that directed the family's movements. Directly behind the central fire was the place of honor. The area to the right was allocated to family members and the left central portion was for guests undeserving of the place of honor. Nearest to the left of the tipi's doorway was the area where the old people begging for food could rest. The pattern of order that directed all movement within the tipi helped the family to visualize it as the cosmos in miniature where movement had to follow culturally prescribed patterns. In commenting on the importance of the tipi as a microcosm, Joseph Epes Brown has said, "Since for every Sioux, every tipi is the world in an image, the fire at the center represents Wakan Tanka within the world."[3] In such a dwelling it is easy to integrate images of the universe with images related to one's personal life. The great myths and legends take on concrete meaning when the fire that draws the attention of all participants in the story-telling session represents Wakan Tanka.

The camp circle also had its prescribed movements. Each tipi had its place within the circle and thus it automatically identified the role of its inhabitants relative to that of other members of the group. As a family gained in prestige, a tipi could be moved but whenever a family could not contribute to the group's welfare, its tipi had to be moved outside the circle.

Because the Sioux visualized every level of social organization as a circle that unified members of the group and marked out the circumference of a prescribed pattern of movement, they could think of their personal identity as a function of the particular place occupied in the circles of social organization. But no one's place was ever static. All of life's activities caused movement among the various circles of being. The one inescapable movement that every person had to submit to was the constant progression of time. The Lakota used spatial imagery to articulate their concept of time. Black Elk has explained this idea.

"Is not the south the source of life, and does not the flowering stick truly come from there? And does not man advance from there toward the setting sun of his life? And does he not arrive, if he lives, at the source of light and understanding which is in the east? Then does he not return to where he began, to his second childhood, there to give back his life to all life and his flesh to the earth whence it came?"[4]

As the Lakota questioned the forces that govern the natural world, they found symbols, images, and patterns of meaning that gave them a relationship to immense creative energies. They could see that the macrocosm and the microcosm stay alive in the same ways. But there was and is still the sense that much has yet to be learned. There is still the sense that the ways of the Great Spirit are a mystery that compels human beings to continue their search in both the physical and the spiritual worlds. And this search for the future brings us to my third point about the introductory narrative: the searchers' response to their new insight is an awed response to mystery. If one gives one's entire being over to exploring the patterns and possibilities in the environment, then new possibilities are always in the making and one is caught up in a forward momentum just as the two characters in the introductory narrative are. They keep going on and on just to see what might be beyond the next hill. This is the restlessness in the search for the unknown that gives creative strength to a person and to a culture. But such restlessness can lead to anarchy as well as to new life for the individual and the group, so the Lakota found ways to safeguard the search for the new without destroying the structure of the old. The individual was taught to penetrate farther and farther into the incomprehensible and marvelous mystery of both the physical and spiritual worlds but always to come back to the group with his or her findings so that the group could integrate the new knowledge with the old.

If we look at the vision quest as a way of responding to the mystery that must intrude upon every individual life, then we can see that the Lakota way of relating the known and the unknown makes the image of the two men moving from hill to hill, horizon to horizon, a symbol of every Lakota's journey through life. The vision quest was a journey to the inner, spiritual landscape that showed the quester the direction to follow in the travels through the physical landscape. "Hanblecheyapi" or "Crying for a Vision" is among the most ancient Lakota rites. As with all of the ceremonies, some of the details varied according to time and place, but the essentials of the rite were part of the life of all the Lakota bands. The person who wanted a vision sought the guidance and instruction of a holy man who tested the strength of character and the knowledge of the person about spiritual matters. Just before leaving camp, the seeker underwent a purification ceremony as protection against evil influences. The actual crying for a dream occurred in isolation usually atop a high butte or hill. Upon arrival at the chosen place, the seeker ritually prepared an area of earth making it a "center of the earth." The person remained on or near the place until a dream came or a mentor advised giving up the quest. Generally the quest included the gift of some object representing a spirit that would be the visionary's helper throughout life.

The events that occurred in isolation definitely enhanced the individual's prestige and they were believed to be evidence of unique powers. But the individual could not actualize even the unique powers of the dream without the help of the community. In most bands, the dreamer had to enact the dream for the tribe before it could become efficacious. In this way the powers of the dream were made part of the general economy of spiritual power and the person was dramatically reminded that he acted on behalf of the group.

The vision gave its seeker the courage to face the mysterious dimensions of life with the calm foreknowledge that comes from a personal relationship to mystery and an inner point of departure for the continuing journey of exploration that is life itself. The light of the vision illumines some of the night of uncertainty for both the individual and the group. Or, to use another set of images, the vision is a way of climbing a hill so high that the visionary has a perspective from which to view the many lower hills stretching toward the horizon of death.

Much has changed in Lakota life since the establishment of reservations, but the people have not lost the sense that their spiritual journey is linked with their travels through their plains environment. In the Lakota world, the west is a direction of change and occasional destruction. Perhaps the brief story about Wakan Tanka can even be interpreted as a comment on the last hundred years of history. Using different words, of course, dozens of leaders have said to their people, "Let's go up the hill towards the west; let's see what's over the hill." What they have seen has been a mystery that could have crushed people with less spiritual strength. But the Lakota go on climbing hill after hill in order to *see* what is over the horizon.

White Buffalo Woman

Lakota

There is a story about the way the pipe first came to us. A very long time ago, they say, two scouts were out looking for bison; and when they came to the top of a high hill and looked north, they saw something coming a long way off, and when it came closer they cried out, "It is a woman!" and it was. Then one of the scouts, being foolish, had bad thoughts and spoke them; but the other said: "That is a sacred woman; throw all bad thoughts away." When she came still closer, they saw that she wore a fine white buckskin dress, that her hair was very long and that she was very young and very beautiful. And she knew their thoughts and said in a voice that was like singing: "You do not know me, but if you want to do as you think, you may come." And the foolish one went; but just as he stood before her, there was a white cloud that came and covered them. And the beautiful young woman came out of the cloud, and when it blew away the foolish man was a skeleton covered with worms.

Then the woman spoke to the one who was not foolish: "You shall go home and tell your people that I am coming and that a big tipi shall be built for me in the center of the nation." And the man, who was very much afraid, went quickly and told the people, who did at once as they were told; and there around the big tipi they waited for the sacred woman. And after a while she came, very beautiful and singing, and as she went into the tipi this is what she sang:

> With visible breath I am walking.
> A voice I am sending as I walk.
> In a sacred manner I am walking.
> With visible tracks I am walking.
> In a sacred manner I walk.

And as she sang, there came from her mouth a white cloud that was good to smell. Then she gave something to the chief, and it was a pipe with a bison calf carved on one side to mean the earth that bears and feeds us, and with twelve eagle feathers hanging from the stem to mean the sky and the twelve moons, and these were tied with a grass that never breaks. "Behold!" she said. "With this you shall multiply and be a good nation. Nothing but good shall come from it. Only the hands of the good shall take care of it and the bad shall not even see it." Then she sang again and went out of the tipi; and as the people watched her going, suddenly it was a white bison galloping away and snorting, and soon it was gone.

This they tell, and whether it happened so or not I do not know; but if you think about it, you can see that it is true.

Eagles Fly Over

Arthur Amiotte

Petaga is a medicine man of the Sioux people. He lives in a little hut of logs and mud near the white sandstone buttes of Payaba Community on the Pine Ridge Reservation. His face is noble, deep-lined with age and bold with wisdom tempered by hard work, weather and uncompromising devotion to living out his vision.

Petaga Yuha Mani—He Walks with Coals of Fire.

I sought him out and he spoke to me like this:

. . . Life is like a huge design. Each part of the design is made up of the happenings, acts and interactions of people with each other and the world. You must know that this design is completed by the intervention of Wakan Tanka. People and this world and all that is in it are only a part of Wakan Tanka. Wakan Tanka is all that is wondrous, awesome, powerful, and infinite, and yet he is also personal, compassionate, loving and tender. Perhaps this is why we call him Great Mystery.

Look at the tiny ants going about their business on the ground in front of us. In this world, everything has its purpose, its time and its place, from the smallest particle to the powerful storms as they sweep and wash the face of the land. Men also come and go, but man is different from the ants for he must learn where his place is and what his life means. That we may do this, our people were given a way of prayer that is called the Buffalo Calf Pipe.

We were given ceremonies in which we pray with the pipe, ways that we may stand before Wakan Tanka so that he will instruct us about our place in his design.

You must know that a medicine man among our people is in possession of a special office. He is a servant of the people and of the gods.

I did not ask for my office. My work was made for me and given to me by the other world, by the Thunder Beings. I am compelled to live this way that is not of my own choosing, because they chose me. I am a poor man; see how I dress and the house I live in. My whole life is to do the bidding of the Thunder Beings and of my people and to pay heed to what the Grand-fathers tell me. You have come to see me, but did you know how to come?

To enter into any ceremony is a most sacred act. It begins in the mind of a person either by himself or because other beings chose him for their purposes. If after he has examined himself well he feels confident that he wants and needs the help of a counsellor, an intercessor, he must fill a good pipe with red willow bark tobacco and seek out the medicine man he wishes to see and whose help he wants. When he approaches the home of the medicine man he should rid himself of all undesirable thoughts so that his mind might be clear to utter his request as a petition prayer.

As a man with a filled pipe approaches a medicine man, he should realize that this man, depending on his predilections and his ability to read the intent of his visitor, has the right to refuse the offered pipe. A petitioner should be prepared to offer the filled pipe four times, each time stepping back and extending the pipe at arm's length. It is important also to hold the pipe bowl in the left hand when offering the pipe as this signifies that the intent is coming from the heart, and is a sign of sincerity and honesty. If the medicine man accepts the pipe on the first or on any other offering, it means he is willing to listen to your request, but it does not mean he will grant it. He will either light the pipe himself or ask you to light it. While he smokes the pipe, you must make your request. Since the pipe is being smoked in a sacred manner, you must make your petition as simply and as honestly as you can, for depending on what you say and how you say it, the medicine man will deliberate and make his decision. When the smoking is finished and after the bowl has been emptied of its ashes, a less formal conversation will follow.

This is the beginning and how it should be done. Go now, prepare yourself, think things through in your mind. In a month you may come back prepared to do things in the proper way . . . .

A storm was coming and there were still a lot of things to do. It had been a very unsettling day, full of anticipation and dread. It had begun with a dream in the early hours: I was sitting against a white chalk cliff—a place that I have seen before, perhaps in my early childhood while exploring near my grandparents' home here on the reservation. In the dream, as I sat, two eagles were soaring in the distance and then began to approach me. As they came closer and swooped down I saw they had huge beaks and large eyes that seemed to penetrate my mind. Diving down in front of me they said, "We have come for you now." Then they swerved and flew upward and away and the dream ended.

When I woke I pondered the meaning of this dream and decided the ceremony had begun and the eagle nation was already waiting for me.

I had to go to Pine Ridge and set up an account at a local store so my relatives would be able to buy meat and other food for the ceremonial meals that would take place while I was gone. I also had to find a wooden bowl, twine, colored cloth, and tobacco to take to the medicine man so his wife could make the rosary-like strings of tobacco offerings wrapped in tiny cloth squares, to enclose the sacred area where I would stand for the Pipe Fast. The day seemed to pass too quickly; I couldn't find a decent wooden bowl, and kept mentally telling the eagles, "I'm coming, I'm coming." Finally I had to settle for an old bowl that I sanded down to the unused wood. Somehow I collected the other things I needed: a quilt and a blanket that had never been used, a large knife, a pail and dipper, yard squares of red, yellow, green, and white cloth, Bull Durham tobacco, an eagle feather attached to a conch shell disc, and of course my pipe, sage, and a braid of sweet grass. One thing that was hard to find was wild chokecherry juice; fortunately one of my neighbors found a jar of canned chokecherries and I could use the juice from that.

The storm was getting closer and there was more sage to gather. My aunt and my grandmother drove with me to my cousin's place and we picked sage. Before we picked it I offered pinches of tobacco and addressed the gray grass, our oldest plant relative, asking it to help me in the task I was going to undertake. I asked it to forgive me for uprooting it and I asked the creation to accept the tobacco as an offering:

> Peji hota, my relative,
> from time immemorial you have helped us.
> It is said you are one of our first and oldest
>   medicines.
> Peji hota, I have come to get you now
> for I wish you to help me and protect me.
> You were here first and know many things.
> I am only a man seeking a way and a place.
>
> Peji hota, forgive me for taking you away
> from this place.

You will be put in another
one in which you will be recognized
by those who already know you.
You will become a ceremony.

Peji ḣota, accept this offering and help me
in the way that is your way
that my relatives and I may know and live.

I had just gotten back to the house when the rain started.
Some relatives came to visit and stayed very late. I had wanted
to sit down at the sewing machine and hem a piece of cloth for
my ceremonial breech cloth, but the electricity went off and we
spent most of the night by candle light. Finally I began to fix the
cloth by hand and my aunt finished it when the power came back
on again about one o'clock in the morning.

I had gotten a puppy from my grandmother's sister for the
sacrifice that had to take place on the evening of the first day of
my fast. After we had kept it for about three weeks, my little son
Andrew had become as fond of it as I had, but I told him that I
would have to take it home later on and that we couldn't keep it
or name it. This night the puppy slept soundly; but in the
distance, yet seemingly close at hand, another puppy was crying. It reminded us of the one that was sacrificed at the first
Eagle Ceremony at Pete Catches'* place, at which the time and
day of my fast was designated for me. That puppy had not been
cooked for the feast following the ceremony proper, but was put
in an old car until the next day. During the ceremony it yelped
and cried; we were told that it wanted to be inside where we
were, but since it could not it was crying and praying that I would
have good weather when the time of my fast arrived. The voice
of that pup was just like the one we were hearing tonight,

---

* *Pete Catches is Petaġa's everyday name. He is called Petaġa only when ritually
addressed.*

nearby yet far-off; and now we felt confident that the weather would be good in the following days, since my first puppy was still crying and praying for me from wherever it is that sacrificed puppies go.

We slept for an hour or two and were up again a little after three. Andrew was sound asleep; he had been told that his father was going away to a meeting. I felt that it was indeed to be the meeting of myself with the richest traditions of our people, a meeting that would begin my spiritual journey through a timeless place; for here were to be joined the ritual and wisdom of the ancients and a contemporary soul adrift in a chaotic world. I hoped I would be worthy and would recognize and understand the truth in the newness and strangeness of what was to come.

My grandmother cooked breakfast and we were on our way before four. At one point a porcupine crossed the highway in front of us, and a little later, three deer.

The ceremony was to take place at Pete Catches' (Petaġa's) country place at Payaba Mission. We found the road passable, even though it had rained very hard the night before. Shortly after we arrived, Catches' brother drove up and began to get the fire ready to heat the stones for the sweat bath. The men all went up to the sweat lodge on the hillside, and the women stayed down by the house.

By this time the fire was burning hard and Catches was now ritually filling his pipe and mine and offering them to the four quarters, the sky and the earth. I was to take mine with me to the hilltop. His would be left inside the sweat lodge for the duration of the fast. His brother tore pieces of the red cloth I had brought and prepared four little tobacco offerings—flags attached to short sticks, which were placed on the earth altar in front of the door which faced west and towards the fire where the rocks were heating. Sage had already been spread on the floor of the lodge. The four colored cloths I brought were also tied on sticks and stuck in the ground outside the door near the earth altar, after they had been purified inside the sweat lodge over the first steam, before the door was closed.

I had already attached the feather to the shell disc, and now Catches tied it to my hair on the back of my head. We stripped and entered the lodge. I hadn't brought a towel so I used my shirt to wipe myself during and after the bath.

Inside I was seated facing the door with the fire pit between me and the door. Catches sat to my left, or on the right as one entered the lodge. Catches' brother placed the rocks in the pit in the center of the lodge with a pitchfork, after which he entered and sat on my other side. A pail of water, the wooden bowl, dipper, knife, and pipes were now arranged in their proper places, my pipe being set before me on the sage. Before the door was closed some prayers were said and the bowl, the knife, and the bowls of the pipes were touched to the heated stones.

After the door was closed, Catches prayed and told of his power, and then told from the beginning the story of my coming there. He repeated my prayer of supplication from the first time I offered him the pipe, before and during the Eagle ceremony. Then the singing began and the Eagle's wings touched me.

Water was poured on the hot stones and steam arose with the praying.

I think it was then that the little bird sound was in the lodge; and now Catches' brother repeated my prayer to Red Hawk, Petaġa's intercessor; then the wings touched me again.

Four times, water was poured on the stones and steam filled the lodge and sweat poured from me as I have never known it to do before.

At the end of some prayers the door was opened and a dipper of water was passed out of the door to someone — I think it was Catches' wife — and when it was handed back, water was offered to me and then to the others, and we drank.

The door was closed again and there were more prayers and again water was poured on the rocks.

We then all came out of the lodge and wiped ourselves. I put on my dark blue breech cloth and moccasins and trousers, and was handed my pipe. I felt that a new kind of existence had begun and that an invisible wall had come between me and the people around me. All I wanted was to be alone.

The cars were now parked by the lodge. My grandmother and aunt were in my car, my aunt driving. I got in and Catches and his group got in their car and led the way to the place. We drove until we came to a windmill near the base of the little range of hills where I was to go. Before we started up the hill I wrapped my pipe in the sage where the bowl and stem come together. Then I wrapped it with two strips of red flannel. The rest of the party each took some of the other things, the blanket, quilt, sage, bowl, and knife. Catches led the way, carrying his suitcase of paraphernalia; I followed him and the rest walked behind us. We stopped four times climbing the hill. About halfway up were four large cherry trees that Catches had cut earlier. He picked up two of them and his brother the other two, and they dragged them the rest of the way up the hill.

The sky was now light with scattered clouds from behind which the sunshine was occasionally reaching past to touch the earth. A slight wind was blowing and changing directions every now and then. As we reached the place I was rather surprised to see an elongated willow structure about the length of a man and three feet high, made of little arches tied with strings of yellow cloth.

We stopped and stood while Catches and his brother prepared the place. With a crowbar apparently brought up the day before, Catches' brother made four holes about ten feet apart, forming a square. Into these holes the cut ends of the cherry trees were placed so they stood erect but not firm. A bed of sage was then laid out in a little circle where I was to stand. In front of the sage, an altar was erected, made of two forked sticks about a foot high with a crosspiece of fourteen inches. The bowl and the knife were set to the left of the altar.

I took off my trousers and moccasins and was led counterclockwise around to the front of the square, which faced west. I was stationed holding my pipe and standing facing the west on the bed of sage. Catches then took a rosary of tobacco bags which his wife had prepared the previous day, and wound on a piece of cardboard. He began unwinding it, first tying it to the cherry tree on the west on which the yard of red cloth had also been tied, then to the tree on the north which had the yard of white cloth on it, to the tree on the east with the yellow cloth, and the one on the south with green. The little red tobacco flags that had been used on the altar before the sweat lodge were stuck in the ground on either side of the stick altar. The tobacco rosary, stretching from tree to tree, reached back to the west tree and surrounded the square defined by the trees standing at each of its corners.

Catches then laid a row of single sage stems in front of the altar. He paid great attention to this and laid them very exactly. When he had finished he lit a braid of sweet grass and sent the smoke over the entire area and the rosary surrounding the space where I was standing. He then backed out of the space and tied the loose end of the rosary to the west tree, thus closing the space. Then he smoked the entire rosary from the outside, going clockwise until he came to the west. When he had done this, the people started to leave, going over the hill and down out of sight. Catches walked clockwise around the square, and as he approached the top of the knoll, a short distance from where I was standing, he sang a short song in an imploring, mournful tone and then disappeared down the hill.

I stood alone with the cool breeze gently blowing, I could not tell from what direction. A warm sense of well-being came over me, and a comfort in my solitude welled up from within. At last what I had longed for since leaving the sweat lodge was a reality. I was alone and quiet, naked before the creation. Catches' words spoken in the sweat lodge floated through my consciousness: "He comes to you young and innocent. Have mercy on him and give him what he seeks." Indeed I felt as though I were newly born. Yet there was a foreboding, a strong feeling of the presence of some other being, as I stared in one direction over the hills and into the sky. I was not sure if all that I was sensing was real.

The sun breaking through the clouds for a moment and warming my back brought me back to what I must now do. Holding my pipe, the bowl in my right hand and my left hand on the stem, I first asked that my prayer be heard, and because I had never prayed in this way I asked that my inexperience and possible mistakes be overlooked and my heart read, for I was there to learn and for that I was offering my prayers in these days of my fast.

Standing facing the west, I first addressed those powers, praying that the forces of the west, of thunder, lightning and the storm, hear me and lend me their strength to have courage in the face of what opposed me; should they wish to come to test me I would accept the challenge, but if not, I asked to be spared suffering from the storms while I was in this place. I asked them for courage and wisdom to face the trials of living and contending with my own judgment so that the difference between right and wrong, good and evil, should be as plain to me as the difference between day and night. I asked all this also for all our people, so that they might see their way out of all their difficulties. I asked that the children especially be given strength to grow and become good people who will preserve our ways and take care of the land. To my amazement, a wind began blowing from the west and made the red flag and all the others flutter as I completed that prayer.

Facing the north, I addressed those powers and asked them also to hear me and grant me strength to face all storms, and to receive with thankfulness the cleansing winds and snows that purge and wash away the old, preparing a way for the new. I asked that their harshness brace my weakness and make me strong and persevering, just as after the winter has come wrapping the world in cold our old selves are washed away and we can be new again in the spring. I asked that all our people be made strong to stand against what is harsh in life.

Facing the east, I asked these powers to hear me, and that the light which is the day that comes from the east should enter me and light my mind to its fullest power. I asked for the light of wisdom to see and understand what I must do and become so that my people may live. I asked for enlightenment for all the people, that they may discover the wisdom and peace of our religion as a light to guide them and bring day where there is so much darkness. I asked for the new life of spring to come to the people so that they may meet life with hope, as the earth greets spring in regeneration.

To the south I prayed that those powers of everlasting spring and summer grant me health to reach my life's harvest and full potential. I asked them to enter me and bring my life's tasks to fruition just as the summer matures the production of the earth. I asked for this power of accomplishment so that my people may live, and I asked for the people that they also may reach their highest and bear their fruit and accomplish what must be done in their time.

Pointing my pipe to the sky, I asked that the mystery of creation, reaching into infinity, bring together all of life in peace. I asked for wisdom to know and understand my part and place on this earth with other people. I asked to know humility and to become a better man so that my people may live better through my efforts and my work as a teacher. I asked for mercy and to be worthy to know the Spirit as it makes itself known to man.

Pointing my pipe to the earth I prayed the earth to give bodily health to all her children. I asked that the powers that live there manifest themselves in me so that I may be healthy and not be hungry. I asked for health for our people and that the babies and children reach old age, that life be long and good for all the people. I asked earth to be generous to her children and I repented that we have not cared for her nor her creation as we should.

At the end of this prayer I faced the west once again and asked that my prayer be heard.

Shortly after I had finished, a yellow butterfly came from behind the square area where I was standing and flew counter-clockwise to the tree on the west. It circled the tree and then fluttered back and forth in front of it, inside the square. I had been told to offer my pipe to any creature that might come to me while I was in that place; so addressing it, I pointed my pipe toward it and said, "My friend, I offer you this pipe in respect for your presence. If you come with good will, to help me, accept this offering; if you are here for other reasons, you should know that this is a sacred place and I beg you to leave it."

I said this while the butterfly circled the tree. When it fluttered to and fro in front of the tree, I somehow knew it had heard me, for it then flew to the tree on the north and circled it and then did the same with the other two trees. Then it came and circled me and almost lit on my pipe but instead left the place, fluttering clockwise around the square and leaving over the hill.

Soon after this I had to leave the enclosure to relieve myself.

Catches had told me that when this was necessary I was to open the rosary attached to the tree on the west, as though it were a little gate, and to go a distance away from the sacred place. I did this and then returned and closed the gate again. Being out of the square for a few minutes was an experience of difference; I knew that I had left a place that was sanctified and was treading on ground that was ordinary and common. I was glad to come back in to the security of the enclosure.

Catches had said that during the days of the fast, the sacred power of all holy places, the sites of other Pipe Fasts and of the Sun Dance of times past, would be brought together and centered in this place which would henceforth always be sacred. No one who believed this could be harmed or touched by anyone while he was there; it is said that even the rain and the hail sometimes do not touch such a spot, while falling all around it. As I stood thinking about this and other things, a little brown bird flew close and sat in a pine tree about ten feet from the square. I addressed it as I had the butterfly; there were other birds in the trees to the north, east, and south, and they chirped as though in response. A feeling of communication and of being a natural part of that place made me feel that I wanted to stay there forever. One of the birds, a blue one, remained long after the others flew away, and returned daily for the next two days, always coming by itself to the same tree where it sat for hours regarding me. I offered it the pipe each time. I did not know then that it would return for the next three years to sit in a tree to the east of me and, in the third year, sing me a song of encouragement, the words of which I would understand on my third pipe fast and sing on my fourth.

As the sun travelled across the sky that day, the wonder of the creation entered my awareness, the relation of microcosm and macrocosm; and I felt the connectedness of everything, as

Catches had said, like a massive design woven by a sacred power, constantly breathed into by the breath of the Great Spirit.

I stood for what seemed a long time, yet in a way time no longer existed as there was nothing with which to compare the length or breadth of my experience, other than the changing appearances of things as they were touched by the changing light of the sun.

For a long time I had had the strange feeling that somebody was approaching me or looking at me, but I was startled to hear from behind me the sound of a man walking. Not quite knowing if it was someone of this world or another, I waited. Presently a man approached on my right side; it was Catches. He had brought up the buffalo skull to be placed on the altar. Very slowly he lit the sweet grass he had brought and going clockwise, smoked the entire rosary again. When he finished he untied the end of the rosary that was fastened to the cherry tree, opened it and came in and asked me how I was. I told him I was fine. He said that the buffalo skull should have been brought up when we first came but no one was available to carry it to the sacred place, as only those who had fasted before were qualified. So he had brought it now because the day was approaching its end and it would remain with me for the duration of the ceremony. He then placed the skull in front of the little rack facing me and proceeded to smoke the interior of it and then to smoke me, with the sweet grass. Then he smoked the tiny flags and the rack and the inside of the rosary, and backed out of the opening, tying it shut. Then he went to the back, standing in approximately the same place where he had stood before he left for the first time, and sang the same song he had sung earlier.

Shortly after he had gone, I began my second round of prayers to each of the quarters of the earth, beginning at the west, as I had been instructed. I went through the entire round as I had done before, and at the end of that prayer it sounded as if a gun had been shot off in the valley below; it reverberated and echoed through the valleys below me. A little later a host of hawks came flying up from the south near where I was, and hovered there and then headed west. Once again I had the awesome feeling that Nature or the great powers had responded in an unusual way to what I had said, and I knew that my prayers were being answered.

As the sun began to set I heard a strange noise coming from beneath the earth, approaching from the south. At first I thought perhaps it was something digging under the ground, but I didn't know, so I offered it my pipe, as I had been told; and shortly thereafter it stopped. When the sun had sunk a little lower, there was a clopping sound that came nearer; once again, not knowing what it was, I waited, and it was a line of cows going by. Two of them, very curious, stopped and looked at me, so I offered them the pipe also. No sooner had I finished the first prayer, the offering to them, than one turned its head and mooed and went the other way; but the other, a black one, a little bit more curious, stood and looked at me for a long time before it turned finally and left.

I sat and waited until the sun was just touching the horizon and I began my third round of prayers, once again beginning at the west and continuing around. By the time I had finished, the day had almost disappeared and the moon was beginning to rise, so I began my fourth round while the blueness of the day was still there on the horizon. When I had finished the fourth round the moon was quite high. I put my pipe on the pipe rack as I had been told to do, and gathered my blanket around me, and sat, again thinking about all that had happened. It was then that an owl began hooting and a woman's voice, rather mournful, began to come from the hill across the valley that began on my right. I didn't know the meaning of this; I wouldn't know till three years later when things I had seen and heard were finally clarified and their meaning revealed.

As the moon rose higher I sat with my blanket gathered around me and imagined what was happening back at Catches' little mud and log house. I could picture in my mind my relatives and Catches' relatives gathered there, the preparations that had been made for the feast that evening, the sacrifice and cooking of my second pup that would be offered that night as a companion to the first one, in order that there might be good weather and a successful vision quest.

When the moon was quite high I decided it was time to make my first round of the night, as I had been instructed also to make four rounds of prayers also during the night. The night is considered one day in Indian tradition: that is, two nights and two days would actually be thought of as four days. In this case I was fasting five days: three days and two nights. I got my pipe from the rack and began my round. Once again, upon completion of the round, the woman's voice, this time very plainly crying, came from the same place where it had come from before. Knowing that I was in a sacred place and that nothing could harm me as long as I was there, I was not afraid; in fact, I was very glad I had received a sign that was so clear to my understanding, so that I knew the fulfillment of my quest was beginning.

I then placed the pipe on the rack and crawled into the little willow lodge to stretch out and rest. My back was a little warm from the day's exposure to the sun, and oddly enough the insteps of my feet were also quite burned. My face felt hot. I hardly knew whether I was asleep or awake, and I had no mysterious dreams that night, except that the eagles that I had dreamed about the night before I began the fast came again soaring, but this time turned abruptly and flew over me. I don't know how long I had been there in either a dreaming or waking state when I decided it was time to make my round again. This I did three more times that night, and by dawn I was surprisingly very relaxed and prepared to meet the sun.

Shortly before I climbed out of the willow structure to get my pipe and begin my morning round and the greeting to the sun, I had the feeling that I was being watched; but I continued anyway and when I finished I stood facing the west, holding my pipe. The sun was now above the horizon and at my back. I decided to sit for a while, and when I placed my pipe on the rack I saw out of the corner of my eye what looked like a hunched-over eagle form. Turning and looking at it closely I saw that it was Catches sitting on the hill behind me, hunched over, with his eagle-bone whistle in his mouth. When I had put my pipe on the rack, he stood and faced the sun and sang a song that morning to the sun, and waved his eagle wing fan in the air above his head and blew the whistle four times. Then he came down to the sacred place, smoked the outside, untied the string and came in, smoked the whole area and then me. Then he asked if I had to relieve myself, which I did, so he walked in front of me, making a little path and waving the smoking sweet grass. He took me some distance from the sacred area and waited till I was finished and then returned me to the place. When we had gotten back he stood on the sage pallet that had been prepared and checked the tiny sage stems that he had arranged the day before, and examined the flags and the tobacco rosary that enclosed the place like a fence, and then asked me again if I was all right, and I told him once again that I was fine. He backed out then, tied the rosary shut and smoked it, and then returned to the hill where he had sung the last two songs; but this time he faced west as he had done the first day, and sang the same song that he had sung the day before. Then he went away over the hill.

I began my second round of prayers, but this time I took off

Untitled, 1982 CARL BEAM

my blanket as the morning sun was bright enough now to warm me. I went on through that day; and upon the beginning of my third round, I noticed a strange appearance in the sky to the south. It was like two parallel rolling clouds that stretched far into the south and far above me. They were not jet streams; they were much larger, and rolling within themselves. It was at this time then that my vision began. I had thought it would be a very mystical experience, one that would be perhaps more of a dream than a vision, and my first reaction was: "How strange! This is not at all what I thought a vision was like." I felt I was perfectly clearheaded; I had not been deprived of food nor of water for that great a length of time. It lasted for what seemed the greater part of that day, gradually revealing a changing series of distinct forms and figures, like a panorama of shifting scenes, whose meaning once again would be revealed to me only upon the completion of my fourth pipe fast.

I cannot tell this vision here, for there is a time and a place reserved for the telling of visions: a sacred setting, the proper songs, the proper preparations. It lasted, as I said, quite a long time; and by the time it was finished I was thoroughly exhausted. I lay down to rest and covered my head because the day was now very hot; and I knew that something had happened to me, because I was alternately sweating and very cold. I wanted to protect myself from the hot sun, for every ray that touched my body burned almost as if it were focussed on my skin with a magnifying glass; yet when I covered myself, I became so hot I had to take off the blanket, and yet after I had it off for a while I got very cold alternately with being burned by the sun. It was a very strange sensation.

It was then I noticed the wind blowing. I don't understand or know how it blew that way, but all the flags would be blowing inward at one moment and then outward at another moment. I covered my head again and prayed that what was happening to me was a sacred and good thing and I asked for help that I could endure this.

Gradually I fell asleep and when I awoke it was late in the day and everything was very peaceful. What awakened me was the little blue bird that had returned to the tree and was singing the song that I spoke of before. Once again I picked up my pipe, only this time I added to my prayers thanks for that vision that had been given to me, and I prayed at the same time that through it and from it good and understanding would come to me and my people, and that the purpose of my fast would be fulfilled.

When I had finished that round, I was doubly exhausted and very weak. I placed my pipe on the pipe rack and sat once again, slipping in and out of sleep. When I drifted into sleep it was not total unconsciousness but was more like dreaming; it was as though there were multitudes of children playing around me and making a lot of noise, and I would wake up to find I was alone still in the sacred place. Then I would doze again and a phase of my childhood would return: myself as a child speaking with my grandmother and my grandfather. There were also times when in the dreams I walked in very strange places, places I don't remember as a child. Eventually I must have rested, because by the time I awoke again the sun was just beginning to set on the horizon, so I began my fourth round for the day. Upon finishing that, I was exhausted once more and I put my pipe on the rack and returned to the willow lodge. Just as I was about to enter it, Catches came again to check to see if I was all right. He went through the same ritual that he had done before, and when he asked me how I was, he could see there was something strange about me and asked me if I should go down now. I told him no, I had this night and the next day still to go and I preferred to stay them out. I told him that I had had visitors and that something mysterious occurred. He saw my swollen feet and my burned

back and my burned chest and face; the skin was beginning to
peel. That evening when he sang the departing song, the man
cried with such compassion that I cried also, not knowing
whether it was for him, the song, or myself.

That night was a very restless one. I prayed four times.
Catches did not come the next morning which was the beginning of my final day. I began the day greeting the sun, before
and at the moment of its climbing over the horizon. I was very
weak and my lips were very dry and felt swollen. As I returned
my pipe to the rack and stood, I noticed there were two cloud
banks, one to the east and one to the west, like huge cliffs, and
they were moving towards each other, so that in my reckoning
they would collide right above me. I prayed to each of them and
told them that if this was the test that was being given me, I was
ready to endure it, for I knew these things were necessary and a
part of nature; for just as there is sunlight and good weather,
there is also the wind and the rain which are also needed for life
on this earth. Besides, I was very hot and dehydrated; I thought
if it rained I would thankfully get some moisture. But these
cloud signs were so forceful they made me fearful also, because
only two or three weeks before the torrential rains in the Black
Hills had caused floods and the loss of many lives. In our part of
the country we frequently have tornadoes and strong wind
storms. So I prayed and asked that I would be strong enough to
endure what was to happen.

It was then that a nausea and a tremendous weakness came
over me, and with that I heard the sound of wind in the pine
trees and the sound of wind at a great distance and also the sound
of the two approaching storms above. I put my pipe on the rack
and lay down on the ground and covered my head, and I must
have fainted. I don't know how long I was lying there; but on
awakening I was lying on my side with my head in the dirt, and
directly opposite my eyes, the tobacco rosary had been broken

in one place. I staggered to my feet and picked up my pipe, and pointing it toward that place where the rosary was broken I offered it to whatever force it was that had broken through, and reminded it that this was a sacred place. I said that if the intentions it had here were good, it should accept this pipe and all it represents, but if they were evil it must depart. On completing that pipe offering, a certain strength and well-being returned to me, but I was becoming very apprehensive about that place.

It was then I began another round of prayers and while I was making it I saw that the cloud banks, which had subsided somewhat from the time I first saw them, now were beginning to build power again and to move toward each other. I thought that certainly this time I was going to be in the eye of a tornado. Upon completion of that round of prayers I became again very weak and nauseated. I returned my pipe to the rack and lay down and covered my head. That time there was a rushing sensation, almost as if I were in the middle of a whirlwind. I didn't know what caused me to cover my head—I would not know that until later—but for some reason I did and lay there praying all the while that I would be strong enough to endure whatever it was that was happening. I lost consciousness again and as I awoke I saw directly in my line of vision that the tobacco rosary had been broken in two more places. I felt very much afraid and I knew that something extraordinary had happened. Then I thought, "Now it is over. The Pipe Fast is finished." Suddenly I had a surge of energy and a strong sense of well-being. I rose and took my pipe and made my round, that time in a kind of joyous thanksgiving for all that had taken place. Indeed a part of what I had seen during the vision prompted me on this final round to make at each quarter, in gratitude, the dance steps up and down of the Sun Dance, for I felt a great sense of joy but also one of responsibility and of awe, almost as if an obligation had been laid upon me.

As I returned from that round to face the west, the eagles flew above, one from each quarter; not all at once, but beginning from the west an eagle flew over me, then one from the north, one from the east, and one from the south. Soon afterward the butterfly that I had seen on the first day returned, and danced about the trees as it had done before, and disappeared. It was after all that that I noticed that the cherry trees had bent over and that the flags were now touching the ground; and it was a verification that the ceremony had indeed come to an end.

I stood then for the remainder of the day until later afternoon with my pipe and as I examined the area around me and myself, it seemed I was in a pitiful condition. Finally I heard steps approaching from the rear, and there was a procession of people coming to take me down. Catches and his brother came around in front of me. I didn't look back to see who was in the group, but stood and held my pipe.

First Catches untied the rosary and went around rolling it up. When he come to the broken parts he stood and pondered for a while and then went on rolling them into a ball. He pulled out the cherry trees and took them and the tobacco pouches and laid them over in the little gully to my right, where the valley began. He took down the willow frame and put that over there also, as well as the rack and the little flags. He smoked me with the sweet grass and then took his eagle wing fan and beating it on his leg several times, very carefully began to wipe me with the fan, making quick brushing motions as if to dust or wipe something off. Then he stood and addressed the west and prayed and gave thanks that this process had gone this far. He gave instructions to his brother to hand the things that I had used to the people that had come with him. Then he told my grandmother to come and put on my feet the moccasins she had brought. She could hardly get them on because my feet were so swollen with sunburn, and the poor little bent-over woman cried very hard. Then out of the corner of my eye I could see that my mother had arrived also. She lived 120 miles from there, and they had called her once I had been placed upon the hill. I am sure she would have objected at first, which is why I had told them not to tell her until after I had been put on the hill. We went then in a procession: Catches first, then a man with the buffalo skull, and after him I walked carrying my pipe. We went down the hill stopping four times, and each time Catches sang a song of thanksgiving.

When we reached the bottom of the hill cars were there waiting, but I told him that I preferred to walk the rest of the way. He asked me if I could, and I said yes. So the rest got in the cars and he walked ahead of me leading the way, and we went back to the sweat lodge.

When we arrived, the rest had already gotten there, and all the ceremonial paraphernalia was gathered by the sweat lodge, because it had to be purified once again. By that time the fire was roaring and the rocks were heating, and I was placed in the lodge to wait. After the rocks had been put in the men entered, once again sitting in the places they had sat in before. I was at the very back facing the door which opened to the west, Catches at my left and his brother at my right.

First of all the bowl and blanket and knife I had used were held above the hot rocks as water was poured on them, so that the spiritual residue could be washed away and they too could return to the world of men. Those things were passed out the door and then the door was closed and the ritual began. This time Catches took sage and wiped my eyes, my nose, my mouth and my ears. Then he blew in my eyes, he blew on my nose, my mouth and my ears, so that they too would be made ready for the common world again. During the ritual the cherry juice was poured into the wooden bowl, and taking the sweet grass Cat-

ches painted the parting in my hair with cherry juice; this is
symbolically my red road. Then he painted four times down the
back of my hair, somehow setting the pattern that I would do
this three more times to complete the cycle that had begun
there.

Then he began his telling of visions—that is, the story of his
power as a man and his qualifications to conduct such rites; and
the little bird sound came, his intercessor, Red Hawk, arrived;
and it was time for me to tell now of the things I had seen and
heard and experienced on the hill. Starting from the beginning
and not leaving out anything that might have meaning, I began
to tell of all that had happened. The intercessor heard this and
left for a while; the door was opened, and I had my first drink,
which was cherry juice. Catches first dipped a braid of sweet
grass in the cherry juice and I sucked the juice from the end of
the sweet grass. This he did four times. After that I took four sips
of the cherry juice. Next I was given four drinks of water. Then
the intercessor returned, the door was closed and the singing
began: translated from the sacred language into one I could
understand, it was said that indeed a legitimate spiritual event
had taken place, and that I was now committed for the next four
years to fasting and participation in the rituals so that my vision
might be fulfilled and made efficacious.

The responsibility weighing on me made me very sad but
also very happy, for I had gone there seeking something and had
come away with something very wonderful, very powerful yet
also very hard to live by. I had something difficult to do in the
years to come.

The door was opened once more, then Catches explained that
the sweat lodge is a true part of the whole rite. He explained that
it was only opened four times in all, twice the first time and
twice the second, and it is the beginning and ending of the

ceremony. As before, at the ending the water was passed out first to the helper and then back in and then to me. Then it was time to come out and wipe ourselves and prepare ourselves for the breaking-of-the-fast meal which had been prepared and was waiting.

As we emerged from the sweat lodge, gliding in and hovering over us came the hugest eagle I have ever seen, and the people down by the house below the sweat lodge had seen it also. It circled and hovered and slowly, slowly passed over the pine trees, and the blessing rain came. There were some broken clouds in the sky, but it was sunlight; and yet a slight rain came at that moment and a very tiny little rainbow opened up on the hillside across the valley from where we were; and we knew again that it was good and that our prayers had been heard.

We went down to the house then where I went among my relatives and shook their hands and embraced the womenfolk; it was such a happy reunion, coming back from a journey so very far away in time, since where I had gone was actually four generations back. We assembled inside the little house and a very traditional meal was served. The first dish that was brought around was the *wasna*, the dried and pounded pemmican mixed with chokecherries. I gave my first handful to the spirits that they might be fed, and it was taken out and offered to them.

I had thought of food occasionally when I was on the hill, but not very much; and now when the time came that I could eat again, I was hardly hungry, and all I could take was a small amount of soup and a little bit of *wasna*.

Later the people began to leave, to return that night for the final ceremony, the one that was to be held in the dark. And I went out and sat on a stump by the woodpile and thought, and thought, and thought: how wonderful it was to be alive in this century yet also able to experience the sacred traditions from the past and to know that the Great Spirit still responds to his twentieth-century children by giving them visions and signs, and a sense of peace, and the knowledge of an all-enduring faith.

The Return

Navajo

*T*he people began in the first world, and came up through three others to emerge into this, the fifth world. But in the world before this, the fourth, the men and women were separated for a while and the women gave birth to monsters, who were the enemy gods. In the fifth world they became very numerous and powerful. When they had devoured nearly all the People, Talking God and the others made two more people out of corn, and two women, one out of turquoise and the other out of white shell. They were Woman Who Changes and White Shell Woman. The gods took the other people away and left the two sisters alone on the sacred mountain in the middle of the land.

They felt lonely. Woman Who Changes lay down on a rock in the sun, and White Shell Woman lay under a waterfall. Four days later they knew they were pregnant, and four days after that they bore sons. The son of Woman Who Changes was born first.

The boys grew very fast. At the end of four days they were the size of twelve-year-olds, and the gods came and raced with them; but the gods could run faster, and got behind them and whipped them with twigs. In four more days the boys were full grown, and when the gods came back to race them again, it was they who won, and who chased the gods with sticks.

Their mothers told them not to go far from the lodge, but each day for four days they wandered far in each of the four directions, and each day they saw a strange bird or animal; so the women knew that the spies of all the enemy gods had seen them. The next day the giant Yéitso, the chief of the alien gods, came to the lodge. White Shell Woman saw him coming and she and her sister hid the boys. Yéitso came and sat down by the door.

"What has made all the tracks around here?" he asked.

"Oh, those tracks I have made for fun," replied Woman Who Changes. "I was feeling lonely so I pretended there were many people around me, and I made the tracks with my fist, like this," and she showed him. Yéitso seemed satisfied and went away.

But White Shell Woman went out to look and saw many of the alien gods hurrying toward the lodge. She ran and told Woman Who Changes, who made a great wind blow in all directions from the lodge so that none of the enemies could advance against it.

The next morning the boys got up before daybreak and stole away. Soon the women missed them but could not trace them in the dark. When it was light enough they went to look for their tracks, but all they could find was four footprints of each of them, so they knew that they had taken a holy trail, on a rainbow, and stopped looking for them.

Meanwhile the boys traveled fast on the rainbow, and soon after sunrise they saw smoke rising from the ground. They looked down the smokehole and saw an old woman, who was Spider Woman. "Welcome, children, enter," said Spider Woman. "Where are you going?" She asked them four times, but they would not answer her. Then she said, "Perhaps you would seek your father?" "Yes," they answered, "if only we knew the way to his house." "Ah," said Spider Woman, "it is a long and dangerous way to the house of your father, the Sun. But I will give you something to preserve your lives, and a charm to subdue your enemies." So she gave them each life-feathers to wear to protect them, and taught them a charm to subdue the anger of their enemies: "Put your feet down with pollen. Put your hands down with pollen. Put your head down with pollen. Then your feet are pollen; your hands are pollen; your body is pollen; your mind is pollen; your voice is pollen. The trail is beautiful. Be still."

The first of the dangers that the boys came to after they left the house of Spider Woman was the Crushing Rocks. When a traveler approached, they would open wide, but as soon as he was between them they would close and crush him to death. These rocks were really people; they thought like men; they were enemy gods. Four times the boys pretended they were going between them and drew back just in time. Then the rocks asked, "Who are you and where are you going?" and the boys answered, "We are children of the Sun, and we seek the house of our father." Then they repeated the charm that Spider Woman had taught them, and the rocks drew back and said, "Pass on to the house of your father."

The second danger was the Cutting Reeds, who showed a clear passage between them and then leapt together and cut the traveler to pieces. Four times the boys deceived them; then the reeds spoke to them, as the rocks had done. They answered and repeated the sacred words. "Pass on to the house of your father," said the reeds, and the boys passed on in safety.

The third danger was the Tearing Cactuses, where the same thing happened, and the fourth was the Boiling Sands, which subsided at the words of the charm. Soon after this they approached the house of the Sun, which was guarded by bears, by serpents, by winds, and by lightnings; but all were subdued by the pollen chant.

The house of the Sun was built of turquoise, and stood on the shore of a great water. When the boys entered they saw, sitting in the west, a woman; in the south, two handsome young men; and in the north, two handsome young women. The young men rose without speaking, wrapped the boys in four coverings of the sky, and laid them on a shelf.

The boys had lain there quietly for some time when a rattle that hung over the door shook and one of the young women said: "Our father is coming." The rattle shook four times, and then Tsóhanoai, the Sun Bearer, entered his house. He took the sun off his back and hung it up on a peg on the wall, where it shook and clanged for some time, going "tla, tla, tla, tla," till at last it hung still.

Then Sun Bearer turned to the woman and asked her in an angry tone, "Who are those two who entered here today?" After he had asked four times, the woman said, "You had better not say much! Two young men came here today, seeking their father. You always tell me that you meet no other woman but me. Whose sons are these?"

She pointed at the bundle on the shelf and Sun Bearer took it down. He first unrolled the robe of dawn, then the robe of blue sky, next the robe of yellow evening light and last the robe of darkness, and the boys fell out on the floor. He seized them and threw them first upon great, sharp spikes of white shell that stood in the east; but they bounded back unhurt, for they held their life-feathers tightly all the while. Then he threw them in turn on spikes of turquoise in the south, on spikes of haliotis in the west, and spikes of black rock in the north; and when they were not hurt, he said, "I wish it were indeed true that they were my children."

Then he said to the four young people, his children who lived in his house, "Go prepare the sweat-house and heat for it a white, a blue, a yellow, and a black boulder." Wind heard him and dug a hole in the bank behind the sweat-house, and whispered to the boys, "Do not hide in the hole until you have answered your father's questions." The boys went into the sweat-house, the hot boulders were put in and the opening of the lodge was covered with the four sky-blankets. Then Sun Bearer called out to the boys: "Are you hot?" and they answered, "Yes, very hot." Then they crept into the hiding place and lay there. After a while Sun Bearer came and poured water through the top of the sweat-house on the stones, making them burst with a loud noise and a great heat and steam. But in a little while the stones cooled and the boys crept out of their hiding place. Sun Bearer came and asked again: "Are you hot?" expecting to get no reply, but the boys answered, "Yes, very hot," and he took the coverings off the sweat-lodge and let them out, saying, "Yes, I think these are my children."

Then Sun Bearer told his daughters to make the boys look like his other sons; and the young women pulled their hair out long and moulded their faces and bodies to look like the other two. Then Sun Bearer told them all to enter the house. As they went in, Wind whispered to them to look down, and they saw a caterpillar who spat out two blue spits. "Each of you take one," said Wind, "and hold it in your mouth so that you can endure the next trial."

Sun Bearer now took a pipe of turquoise and filled it with tobacco, lit it from the sun hanging on the wall, and gave it to the boys to smoke. They smoked it, passing it from one to the other until it was finished. They said it tasted sweet; and it did them no harm. When the pipe was smoked out and Sun Bearer saw it had not killed them, he was satisfied, and said: "Now, my children, what do you want from me?"

The boys answered: "Father, the land where we dwell is filled with alien gods who devour the People. Give us weapons to destroy our enemies."

Sun Bearer said: "Yéitso, chief of your enemies, is also my son. Yet I will help you to kill him, and I shall hurl the first bolt. Here are weapons to help you in war." He gave to each of them a shirt, leggings, and moccasins of flint, arrows of lightning and a great stone knife.

"These are what we want," said the boys, and put on the armor, and streaks of lightning shot from every joint.

The next day Sun Bearer led them out to the edge of the world, and there were sixteen wands leaning from the earth to the sky: four were of white shell, four of turquoise, four of haliotis and four of red stone. Wind whispered to the boys, "The red wands are for war, the others for peace," and when Sun Bearer asked them on which they wished to ascend, they said, "On the wands of red stone."

They climbed up to the sky-hole in the center of the sky with their father, on the wands of red stone. From there, Sun Bearer asked them to show him where they lived. The older brother could not tell, but the younger was able to point out the sacred mountains that marked the boundaries of the land of the People. Then Sun Bearer spread out a streak of lightning, and the boys stood on it and shot down to the top of Tsótsil, the mountain of the South, which the gods had fastened to the earth with a great stone knife and adorned with turquoise, dark mist, she-rain and all kinds of wild animals.

The next day they went on, and decided to try out one of the weapons their father had given them; so they shot one of the lightning arrows, and made a great cleft in Tsótsil, which remains to this day. Soon they heard the sound of thunderous footsteps and saw the head of Yéitso peering over a high hill in the east. He disappeared and appeared again in the south, then in the west, then in the north over Tsótsil, each time for a little longer and showing more of his body. Then he came down to the lake to drink, and saw the reflection of the boys in the water. They were standing on a rainbow, and when Yéitso hurled four lightning bolts one after the other, they straightened the rainbow so that the first bolt passed over their heads, then bent it so the second went under their feet, the third again over their heads, and the fourth, although he threw the bolt very high, also passed under their feet. At this moment the lightning promised by Sun Bearer descended from the sky on the giant's head; he reeled but did not fall. Then the brothers loosed four lightning arrows; with the first, he bent to the east, with the second to the south, with the third to the west, and the fourth to the north. Then he fell to his knees and on his face, stretched out his limbs and moved no more. His blood flowed out and turned to stone, and it can be seen to this day in the valley below Tsótsil.

And the younger brother was called Child of the Water, and the older brother, Slayer of the Alien Gods.

New Year Ceremony, 1969   TOM TWO ARROWS

Sun Dance

Joseph Epes Brown

*It is a recurrent pilgrimage, and it is made with propriety, a
certain sense of formality. I understand a little more of it each
time. I see a little more deeply into the meaning of formality, the
formality of meaning. It is a religious experience by and large,
natural and appropriate. It is an expression of the spirit.*

—N. Scott Momaday
"To the Singing, to the Drum"
Natural History, February, 1975

A people's vision that speaks of Life, of sacrificial means for the
recurrent renewal of life, and of suffering for identity with the
source of life, is a vision that can neither be destroyed, denied,
nor ignored, even though such has been attempted.

Today as in the past, the annual "Sun Dance" ceremonies of
the Plains Indians of North America give to these peoples, as
indeed to all peoples, a message through example: affirming the
power of suffering in sacrifice, revealing in rich detail the mystery of the sacred in its operations, in all life, and throughout all
creation. It is here implied that where there is no longer affirma-
tion nor means for sacrifice, for "making sacred," where man
loses the sense of Center, the very energy of the world will run

out. Such traditions affirm for those who listen (and just as inevitably for those who do not), that where the sacred in the world and in life comes to be held as irrelevant illusion, where evasion of sacrifice in pursuit of some seeming "good life" becomes a goal in itself, then, in the empty and concomitant ugliness of such a life and such a man-manipulated world, that ordering cycle of sacrifice will and must be accomplished by Nature Herself so that there may be renewal again in the world.

In accordance with the mood and perspective of this statement, ethnographic description of the particulars of a Lakota, Arapaho, Gros Ventre, Blackfeet, Cree, Cheyenne, or Crow/ Shoshone Sun Dance is neither appropriate nor necessary. For they share a single language of sacred act and vision, expressed in rich and varied dialects, and a composite statement is suggested to convey the essential elements common to them all.

Already in the cold darkness of winter's night there are preparations in the Plains for spring's advent and that celebration variously called "Dance for World and Life Renewal," "Dance Watching the Sun," or "The Thirst Dance." Sponsors come forward, advance vows are made by prospective participants, sacred materials gathered, songs of power are learned, transmitted again from elder to younger, and members of those guiding Societies meet and prepare for the "moon of grass growing," spring's time when the power of the sun will return to renew the life of the earth, to bring new strength, goodness, and joy to all of life's beings. It is the one annual occasion when bands or clans, or even several allied nations, may come together to celebrate in solemnity and joy a sacred event, the beginning of a new cycle of life, to insure that the energy of this world and life will be renewed so that the cycle may continue. For three or four days of life-shaping formal rites and ceremonies, and in the additional camp days of preparation and endings, individual and group will better know the power of suffering in sacrifice, yet also, in joyful celebration of life and life's season, a little of the mysteries of this life, thus also of the mysteries of death.

Out of the timbers brought from the mountains, to construct the circular ceremonial lodge, the lodge of "new birth," "new life," the "thirst lodge," is to re-enact the creation of world and cosmos. In horizontal orientations, the lodge doorway situated at the East is the place whence flows life in light; from the South comes growth in youth; from the West comes ripeness, full fruit, the middle age of man; and in the North is completion, old age leading to death which again leads to new life. At the center of the lodge the most sacred sacramental cottonwood tree—rooted in the womb of earth as mother and stretching up and out to the heavens—is axis of the world and male generative principle. Into and out from this central point and axis of the lodge flow the powers of the six directions; when man in awful ceremony is actually tied to this Tree of the Center by the flesh of his body, or when women make offerings of pieces cut from their arms, sacrifice through suffering is accomplished that the world and all beings may live, that life be renewed, that man may become who he is.

The qualitatively defined powers of the directions, the effective actualization of sacrifice, cannot be operative so long as man retains impurity. So it is that participants initially purify themselves in the little universe of the round sweat lodge where forces generously released from the rocks of earth, from air, fire, and water, cleanse man and give new life. Indeed, in the days and nights of ritual and ceremony which follow, means are used to maintain participants in a state of purity, through sacrificial concentration on Sun or Center, or through the purifying agency of smokes from tobacco, from burning sweet grass and other wild grasses, from sweet sage and cedar.

Special persons are chosen for specific ritual functions; they become what they personify: "Earth Maker," "Lodge Maker," and the venerable sacred woman of purity who is the earth herself in all her powers and with all her blessings. Without the presence of this most sacred woman there can be no Sun Dance, for the duality of cosmic forces, the complementarity of male and female, are essential to the creative act, are central to realization of totality. To better translate cosmic realities and process into immediate visible and effective experience, on the bodies of participants are painted with prayer and earth-colors the forms of sun, moon, stars, hail, lightning, the varied elements of nature.

At certain times special altars are constructed upon the earth with simple means but of profound import: a place on the earth is cleared and made sacred, directions of the world are delineated always in reference to Center; man's relationship to the cosmos is established, his true "path of life" defined. Ceremonial pipes, themselves portable altars, are ever present with these earth altars. The pipe or straight pipe-stem is associated with the central sacred tree, as both are axes, both trace the Way, both express the male generative principle, and both speak of sacrifice.

Dancers wear and use whistles made of the wing-bone of the eagle to which eagle plumes are attached. In recreating the cry of eagle to the powerful rhythm of song, dance, and drum, the Eagle is present in voice and being, man's vital breath is united with the essences of sun and life. Through such ritual use of sacred form man becomes Eagle, and the eagle in his plumes is the Sun. So it happens at each morning's greeting of the new sun, dancers face the East holding their eagle plumes towards the sun's first rays, bathing the plumes in the new light of life, then placing the plumes in movements of purification to the head and to all parts of the upper body, dancing the while to the rhythm of heroic song. Dignified movements of dance facing sun or Tree are sustained in the suffering of thirst day and night through the beat of the drum, the heart and life of the world, now one with man's own heart and life. The strength of such identity of rhythm, it has often been said, carries on within man's being many months after such celebrations are completed.

Through rich and varied means specific forms of life are celebrated, honored, within the lodge. Living decorated trees may be planted, moisture bearing cattails are offered by friends and relatives for the dancers' bed, or chokecherry bushes are planted in conjunction with sacred rites and altars. High in the fork of the sacred tree there is an offering nest for Thunderbird; some form or aspect of the bison is hung upon the tree, and an eagle, or rawhide effigy of man himself. Small children may even sometimes fashion and bring into the lodge little clay animals two by two: elk, deer, rabbits, kitfox, dogs, otter, even grasshoppers. Thus present within the lodge is that which grows from the earth, those who live in the waters, those who walk on the earth, and those who fly above the earth. The powers of all things and all beings are present here in this holy place.

The Sun Dance, thus, is not a celebration by man for man; it is an honoring of all life and the source of all life, that life may go on, that the circle be a cycle, that all the world and man may continue on the path of the cycle of giving, receiving, bearing, being born in suffering, growing, becoming, giving back to earth that which has been given, and so finally to be born again. So it is told that only in sacrifice is sacredness accomplished: only in sacrifice is identity possible and found. It is only through the suffering in sacrifice that finally freedom is known and laughter in Joy returns to the world.

> here am I behold me
> I am the sun
> behold me
> —*Lakota Sunrise Greeting Song*

The Road to the Center

Arthur Amiotte

In the mythic beginning of the Lakota world, its sacred and temporal dimensions were one, and the Lakota still recognizes himself as a microcosmic reflection of the macrocosm. If he can live in concert with the holy rhythm of that which causes all life to move, he is then assisting in the ongoing process of creation. To maintain his participation in this process, he needs annually to make the journey to the Center of the World, which is the place of his beginning and the origin of all things. There he can renew his relation with the sacred rhythm in the ceremony known as the Sun Dance.

Especially at this time, since many of the Lakota are scattered, people must sometimes travel great distances to return to their homeland to take part in the event. But before it can take place, another journey has to be made, though not by all. The sacred Center changes annually—the place of the holy Tree through which the worlds of above and below are joined—and it must first be found by traditionally initiated shamans and priests. These are people who have sought through many disciplines to empty themselves of the profane and accumulate the sacred energy of the gods, in order to become intercessors for their fellow-beings. They have, as it is said, "the right to paint their hands red," and are instruments through which the power of the sacred world will be funneled into this, the temporal one.

On the appointed day, near the time of the summer solstice, four such priests, having passed through the purification rites of the sweat lodge, set out to find the holy place. Due consideration must be given to the physical setting: it must accommodate a circular camp of hundreds of people; fuel and water must be available, also an abundance of male sage, the purifying herb, and cottonwood trees must grow nearby. An expansive plain of level ground with a relatively unobstructed horizon is considered best. In modern times, pains must be taken to avoid sites where man-made structures are glaringly visible.

The priests carry with them a pointed cottonwood stake about three feet long, a portion of precious red cloth (antique Hudson's Bay trade cloth), sacred powdered paints, a pipe and tobacco, sweetgrass and sage for incense, a great length of cord, formerly of bison rawhide, now of deerhide, and eight tipi stakes of chokecherry wood, representing the fruitfulness of the earth.

When an appropriate place has been selected after considering four potential ones, the four priests walk toward what will be the central sacred place, singing warrior scouting songs or songs of the old warrior societies, particularly those that are designed to encourage bravery. They stop four times, the fourth time being at the exact place where the tree will eventually be placed. The four priests then sit down and face the west for a short period of silence.

They then proceed to talk and chat in a lighthearted way about such things as would be discussed by people who have not seen each other for a long time, inquiring how their family members are, and jokingly teasing each other about old and new lovers, invented sexual exploits, and all kinds of ribaldry and gluttony. This seems to be a reversal of what they have actually been doing in preparation for the event. It also appears to be an enactment of chaos and the profanity of an unbridled gross life as compared to the sacred life in which there is divine order, restraint, and harmony. This may refer, among other things, to the undifferentiated chaos which existed before the gods brought about the world as we know it and interjected into it the sacredness and harmony that we strive to attain.

When this phase is finished, the actual ritual of making the place begins. The pipe is ritually filled to the singing of the pipe-filling song:

> Friend do it this way
> Friend do it this
> Friend do it this way and all that you ask for will be given
> you
> From this center where you stand
> with this sacred pipe
> make an offering
> send a voice from within
> to your grandfather
> and all that you ask for will be given you
> Friend do it this way
> and all that you ask for will be given you.

As it is filled, each pinch of tobacco is first held over smoking and burning sage and then a smoking braid of sweetgrass, thus sanctifying it. Burning sage expels any evil influence, burning sweetgrass infuses with positive power. Each pinch is offered to each of the directions, beginning with the west, imploring the force present there to be present in the pipe bowl, the center of the world. Tobacco is also offered to that which is above and below.

The relationship of the human body and spirit to the gods or their manifestations is seen in the comparison of the body to the sacred pipe: both consist of the same material substances, and both have a central axis, with an upper and lower part. The pipe is also identified with the Sun Dance tree—the axis of the universe. The top of the Tree is at once itself, the sun, and the masculine principle; its middle, the crotch to which will be tied the offering bundle containing the tools of human culture, and the ropes of sacrifice from which will flow the renewing creative energy of the god-tree-sun; its base, embedded in the earth, the female principle and foundation. During the ritual centering of the Tree, in southern Sioux tradition, a pipe is actually embedded inside the excavation—an idea similar to that of the sacrificial body of man through interment becoming one with all that is.

When the pipe is filled, it and its offerings are once again offered to each of the directions. Following this, the formal prayer is made by one of the priests. The prayer is not only a request to the Lakota cosmos to become present here in this place, but also a recital of why this is being done. The part of the Lakota mythology dealing with the beginning of the world and how it was created is retold, and how the four directions came to be; how mankind dwelt in the mythological underworld and how man and the bison, bear, and other animals were once one and the same. The story of the coming of the sacred pipe is told, and how through it and its teachings man may once again realize the other world so that he may truly live in this one. It is then requested of the gods to sanctify mankind and this ground, for this place will be made a sacred place where man will join himself with them and they may dwell together again for a little while. Together, gods and mankind will create the true world as it is, so that man may enter the sacred reality of the presence of the gods.

Upon completion of the narrative, a knife is purified over the smoke of the sage and sweetgrass. Beginning at the west side of the place before which the men are now seated in a circle, an incision is made and a small portion of sod is lifted and placed to the west. The song of making the sacred place is sung:

> Four times to the earth I sent a voice [prayer]
> A place I will prepare
> Oh . . . people [tribe] behold!

This same song will be sung during the making of the sacred altar of the Sun Dance proper, which is called the *Unma Wiconi*, the other world.

At each of the directions, sod is lifted up after feigning three times and completing the act on the fourth. Finally two pieces are lifted from the center. The cutter of the sod has previously painted his hands red and purified them over the smoke of the sage and sweetgrass. All the while the cutting is being done, one of the priests has been standing on the eastern side of the group, holding the pipe and praying audibly, as each sod is lifted, to each of the directions, imploring them to be present now in this place. Finally the remaining sod is lifted and placed to the west, forming a small mound. Now a circle is revealed, about sixteen to eighteen inches in diameter, a little larger than the base of the tree which will be placed there. A circle of soft mellowed earth, which is further softened and cleared of any remaining roots and plant particles, will become the center of the world.

The cleared circle is smoothed and brushed with an eagle feather drawn from the back of the head of one of the priests. The priests then stop for a short rest period. They smoke not the ceremonial pipe but common small everyday smoking pipes or modern cigarettes.

The initial lifted sods placed at each of the directions would form a square if connected by lines; however, they are not.

Instead, the sod is removed to form a circular mellowed earth shape. The mellowed earth altar of the Sun Dance proper, however, is in the shape of a square or rectangle with a circle divided into four quarters by a cross. Actually a linear groove is made moving from the center and around the outside edge, into the center and back again to the edge at each of the directions, continuing around to the west and returning to the center. The maker thinks about and re-enacts in his mind that part of the mythology that traces the journey of the four sons of Tate, the wind, as they went about the edge of the world establishing the four directions and returning to their father's tipi at the center of the world; for their father, Tate, is a companion to the one above and one who can commune with the one above, having lived there originally but having come to the world that the world might be made more complete.

Tobacco is next placed in the grooves, thereby placing all living things on the earth. Finally precious red paint is placed in the grooves on top of the tobacco, imbuing the earth with the hue of life, blood of the gods and man which speaks of sacrifice, tradition, and order, the red way; a good red day in the world.

A priest then touches the pipe to the prepared stake and declares that these two are really one and the same and that this time is really the same time which will occur in the near future when the tree will be placed here. The long cord is attached to the top of the stake along with the red cloth offering. The end of the pipe bowl is touched to the center of the mandala and then the pointed end of the stake is placed at its center and driven in firmly with a stone or stone hammer.

One of the priests then unrolls the cord as he walks to the west, stopping four times as he approaches a distance determined by his judgment of how large he thinks the diameter of the actual future lodge should be—in modern times, from eighty to one hundred feet. He re-enacts in his mind how the great Inyan, the original rock of the universe, the Tunkasila, opened himself to release his blood which flowed and spread around him in a great disc to form Maka, the earth.

Lodgemaker also reflects on the mythical journey of the sons of Tate. As he approaches what will become the western edge and one of the entrances of the sacred lodge, he stops and drives two tent stakes into the ground, thereby creating the two sides of what will be one of four doorways to the sacred area. He makes a preliminary hole before driving in the stake on each side, into which he puts a pinch of tobacco first. He creates spaces — doorways — rather than walls, signifying that space, that which is invisible, is really something — much like the "somethingness" of the sacred reality which is most often invisible. Lodgemaker then proceeds clockwise around the perimeter of what will be the lodge, using the cord as a means to establish the other three directions equidistant from the center.

To be in concert with the world as it will be at or near the time of the summer solstice, the directions are not established as true according to the compass but rather in line with where the sun will rise and how the world really is at a specific time. Thus, as the sun rises on that day, it will travel a sacred road into the east entrance of the dwelling fashioned for it. Directly opposite this entrance and on the rear or west side of the sacred lodge is the fire without end, the power of the sun itself, where the stones for the purification lodge will be heated. The distance of the fire from the west entrance of the sacred lodge is approximately the same as the diameter of the lodge. An actual break in the wall of the sacred lodge will be provided on the west side so that the sunrise, the tree, the mellowed earth altar, and the fire will all be directly aligned, each a manifestation of the Wakan, all linked in their common energy.

This preliminary ritual having been completed, the four priests gather their materials including the long cord, but leave the center and other stakes, and walk backward toward the east entrance, stopping four times and going out through the invisible gate. Before they leave, however, they sit at the east entrance and smoke the ceremonial pipe, offering prayers for good weather and that the newly consecrated place will remain unblemished by negative influences and free from those who might abuse it. Finally before leaving, a smoking piece of sweetgrass is walked around the outside perimeter of the sacred circle, incensing it and giving it an invisible sacred protection.

Upon their arrival at their homes, the four men enter the purification lodge and cleanse themselves of the residue from having been to the sacred world, a re-created sanctuary. They are then ready to return to the mundane tasks of the profane world, and to continue preparations for the days to come when, at the designated time, the people will arrive in great numbers to celebrate having arrived at their sacred center, still located in their ancestral land.

Lakota mythology tells us of the failure of men to remain responsive to the gods in some primordial time, when they lived in permanent dwellings and harvested fruit from gardens, but fell from grace despite the luxury provided by such a life. After several hundred years of a nomadic hunting life, and a hundred years of sedentary coexistence with foreigners, the Lakota sacred traditions have remained uninstitutionalized as "organized religion." Today, they formally and consciously reject permanent sacred architecture as suitable or as having any lasting significance. The transparency of the world of matter and the transmutability, birth-lifetime-death, of all things including the earth itself, precludes the thought that material permanence has very much to do with sacred space. Rather, by not being in a

structure, one is in the sacred temple—*templus*—which is the
world itself, with the actual dirt of the earth as the floor and the
vast blue dome of the actual sky as the ceiling. Any material
representation could potentially be a profanation of that which
already exists in a sacred manner and is readily available around
one. Thus, once a year at the height of the life cycle of the earth
and sun, the temple is complete. The re-creation of the world at
this time appears visible in the temporary Sun Dance lodge,
which can never be used again, and serves only as a *temporary
device* to assist men to realize that there is a sacred world whose
center is everywhere, including inside himself; and that our
whole life is the journey towards it.

Sweet Medicine's Prophecy

Cheyenne

One man who sat in the circle in the lodge spoke to Sweet Medicine, who for a long time had been sitting in silence with his head hanging down, as if discouraged. He said: "Friend, what is your trouble? Why are you sorrowful?" Sweet Medicine answered: "Yes, it is true I am troubled. Listen to me carefully. Listen to me carefully." He said this four times. "Our great-grandfather spoke thus to me, repeating it four times. He said to me that he had put people on this earth, all kinds of people. He made us, but also he made others. There are all kinds of people on earth that you will meet some day, toward the sunrise, by a big river. Some are black, but some day you will meet a people who are white—good-looking people, with light hair and white skins." A man spoke up, and said, "Shall we know them when we meet them?"

"Yes," said Sweet Medicine, "you will know them, for they will have long hair on their faces, and will look differently from you. They will wear things different from your things—different clothing. It will be something like the green scum that grows on waters about springs. Those people will wander this way. You will talk with them. They will give you things like isinglass [*i.e.*, things that flash or reflect the light, mirrors] and something that looks like sand that will taste very sweet. But do not take the things they give you. They will be looking for a certain stone. They will wear what I have spoken of, but it will be of all colors, pretty. Perhaps they will not listen to what you say to them, but you will listen to what they say to you. They will be people who do not get tired, but who will keep pushing forward, going, going all the time. They will keep coming, coming. They will try always to give you things, but do not take them. At last I think that you will take the things that they offer you, and this will bring sickness to you. These people do not follow the way of our great-grandfather. They follow another way. They will travel everywhere, looking for this stone which our great-grandfather put on the earth in many places.

"Buffalo and all animals were given by our great-grandfather; but these people will come in, and will begin to kill off these animals. They will use a different thing to kill animals from what we use—something that makes a noise, and sends a little round stone to kill.

"Then after a while a different animal will come into the country. It will have a head like a buffalo, but it will have white horns and a long tail. These animals will smell differently from the buffalo, and at last you will come to eating them. When you skin them, the flesh will jerk, and at last you will get this same disease. At last something will be given to you, which, if you drink it, will make you crazy. These people will have something to give to animals to eat which will kill them.

"There will be many of these people, so many that you cannot stand before them. On the rivers you will see things going up and down, and in these things will be these people, and there will be things moving over dry land in which these people will be.

"Another animal will come, but it will not be like the buffalo. It will have long heavy hair on its neck, and a long heavy tail which drags on the ground. It will come from the south.

Arrowhead, 1988 JAUNE QUICK-TO-SEE SMITH

"When these animals come, you will catch them, and you will get on their backs and they will carry you from place to place. You will become great travelers. If you see a place a long way off, you will want to go to it, so at last you will get on those animals with my arrows. From that time you will act very foolishly. You will never be quiet. You will want to go everywhere. You will be very foolish. You will know nothing.

"These people will not listen to what you say; what they are going to do they will do. You people will change: in the end of your life in those days you will not get up early in the morning; you will never know when day comes; you will lie in bed; you will have disease, and will die suddenly; you will all die off.

"At last those people will ask you for your flesh [he repeated this four times], but you must say, 'No.' They will try to teach you their way of living. If you give up to them your flesh [your children], those that they take away will never know anything. They will try to change you from your way of living to theirs, and they will keep at what they try to do. They will work with their hands. They will tear up the earth, and at last you will do it with them. When you do, you will become crazy, and will forget all that I am now teaching you."

Out of Chaos

Vine Deloria, Jr.

*I*ndian exile, because of its impact on ceremonial responsibilities, includes a religious dimension which modern political exile lacks. If we understand ceremony and ritual, performed as a condition of living in certain places, as the critical element which distinguishes each Indian group, then the cultural life of the people, its continuance or destruction, is the important fact in considering whether an exile has occurred. So while the Sioux, Apache, Blackfeet, and Crow, for example, all live within their original lands, persistent efforts to change their culture and exclusion from sacred places has produced a profound sense of exile.

When we talk about exile today we are more likely to have a political situation in mind; but the original use of the word is considerably more enlightening. The roots of the idea of exile are most prominently displayed in a religious or mythic context. Moses and Oedipus immediately come to mind—as well as a host of other historical and mythological figures—all experiencing exile or suffering the sense of alienation which such a status entails. The religious aspect of exile, in contrast to its political meaning, involves many intangible factors which help us change and enhance our knowledge of the world.

The mythic and traditional idea of exile entails the expulsion of the chosen one from his comfortable and often exalted position in society. He is then thrust into a barren place where he has to abandon his former knowledge of this world. He learns humility and faith, comprehends the transcendent nature of ultimate reality, and is initiated into the mysteries and secrets of the other, higher world. Then the exile returns to his society armed with his superior knowledge, and creates fundamental and lasting reforms, so that society marks its distinctive identity from the time he received his exilic commission.

Considering all the modern racial and ethnic groups to whom the idea of exile might be applied, none appears more deserving or representative of this status than North American Indians. In the half-millennium since the discovery of the western hemisphere, almost all Indian tribes have been forcibly removed from their ancestral homelands and subjected to cultural and religious indignities comparable in many ways to the manner in which the old culture heroes were stripped of their beliefs and presuppositions. At least this view is the popular explanation of the condition of Indians in modern American society. But there is considerably more to the story.

We immediately remember the removal of Indians from the Ohio valley and deep South as the most prominent historical instance of Indian exile. The bitter picture of thousands of Cherokees, Creeks, and Choctaws, their heads bowed in sorrow, walking west in the driving rain of a cold winter is deeply etched on our consciousness. Federal policy to clear the country east of the Mississippi of Indians was carried out with almost scientific precision, even gathering small bands of Winnebagos in Wisconsin and moving them a few hundred miles to Nebraska. Removal was understood as a sensible solution to the Indian problem until the 1890s; plans were even suggested to gather all the tribes in western Oklahoma, ring the area with forts, and maintain a massive concentration camp until such time as the Indians had either acculturated or vanished.

When we look at a map of the United States, however, we find that there were tribes that escaped this fate. Beyond the Mississippi-Missouri border, tribes were generally settled on reservations within their aboriginal homelands; and if we note that many groups are still living within their original occupancy areas, we might argue that exile is not an appropriate description of the condition of western Indians. But we would be mistaking the possession of the title to lands for the right to live on them freely, and substituting our own political concepts for the rich feeling toward lands that has always characterized Indian society.

Within the western context we are always inclined to see land as a commodity and think first of its ownership; in contrast, the traditional Indian understanding of land focuses on its use, and the duties people assume when they come to occupy it. When an Indian thinks about traditional lands he always talks about what the people did there, the animals who lived there and how the people related to them, the seasons of the year and how people responded to their changes, the manner in which the tribe acquired possession of the area, and the ceremonial functions it was required to perform to remain worthy of living there.

The idea of lands, therefore, tells us the difference between Indian and non-Indian views so we can determine whether or not an exile has occurred. Whites acquire land through purchase and sale, and land is a quantifiable, measurable entity; their primary responsibility as landowners is simply to prevent a loss of value; hence any responsibility the landowner may have is only to himself. Indian tribes acquire land as a gift from higher powers, and in turn they assume certain ceremonial duties which must be performed as long as they live on and use the land. Removing an Indian tribe from its aboriginal territory, therefore, results in the destruction of ceremonial life and much of the cultural structure which has made ceremony and ritual significant. So the western tribes, although not completely removed from their lands in a geographical sense, experienced exile in much the same way as did their brothers from the east. Restrictions in the manner in which people use lands are as much a deprivation of land as actual loss of title.

A good example of this intangible, cultural/religious exile can be seen in the struggle of Taos Pueblo during this century to regain the Blue Lake area. Deprived of exclusive use of the lake, located near the Pueblo and central to its ceremonial life, when a national forest was established at the turn of the century, the Pueblo was given a "use permit" that only enabled it to visit the lake and conduct ceremonies but did not give it exclusive use. When the Pueblo filed its claims in the Indian Claims Commission, it carefully segregated the claim for the Blue Lake area and asked for restoration of the land to the Pueblo instead of a financial payment for its loss. After an intensive struggle in Congress the Pueblo finally succeeded in getting a bill passed in which the United States recognized in the Pueblo the title to the lake area.

It might appear to the casual observer that title was the primary concern of the Pueblo during this argument and that the Pueblo was only acting in the same manner as any other land owner faced with similar circumstances. Such was not the case. Rather, from the Pueblo point of view, its religious responsibilities to the lake and surrounding lands were paramount and could only be carried out in their totality by the complete exclusion of all other activities from the area.

Obligations demanded by the lands upon which people lived were part of their understanding of the world; indeed, their view of life was grounded in the knowledge of these responsibilities. Tribal ritual life was intimately related to the seasons of the year. Other species shared the land and also responded to the annual rhythms of nature. Thus the people perceived that a social contract existed between men and the other animals. The human ceremonial life confirmed the existence of this equality and gave it sustenance. One could, perhaps, list the tribes according to the complexity of their ceremonial year and project their approximate longevity. We need not distinguish sedentary agricultural tribes from migratory hunting and fishing tribes. Indians had an intimate and precise knowledge of the habits and personality of both plant and animal life and therefore successful relationships with fish and game were no less indicative of the responsibility to land than were successful agricultural activities.

Migratory tribes suffered a considerably greater exile than did agricultural tribes when the Indians were restricted to the reservations. Some of the most important ceremonies needed to be conducted at certain sacred places at specific times of the year. While tribes could hold ceremonies at the proper time, they could not always hold these rituals at the proper place. Sometimes the sacred materials essential to the ceremony could only be obtained at these sacred places and so different materials had to be substituted. These conditions changed ceremonial life considerably, introducing a process of erosion which has since eaten away the substance of rituals and responsibilities. One might even say that the ceremonial year of the migratory tribes was highly dependent upon sacred places whereas the sacred calendar of sedentary tribes had long since become dominant over special places for enactment. On this basis, perhaps, we can determine both the longevity of a tribe and the degree of trauma which confinement produced.

Not only did their geographic confinement work to destroy

the sacred calendars of tribes, but the effort to perpetuate a traditional life within the confines of the reservation was vulnerable to overtures by the federal government, seeking to make the people abandon old ways and adopt new practices which were carefully orchestrated by a new sense of time—a measured time which had little to do with cosmic realities. It is debatable which factor was most important in the destruction of tribal ceremonial life: the prohibition of performance of traditional rituals by the government, or the introduction of the white man's system of keeping time. The answer to this question can be found in an analysis of the impact of each factor on individual tribes.

Many of the old people among the Sioux felt that the government prohibition of the ceremony of the "keeping of the soul," an important condolence ceremony which linked generations of the tribe together in a more comprehensive cosmic reality, brought about the real destruction of ceremonial life in that tribe. On the other hand, in the Pacific Northwest the government tried to impose an agricultural system, and the farming calendar conflicted directly with fishing activities, producing the same erosion of ceremonial life. Prohibition of the potlatch was not nearly as important as the government's insistence that the Indians become farmers and the orientation of all programs to achieve that end.

Certainly the combination of these factors must be present in the immediate past of every tribe. We can safely suggest that the new sense of time introduced into Indian life produced a sense of alienation which made Indians strangers in a land that was becoming increasingly strange—as whites changed it to suit themselves—and that the old ceremonies might have provided an emotional bulwark against this alienation, but their prohibition only increased the feeling of exile among the people of the tribe.

Unless time is understood as sacred, experienced in all its fullness, and so dominant a consideration in the life of a people that all other functions are subservient to it, it is impossible to have a complete and meaningful ceremonial life. Rituals lose their efficacy because they are performed within a secular time which does not always make room for them or give them the status they deserve. They soon take on the aspect of mechanical adjustments made to solve problems which occur within that kind of time. Forced adaptation to secular, mathematically measured time has produced a fundamental sense of alienation.

Although the loss of land must be seen as a political and economic disaster of the first magnitude, the real exile of the tribes occurred with the destruction of ceremonial life and the failure or inability of white society to offer a sensible and cohesive alternative to the traditions which Indians remembered. People became disoriented with respect to the world in which they lived. They could not practice their old ways, and the new ways which they were expected to learn were in a constant state of change because they were not a cohesive view of the world but simply adjustments which whites were making to the technology they had invented.

Had whites been able to maintain a sense of stability in their own society, which Indians had been admonished to imitate, the tribes might have been able to observe the integrity of the new way of life and make a successful transition to it. But the only alternative that white society had to offer was a chaotic and extreme individualism, prevented from irrational excesses only by occasional government intervention. The experiences of Indians since the 1880s have been uniform in the sense that they have been confined within the boundaries of white individualism and whenever and wherever they have attempted to recapture the old sense of community, technology and domestic American politics have combined to beat back their efforts.

There is no question that American Indians have been mired in a century-long exile. Almost anything that has happened to Indians in the decades since the establishment of the reservations can and must be seen in this light. Individual incidents are but minor episodes indicating the extent of the pattern that has encompassed tribal life. We find little of the ebb and flow of sentiment and understanding which keeps a community healthy and growing, only apparent movement back and forth between the poles of political independence and dependence. In Indian cultural and religious life we have seen a unilateral shedding of old forms coupled with a paralyzing inability to create new customs and traditions which have a relationship with the past. While Indians have copied many ways of white society, on the whole they have done so badly and sporadically. Tribal governments, for example, do not behave like the old tribal councils, nor, unfortunately, do they perform like modern municipal governments. Their activities suggest some strange hybrid institution which has no knowledge of its constituents or responsibilities.

What, if anything, can Indians do to escape or overcome this condition? Originally, as we have seen, exile had a specific religious direction which suggested that exilic alienation was necessary to prepare an individual for a significant mission. The Old Testament, if we can accept some of its prophetic ideas, saw the exile of the Jews as the means of preparing them to move forward from a parochial, tribal religion and become advocates of a more universal interpretation of the meaning of human social life. Their exile did not produce a new religious understanding so much as it enabled the people to see themselves as representatives of a tradition which had within itself the potential to become an exemplary society, at peace with its neighbors and its environment. We may not be able to apply this model completely to the situation in which American Indians find themselves; but it is certainly important to our discussion of exile to try to do so.

We might, therefore, expect American Indians to discern, out of the chaos of their shattered lives, the same kind of message and mission that inspired the Hebrew prophets. Indians would, in this situation, begin to develop a new interpretation of their religious tradition with a universal application. They would further begin to seek out areas in which they could communicate with sympathetic people in the larger society, and put their own house in order. A process of intense commitment to certain social goals might then emerge in which the traditional values of pre-contact days would be seen as religious principles having a universal application. Most important, Indians would begin to probe deeper into their own past and view their remembered history as a primordial covenant.

It would be important and significant if we could report, in the activities of Indians today, the emergence of such behavior and beliefs. Unfortunately the nature of modern society precludes, or at least substantially inhibits, the development of new religious realities and statements. The vast majority of people, including Indians, believes that the world is primarily a physical thing, and the existence or importance of spiritual realities is given but token acknowledgement. Indians are the popular American minority group and the white majority deeply believes that Indians *already* have the secret mysteries which will produce a wise and happy life. Therefore Indians are plagued with a multitude of wellwishers and spectators hoping to discern, from within the Indian communities in which they visit, some indication of the substance of religious experience. This inundation of pilgrims makes it impossible for Indians to experience the solitude and abandonment which exile requires in order to teach its lessons.

Finally, modern American life is comparable to a large and bountiful Christmas tree. It promises only joy and fun, and never suggests a period of doubt when ultimate realities are experienced and understood. Indians are wandering in this plush fantasy desert in the same way as sensitive non-Indians. It will require considerably more thought and significantly less recreation and entertainment before Indians will be able to discern in their own traditions the substance and energy which lies dormant.

The exile of today is filled with frustration because it is being experienced in the midst of many other intensely competitive factors, all of which require energy and attention and none of which provide any lasting sustenance. It may be that technology has so insulated human society that the religious context of exile is now a thing of the past, incapable of realization in a wholly artificial world. If so, we have lost an important key to unlocking the potential which human social existence suggests. It may be that American Indians contain the last best hope for spiritual renewal in a world dominated by material considerations. The multitude of non-Indians arriving at reservation doors seeking answers would seem to indicate an intuition in many hearts that Indians do give us the last hope for resurrection. Perhaps out of the confusion of modern Indian society will come a statement about the world that we have come to expect when exiles return.

Untitled, 1984 JAUNE QUICK-TO-SEE SMITH

Our Mother Earth

Oren Lyons

A thousand years ago a man came from the west. And he came across the water, and he brought a great message of peace. He came across the water, the great lake that you now call Ontario; he stopped on the shores, and he visited the various nations who were at war and who had forgotten how to live together. He came with a great message of peace; and he gathered the strongest and the fiercest of leaders in the Great Council. And it took many years; but with the help of Hiawentah, whom you call Hiawatha, together they created the Houdenosaunee, the great league of peace—one thousand years ago. And the principles were set down, at that time, of how to conduct ourselves, of how to raise the chiefs, how to raise the clan mothers; and how to set men in council, so that they could first perform the ceremonies as the spiritual being, the center, of the nation. The ceremonies were the first obligation of the chiefs, and the faith keepers, and the clan mothers. And then they were to sit in council for the welfare of the people.

A thousand years ago we were given this message by the Creator; we were given a government by the Creator. This government was not manufactured from the minds of men, it was *given* to us; and we were to cherish it. And each generation was to raise its chiefs and to look out for the welfare of the seventh generation to come. We were to understand the principles of living together; we were to protect the life that surrounds us; and we were to give what we had to the elders and to the children. The men were to provide; and the women were to care for the family, and be the center, the heart, of the home. And so our nation was built on the spiritual family, and we were given clans: the turtle — the eagle — the deer — the beaver — the wolf — the bear — the snipe — the hawk: symbols of freedom. We were given an understanding of how free people live. And we were told to protect the freedom of every individual; we were told that sovereignty began with the individual, and you protect that. And so a free nation stood, and a great peace prevailed.

Many years later there landed, on our shores to the east, our white brother. And he brought with him things that we could not contend with. We were told at an earlier time that the name Ga-nya-di-yo, whom you call Handsome Lake, would be important; and so it came to pass that in the year 1800 we were given a third and final message of how to deal with the things that were brought across the water — when our men were drunk; when our home fires were out; when the dogs walked in the ashes; and the children and the women hid in the woods because of what the whisky and the liquor did to our men. And we were given a message at that time; and this message told us about Ga-nya-di-yo; and again the Creator took pity on us, He felt sorry for us, and He gave the third message of how to deal with the whisky and with gambling, how to deal with the Bible and the missionaries. We were told at that time what would happen to this earth. And as Ga-nya-di-yo walked with the Four beings, the Four Protectors, who had been sent by the Creator to look out for mankind, they pointed out to him, here and there, "What do you see?" "I see a woman, so fat that she can't rise, yet she continues to stuff her mouth, she continues to eat like a glutton." And they never said whether that was right or wrong; they asked him, what did he see? And so they went, and he was given this opportunity to see, and to be told that one day the water would not be fit to drink, that indeed the water would burn, that the trees would begin to die from the tops down; that the chief of all trees, the maple, would signal to us the time of the deterioration of life, when the end would be near. He told us, and pointed out the variety of events that would occur: the sickness of our children and of the elders, and of what money would do — the greatest sickness of all.

Now we are faced with these things, as leaders of our people, as people given a great responsibility; we in this generation must deal with all of these elements.

When the Creator gave His Great Law and planted the great tree of peace, He uprooted it, and He threw under it all the weapons of war. He said: You are now a nation of peace; and I will give you *oyankgwa-oohway,* the sacred tobacco; and that will be your strength. That will be what you depend on, the spiritual power of prayer, a belief: the belief of your people. And if you have one mind, and you consider this again, it is the power that you have. So it happens when you burn the tobacco and use the sacred cornmeal that all of the animals stop and they listen; they turn, and they listen to these words.

Our brothers, the bears and the wolves and the eagles, are Indians. They are Natives, as we are. At one time we spoke their language; at one time we conversed, a long time ago. The two-leggeds have fallen from grace. Those animals and those wingeds, they live in a state of absolute grace; they can do no wrong. It is only we who have been given a choice, so clearly pointed out by the Four Beings: this is the way it is, they said, and what do you see here? They did not tell him: Do this or do that; they said, This is the way it is: what you do will be up to you. And that is what the Creator gave to us, the choice: a great gift, the mentality that we have. And among us there are even people with other gifts—a gift of art, or a gift of speech, or a gift of a smile that can make everyone laugh. Whatever it is, each of us was born with a mission. We were born with a mission, and we must know what it is and develop it and *do* it. And that's a choice—that is *your* choice.

We went to Geneva—the Six Nations, and the great Lakota nation—as representatives of the indigenous people of the Western Hemisphere. We went to Geneva, and we spoke in the forum of the United Nations. For a short time we stood equal among the people and the nations of the world. And what was the message that we gave? There is a hue and cry for human rights—human rights, they said, for all people. And the indigenous people said: What of the rights of the natural world? Where is the seat for the buffalo or the eagle? Who is representing them here in this forum? Who is speaking for the waters of the earth? Who is speaking for the trees and the forests? Who is speaking for the fish—for the whales— for the beavers—for our children? *We* said: Given this opportunity to speak in this international forum, then it is our duty to say that we must stand for these people, and the natural world and its rights; and also for the generations to come. We would not fulfill our duty if we did not say that. It becomes important because without the water, without the trees, there is no life.

New York City—you live here; you can't get a clean drink of water here. The water you drink is filthy. You don't know what clear spring water is like, because you have to drink what comes out of the tap. And eventually it will kill you. Eventually, you will not be able to clean that water; nor your children, nor your grandfather, nor your grandmother . . . . You think about it . . . . When you are sick and when your children are sick, you remember what the Indian said to you about water.

We are indigenous people to this land. We are like a conscience. We are small, but we are not a minority. We are the landholders, we are the landkeepers; we are not a minority. For our brothers are all the natural world, and by that we are by far the majority. We want you to understand the opportunity now. It is no time to be afraid—there is no time for fear. It is only time to be strong, only a time to think of the future, and to challenge the destruction of your grandchildren, and to move away from the four-year cycle of living that this country goes through, from one election to another, and think about the coming generations.

We spoke about human rights and we spoke in defense of all people and of all children. But remember that as long as we are burning tobacco, as long as the Indian nations exist, so will you. But when we are gone, you too will go.

Dahnato. *

* *Now I am finished.*

Notes

All the articles and stories presented in this volume were originally published in PARABOLA Magazine except where otherwise noted. PARABOLA publication information is given in the form: Volume:issue (date).

BECOMING PART OF IT

VII:3 (Summer, 1982)

Originally given as an address at the American Museum of Natural History in January, 1982, as part of a program entitled "I Become Part of It," presented by the Society for the Study of Myth and Tradition.

THE TREES STOOD DEEP ROOTED

II:2 (Spring, 1977)

1 Ruth Underhill, *Singing for Power: The Song Magic of the Papago Indians of Southern Arizona* (Berkeley and Los Angeles: University of California Press, 1968).

2 N. Scott Momaday, "Man Made of Words," in *Indian Voices: The First Convocation of American Indian Scholars* (San Francisco: The Indian Historian Press, 1970), pp. 49-62.

3 Leland C. Wyman, *Blessingway* (Tucson: The University of Arizona Press, 1970).

4 Washington Matthews, "Night Chant, A Navajo Ceremony," in *American Museum of Natural History Memoirs*, Vol. 6 (New York: 1902).

5 Saul Bellow, *Mr. Sammler's Planet* (New York: The Viking Press, 1969).

THE ROOTS OF PEACE

V:3 (Summer, 1980)

From *The Great Law of Peace of the Iroquois Nation.*

DOING YOUR THINKING

IV:4 (Fall, 1979)

1 Harry K. Roberts, "Lonesome Trail," *The Windbell*, Vol. 16, No. 1, 1979, p. 34.
2 Raymond White, "Religion and Its Role Among the Luiseño," in *Native Californians: A Theoretical Retrospective*, eds. Lowell Bean and Thomas C. Blackburn (Socorro, N.M.: Ballena Press, 1976), p. 356.

GLUSKABE AND THE FOUR WISHES

X:4 (Fall, 1985)

THE DEMANDS OF HARMONY

II:4 (Fall, 1977)

THE COMING OF THE LIGHT

VIII:4 (Fall, 1983)

Reprinted from Jack Frederick Kilpatrick and Anna Gritts Kilpatrick, "Eastern Cherokee Folktales," in *Bureau of American Ethnology, Anthropological Papers 75-80, Bulletin 196* (Washington, D.C.: Government Printing Office, 1966).

"IT'S WHERE YOU PUT YOUR EYES"

IV:4 (Fall, 1979)

1 Washington Matthews, "Mythic Dry-Paintings of the Navajos," in *American Naturalist*, Vol. XIX (1885), pp. 931-939.

2 For a fuller analysis of a single sand painting see my "Whirling Logs and Colored Sands," in *Native American Religious Action* (Columbia: University of South Carolina Press, 1987), pp. 47-57.

3 Ted Brasser, "North American Indian Art for TM," in *The Religious Character of Native American Humanities* (Published privately by the Department of Religious Studies, Arizona State University, 1977), pp. 126-143.

4 Don Talayesva, *Sun Chief: An Autobiography of a Hopi Indian* (New Haven: Yale University Press, 1942), p. 184.

5 Emory Sekaquaptewa, "Hopi Ceremonies," in *Seeing with a Native Eye*, ed. Walter Holden Capps (New York: Harper & Row, 1976), p. 39.

6 LeRoi Jones, "Hunting is Not Those Heads on the Wall," in *Home: Social Essays* (New York: William Morrow, 1972), pp. 173-178.

7 Robert Thompson in *African Art in Motion* (Berkeley and Los Angeles: University of California Press, 1974). Others have shown how true this is for African art.

8 Edmund Carpenter, *Eskimo Realities* (New York: Holt, Rinehart and Winston, 1973), p. 202. Another sensitive book introduced by Carpenter is: Bill Holm and Bill Reid, *Indian Art of the Northwest Coast: A Dialogue on Craftsmanship and Aesthetics* (Seattle: University of Washington Press, 1975).

9 The phrase "It's where you put your eyes" is taken from a Sesame Street song.

WHY ANT HAS A SMALL WAIST

VI:1 (Winter, 1981)

DANCING WITH DASH-KAYAH

VI:3 (Winter, 1981)

1 Joseph Campbell, *The Masks of God: Primitive Mythology* (New York: Viking Press, 1970), p. 25.

2 Joseph Epes Brown, "The Roots of Renewal," in *Seeing with a Native Eye*, ed. Walter Holden Capps (New York: Harper & Row, 1976).

3 Dennis and Barbara Tedlock, eds., *Teachings from the American Earth: Indian Religion and Philosophy* (New York: Liveright, 1975).

HOW GLUSKABE STOLE TOBACCO

IX:2 (Spring, 1984)

DISENCHANTMENT

I:3 (Summer, 1976)

1 Victor Turner, *Chihamba The White Spirit: A Ritual Drama of the Ndembu*, Rhodes-Livingstone Paper No. 32 (New York: Humanities Press, 1962).
2 Dorothy Eggan, "The General Problem of Hopi Adjustment," in *American Anthropologist* 45 (1943), p. 372.
3 R.H. Matthews, "The Burbung of the Wiradthuri Tribes," in *The Journal of the Anthropological Institute of Great Britain and Ireland*, XXV (1896), pp. 295-317 and A.W. Howitt, *The Native Tribes of South-East Australia* (London: Macmillan, 1904), pp. 516-563.

THE ELK SKULL

I:4 (Fall, 1976)

BOUNDARIES OF BELIEF

IV:1 (Winter, 1979)

1 Ruth Benedict, *Zuñi Mythology*, 2 vols. Columbia University Contributions to Anthropology Vol. XXI (New York: Columbia University Press, 1935), Vol. 1, pp. 43-49.
2 Dennis Tedlock, *Finding the Center: Narrative Poetry of the Zuñi Indians* (Lincoln: University of Nebraska Press, 1978), pp. 87-132.
3 John G. Bourke, *The Urine Dance of the Zuñi Indians of New Mexico* (Privately printed, 1881), pp. 5-6.
4 Matilda Coxe Stevenson, *The Zuñi Indians: Their Mythology, Esoteric Societies, and Ceremonies*, Twenty-third Annual Report of the Bureau

of American Ethnology (Washington, D.C.: Government Printing Office, 1904), p. 437.

5 Frank Hamilton Cushing, *Zuñi Breadstuff.* Indian Notes and Monographs Vol. VIII (New York: Heye Foundation, 1920), pp. 621-622.
6 Stevenson, *op. cit.*, p. 437.
7 Bourke, *op. cit.*, pp. 3-4.

BLUE JAY

II:4 (Fall, 1977)

Reprinted by permission of the Colville Confederated Tribes.

ONE MORE SMILE FOR A HOPI CLOWN

IV:1 (Winter, 1979)

HOW SALMON GOT GREASY EYES

IV:1 (Winter, 1979)

Recorded for PARABOLA Magazine by Jim Metzner. This story is part of a long cycle of stories about the creation of people which is traditionally told at night during the winter months.

OUR OTHER SELVES

VII:2 (Spring, 1982)

1 John G. Neihardt, *Black Elk Speaks* (New York: Simon & Schuster, 1972), pp. 15-16.
2 Britannica World Language edition of Funk & Wagnall's Standard Dictionary.

THE BLACKFOOT GENESIS

VIII:2 (Spring, 1983)

Adapted from George Bird Grinnell, *Blackfoot Lodge Tales: The Story of a*

Prairie People (Lincoln: University of Nebraska Press, 1962).

THE BISON AND THE MOTH

VIII:2 (Spring, 1983)

THE FOX AND THE BUFFALO

VI:4 (Fall, 1981)

Adapted from Gene Weltfish, *Caddoan Texts, Pawnee South Band Dialect* (New York: Publication of The American Ethnological Society, Vol. XVII, 1937). Adaptation © 1981 Brian Swann, Green Tiger Press.

THE SPIRITUAL LANDSCAPE

II:3 (Summer, 1977)

1 See James R. Walker, *Lakota Myth* (Lincoln: University of Nebraska Press, 1983), pp. 193-245.
2 See *Lakota Myth*, pp. 16-24.
3 Joseph Epes Brown, *The Sacred Pipe* (Norman: University of Oklahoma Press, 1953), p. 23.
4 John G. Neihardt, *Black Elk Speaks* (Lincoln: University of Nebraska Press, 1961), pp. 203-204.

WHITE BUFFALO WOMAN

VII:3 (Summer, 1982)

From John G. Neihardt, *Black Elk Speaks* (Lincoln: University of Nebraska Press, 1961).

EAGLES FLY OVER

I:3 (Summer, 1976)

THE RETURN

I:3 (Summer, 1976)

Retold from Washington Matthews, *Navaho Legends*, published as Vol. V of the *Memoirs of the American Folk-Lore Society* (New York: Houghton, Mifflin & Co., 1897).

SUN DANCE

III:2 (Spring, 1978)

THE ROAD TO THE CENTER

IX:3 (Summer, 1984)

From a work in progress documenting the entire process of the Sun Dance.

SWEET MEDICINE'S PROPHECY

VII:2 (Spring, 1982)

From George Bird Grinnell, *The Cheyenne Indians: Their History and Ways of Life* (Lincoln: University of Nebraska Press, 1972).

OUT OF CHAOS

X:2 (Spring, 1985)

OUR MOTHER EARTH

VI:1 (Winter, 1981)

Delivered as a talk at the Cathedral of St. John the Divine, New York City, May 24, 1978.

Notes on Illustrations

Cover

Jaune Quick-to-See Smith:

Charlo 84-4, 1984, pastel on paper, 30" x 22." Collection of Dr. and Mrs. Joseph N. Cunningham. Photograph by Karen Bell.

Frontispiece

Kevin Red Star:

Bird's Head Shield, 1981, acrylic and mixed media on canvas, 32" x 42." Artifact no. 25-591. Gift of Mr. and Mrs. L.D. Horodewski. Photograph by Julia V. Smith, courtesy of the Museum of the American Indian, Heye Foundation, New York.

Page 17

Jaune Quick-to-See Smith:

Untitled, 1984, pastel on paper, 30" x 22." Courtesy of the Bernice Steinbaum Gallery (New York, New York).

Page 42

Rick Bartow:

Coyote Running, 1985, graphite and conte crayon, 19 ½" x 15." Courtesy of John Slocom. Photograph by David Cohen.

Page 58

Betty Bia:

Mother Earth and Father Sky, 1968, handspun native wool, 17" x 18 ½."
(Catalog w-68.40.16). Photograph courtesy of the United States Department of the Interior, Indian Arts and Crafts Board.

Page 86

Edna Jackson:

Spirit Mask, 1988, cast cedar paper, cedar paper, devil's club paper, linen roving, silk thread, seal gut and acrylic on canvas, 28" x 24." Photograph courtesy of the United States Department of the Interior, Indian Arts and Crafts Board, Southern Plains Indian Museum and Crafts Center.

Page 95

Rick Bartow:

Owl and Man Talking, 1987, monoprint, 30" x 20." Courtesy of Jamison/Thomas Gallery (Portland, Oregon). Photograph by David Cohen.

Page 114

Rick Bartow:

Coyote's Journey, 1988, pastel and graphite on paper, 40" x 26." Courtesy of Jamison/Thomas Gallery (Portland, Oregon). Photograph by David Cohen.

Page 130

David Paladin:

Blue Winter Kachinas, 1978, acrylic on canvas, 24" x 36." Reprinted with permission of Lynda Paladin. Photograph courtesy of the University of Arizona Museum of Art (Tucson, Arizona).

Page 153

Dan Namingha:

Longhair Kachina, 1987, acrylic on canvas, 64" x 48." Photograph courtesy of the artist.

Page 168

Jaune Quick-to-See Smith:

Untitled, 1984, pastel on paper, 30" x 22." Courtesy of the Bernice Steinbaum Gallery (New York, New York).

Page 183

Frank LaPena:

Deer Rattle—Deer Dancer, 1981, acrylic, 34" x 48." Photograph courtesy of the artist.

Page 223

Carl Beam:

Untitled, 1982, oil on canvas, 29 ¼" x 39." Artifact no. 25-2521. Gift of Mr. and Mrs. L.D. Horodewski. Photograph by Julia V. Smith, courtesy of the Museum of the American Indian, Heye Foundation, New York.

Page 240

Tom Two Arrows:

New Year Ceremony, 1969, casein on illustration board, 33 ⅛" x 27 ⅜." (Catalog w-69.50). Photograph courtesy of the United States Department of the Interior, Indian Arts and Crafts Board.

Page 257

Jaune Quick-to-See Smith:

Arrowhead, 1988, pastel and acrylic on paper, 30" x 40." Courtesy of the Bernice Steinbaum Gallery (New York, New York). Photograph by Karen Bell.

Page 269

Jaune Quick-to-See Smith:

Untitled, 1984, pastel on paper, 30" x 22." Courtesy of the Bernice Steinbaum Gallery (New York, New York).

Special thanks to Lloyd Oxendine, curator, the American Indian Community House (New York, New York).

Profiles of Authors

Arthur Amiotte, Oglala Teton Sioux, has studied the Lakota traditions with the elders of his people. He mastered and has practiced many of the sacred rites, as well as traditional crafts with fabrics, beads, and quill work, which he has incorporated into his work as a contemporary artist. His work has been widely exhibited and he has taught and lectured in many places.

Joseph Epes Brown was a friend and pupil of Black Elk and recorder of his account of the Seven Rites of the Oglala Sioux (*The Sacred Pipe*, University of Oklahoma, 1953). An influential authority on the Plains Indians, he teaches religious studies at the University of Montana. His books include *The Spiritual Legacy of the American Indian* (Crossroad, 1964).

Joseph Bruchac's ancestry is part Abenaki, part Slovak. He is the editor of *The Greenfield Review*, and publishes and distributes books through the Greenfield Review Press. He is a storyteller and writer; his many works include *The Good Message of Handsome Lake*, (Unicorn Press, 1979), *Near the Mountains*, (White Pine Press, 1987), several volumes of Iroquois and Abenaki stories, and the introduction to and editing of an anthology of American Indian poetry called *Songs from the Earth on Turtle's Back* (Greenfield Review Press, 1983). His most recent work is *Survival This Way: Interviews with American Indian Poets* (University of Arizona Press, 1987).

Thomas Buckley has done research in native northwestern California since 1970. He is presently associate professor of anthropology at the University of Massachusetts in Boston. His most recent book, with Alma Gottlieb, is *Blood Magic: The Anthropology of Menstruation* (University of California Press, 1988).

Vine Deloria, Jr., Standing Rock Sioux, is former director of the National Congress of American Indians, and is presently professor of law and theology at the University of Arizona. He is the author of a number of books, including *Custer Died for Your Sins* (Avon, 1970), *The Metaphysics of Modern Existence* (Harper & Row, 1976), and *God Is Red* (Dell, 1983).

Sam Gill is a professor of religion at the University of Colorado in Boulder. Among his books are *Songs of Life: An Introduction to Navajo Religious Culture* (E.J. Brill, 1979) and *Sacred Words: A Study of Navajo Religion and Prayer* (Greenwood, 1981); and more recently, *Mother Earth: The American Story* (Chicago, 1987) and *Native American Religious Action* (Columbia, S.C., 1987).

Elaine Jahner is a professor of English and Native American studies at Dartmouth College. She is co-editor with Raymond J. DeMallie of *Lakota Belief and Ritual* (University of Nebraska Press, 1980), editor of *Lakota Myth* (University of Nebraska Press, 1983), and author of numerous studies of Native American literature.

Oren Lyons is a member of the Wolf Clan of the Onondaga Nation, the Firekeepers of the Haudenosaunee. He is associate professor in the Department of American Studies in the State University of New York at Buffalo, and publisher of *Daybreak*, an American Indian news magazine dedicated to the seventh generation.

Emory Sekaquaptewa is a member of an eminent Hopi family and teaches at the University of Arizona. He is presently at work on a comprehensive dictionary of the Hopi language, on a major grant from the National Endowment for the Arts.

Terry Tafoya is Taos Pueblo on his father's side, Warm Springs on his mother's. He is a storyteller, writer, and psychologist, with degrees from the University of Washington in communications and higher education, and has worked in the field of Native American health and education in this country and in Canada.

Barbara Tedlock is associate professor of anthropology at the State University of New York at Buffalo. She has published three books: *Teachings from the American Earth: Indian Religion and Philosophy* (Norton, 1975), *Time and Highland Maya* (University of New Mexico, 1982), and *Dreaming: Anthropological and Psychological Interpretations* (Cambridge, 1987). Recently she has completed a book manuscript titled *The Beautiful and the Dangerous: An Account of Field Work at Zuñi Pueblo*.

Barre Toelken is director of the American Studies Graduate Program and of the Folklore Program at Utah State University. A past-president of the American Folklore Society and a former editor of the *Journal of American Folklore*, he is currently chair of the Western Folklife Center's Board of Directors and is co-chair of the Board of Trustees of the American Folklife Center in the Library of Congress.

Profiles of Artists

Rick Bartow, Yurok, is an artist represented by Jamison/Thomas Gallery in Portland, Oregon. Recent solo exhibitions include *Works on Paper*, 1988, Jamison - Thomas Gallery (Portland, Oregon/ New York, New York) and *Man in a Box*, 1987, Jamison - Thomas Gallery (Portland, Oregon/ New York, New York), Partlow Gallery (Olympia, Washington), and American Indian Contemporary Art Gallery (San Francisco, California).

Carl Beam, Ojibwa, is an artist working in Ontario, Canada. He is represented by the St. Joseph Island Artisan Gallery in Richards Landing, Ontario. He has recently been included in two group shows at the St. Joseph Island Artisan Gallery and in 1984 had an exhibition called *Altered Egos: Multimedia Work of Carl Beam*, Exhibition Center and Center of Indian Art (Thunder Bay, Ontario).

Betty Bia, Navajo, is a weaver who specializes in textiles based on sacred designs of sand painting and in the advancement of the technological aspects of this tribal form.

Edna Jackson, Tlingit, is an artist living and working in Kake, Alaska. Her images represent "contemporary legends." Her work was recently exhibited in a one-person show curated by Lloyd Oxendine at the American Indian Community House in New York, 1988.

Frank LaPena, a Wintu Nomtipom artist, is currently a professor of art and director of the Native American Studies Program at the California State University at Sacramento. His work has been exhibited throughout the United States and Europe. His most recent exhibition was a one-person show at the Sierra Nevada Museum of Art in November 1988.

Dan Namingha, Hopi, is a painter living and working in New Mexico. His most recent solo exhibitions include *Dan Namingha*, 1988, Gerald Peters Gallery (Dallas, Texas); *Images of the Southwest*, 1988, National Academy of Sciences (Washington, D.C.); and *Tewa-Hopi Reflections*, 1987, Heard Museum (Phoenix, Arizona).

David Chethlahe Paladin, 1926-1984, was a Navajo artist and shaman. He was recently honored in an exhibition called *David Paladin: Altered States* curated by Joshua Goldberg at the University of Arizona Musuem of Art.

Kevin Red Star, Crow, is an artist living and working in Billings, Montana. He comes from a long tradition of visual artists and his work has been exhibited throughout the United States.

Jaune Quick-to-See Smith is a member of the Flathead tribe of Montana. She is a painter who exhibits internationally and is a spokeswoman for both traditional and contemporary Native artists. She has founded two cooperatives: the Coup Marks on the Flathead Reserve and the Grey Canyon Artists in Albuquerque. She has lectured and done consulting as well as curated exhibitions for the Native community. Smith's writing, poetry, and illustrations have been published in numerous periodicals and books. She has also served on the boards of the Institute of American Indian Art (Santa Fe), American Indian Contemporary Art Gallery (San Francisco) and ATATL (Phoenix).

Tom Two Arrows, Onondaga-Delaware, was born in Albany, New York. Working as an illustrator, a textile designer, and painter, he has had a commercially successful career as a contemporary American Indian artist. He has also devoted himself to a life-long study of Iroquois myth, ceremony, traditional craft, music, and dance.

Profiles of Editors

D.M. Dooling is the founder and editorial director of PARABOLA Magazine and president of the Society for the Study of Myth and Tradition. She has contributed numerous articles and interviews to PARABOLA over the past 14 years. She has also edited the following PARABOLA books: *The Sons of the Wind: The Sacred Stories of the Lakota*; *A Way of Working: The Spiritual Dimension of Craft*; and *Leaning on the Moment: Interviews from PARABOLA Magazine*.

Paul Jordan-Smith is a senior editor of PARABOLA Magazine, with responsibility for "Epicycles," a section of the magazine devoted to traditional stories, myths and legend. He has contributed numerous articles to PARABOLA and has retold many stories and myths for "Epicycles." He has been an editor of PARABOLA since its inception.

Typeset in Caslon 540 and Cochin Black
Production Coordinator: Kate Gleason
Art Research: Daniella Dooling